The Politics of Federal Reorganization

Pergamon Titles of Related Interest

Bryner   BUREAUCRATIC DISCRETION:
Law and Policy in Federal Regulatory Agencies

Carter   CONTEMPORARY CONSTITUTIONAL
LAWMAKING:
The Supreme Court and the Art of Politics

Hart   THE PRESIDENTIAL BRANCH

Levin/Ferman   THE POLITICAL HAND:
Policy Implementation and
Youth Employment Programs

Shooshan   DISCONNECTING BELL:
The Impact of the AT&T Divestiture

Pergamon Government & Politics Series

The Politics of Federal Reorganization

Creating the U.S. Department of Education

Beryl A. Radin
University of Southern California
Washington Public Affairs Center

Willis D. Hawley
Vanderbilt University

PERGAMON PRESS

NEW YORK · OXFORD · BEIJING · FRANKFURT
SÃO PAULO · SYDNEY · TOKYO · TORONTO

U.S.A.	Pergamon Press, Maxwell House, Fairview Park, Elmsford, New York 10523, U.S.A.
U.K.	Pergamon Press, Headington Hill Hall, Oxford OX3 OBW, England
PEOPLE'S REPUBLIC OF CHINA	Pergamon Press, Room 4037, Qianmen Hotel, Beijing, People's Republic of China
FEDERAL REPUBLIC OF GERMANY	Pergamon Press, Hammerweg 6, D-6242 Kronberg, Federal Republic of Germany
BRAZIL	Pergamon Editora, Rua Eça de Queiros 346, CEP 04011, Paraiso, São Paulo, Brazil
AUSTRALIA	Pergamon Press Australia, P.O. Box 544, Potts Point, N.S.W. 2011, Australia
JAPAN	Pergamon Press, 8th Floor, Matsuoka Central Building, 1-7-1 Nishishinjuku, Shinjuku-ku, Tokyo 160, Japan
CANADA	Pergamon Press Canada, Suite No. 271, 253 College Street, Toronto, Ontario, Canada M5T 1R5

First printing 1988

Library of Congress Cataloging-in-Publication Data
Radin, Beryl.
The politics of federal reorganization.
(Pergamon government & politics series)
Bibliography: p.
Includes index.
1. United States. Dept. of Education.
2. Education and state—United States.
3. Politics and education—United States.
I. Hawley, Willis D.   II. Title.   III. Series.
LA210.R.24   1987   379.73   87-6972

British Library Cataloguing in Publication Data
Radin, Beryl A.
The politics of federal reorganization:
creating the U.S. Department of Education.
—(Pergamon government & politics series).
1. United States, Department of Education.
I. Title.   II. Hawley, Willis D.
379.73   LA210

ISBN 0-08-033978-6 (Hardcover)
ISBN 0-08-033977-8 (Flexicover)

Printed in Great Britain by A. Wheaton & Co. Ltd., Exeter

 # CONTENTS

PREFACE

This study was begun in early 1978 when the establishment of a separate cabinet-level Department of Education was in doubt. When we began interviewing individuals about the effort, they were not always sure whether we were interviewing them about the creation of a department or asking them to tell the story of a proposal that did not materialize. But legislation establishing the Department was enacted and it became a reality. For a few months it seemed obvious that one should study this effort, during this time we had no problem justifying this research to others.

And then came the 1980 election. Ronald Reagan's proposals to abolish the Department of Education suggested that we might be writing about the short unhappy life of a federal department. For nearly a year, the study was in limbo until we could determine whether our research had to be framed in a different context than the one which we had constructed. By the end of 1982, we decided that a Department of Education would continue to exist and that it was useful to write about its creation and early implementation.

The study is based on four sources of information. First, we examined a large number of written materials that dealt with the issue. These included letters, memoranda, reports, minutes from meetings, and other non-public but written accounts of the process. Publicly available information such as testimony, hearings and events reported by the press were also examined.

The second source of information for the study was provided by observers of the decision-making process. Over 200 personal and telephone interviews were conducted over a four-year period with the actors and observers of the policy process through which the Department of Education was created. These included legislators and their staffs, individuals within the Executive Office of the President, political and career staff within the executive branch, representatives of interest groups, and other informed individuals.

The third source of information came from the direct experiences of the authors of this volume. Willis Hawley served as the Study Director for the Department of Education study group within the President's Reorganization Project of OMB and later as a consultant in subsequent stages of the process. While not a direct participant in the Department of Education activity,

Beryl Radin was involved in another part of the PRP project which provided her with an inside view of those reorganization activities.

Finally, we relied on the academic literature in related policy and administrative fields for our fourth source of information. We explored work dealing with the characteristics and dimensions of the stages of the policy process. We investigated the literature on reorganization in general, and federal government reorganization in particular. We attempted to place our case study in the context of the literature on the presidency. Our interest in policy analysis and the relationship of policy analysts to their clients was informed by that aspect of the scholarly literature. Finally, both of us had written on education policy and we revisited some of the literature that dealt with federal education policy.

The study was generously supported over a number of years by the Spencer Foundation. We began to conceptualize this work when the Department seemed but a gleam in a candidate's eye. When the Department did become a reality, the Spencer Foundation was willing to assist us to bring our concept to life. The 1984 publication of a chapter in Michael Nelson's volume, *The Presidency and the Political System*,[1] encouraged us to complete the work on a book-length manuscript.

We are indebted to Marilyn Zlotnik and Lori Fox who served as research assistants during the course of the data collection and organization of this book and, in the process, helped us understand the vagaries of Washington organizational politics. We are especially grateful for Marilyn Zlotnik's initial draft of the enactment chapter. In addition, a number of individuals who were involved in the activities leading to the creation of the Department as well as its early implementation were extremely generous in giving advice and counsel to us as we carried out this project.

NOTE

1.   Willis D. Hawley and Beryl A. Radin, "The Presidency and Domestic Policy: Organizing the Department of Education," in Michael Nelson, editor, *The Presidency and the Political System* (Washington, D.C.: Congressional Quarterly Press, 1984): 449-470.

Chapter 1 INTRODUCTION

As Ronald Reagan completed the first half of his second term as President of the United States, his Secretary of Education, William Bennett was among the most visible and active members of the cabinet. Secretary Bennett used his position as a cabinet official to comment on various aspects of American education and schooling, drawing on the press and public attention that is accorded to an individual of cabinet rank.

For some observers of the political scene, this was a situation filled with irony. Ronald Reagan had campaigned on a platform committed to the abolition of a federal education department and had attempted to use his considerable political clout to make that promise a reality. Nevertheless, the U.S. Department of Education not only survived but, by 1986, even those who had been previously committed to its destruction were taking the existence of the department for granted.

On October 17, 1979 President Jimmy Carter signed a law enacted by Congress that created the U.S. Department of Education and, thus, put another seat at the cabinet table. Carter's signature was the culmination of a long and rocky battle to give full departmental status to the federal presence in education.

Although most twentieth century presidents—indeed, most chief executives at all levels of American government—have made government reorganization a part of their search for executive control, perhaps no president since Herbert Hoover took the subject as seriously as did Jimmy Carter. Each chief executive comes into office riding a political wave but, as the excitement generated by election victory subsides and inaugural day approaches, each begins to worry about the process of governance. The form of that governance seems to create its own fascination—and Jimmy Carter's preoccupation with the structures of government was extremely strong.

As Governor of Georgia, Carter had a particular interest in reorganization and the creation of a separate cabinet-level Department of Education had a special meaning to him. Carter's campaign owed at least a part of its success to the support of the National Education Association—the national organization

1

of teachers, education specialists and administrators with an active membership in every congressional district throughout the United States. Carter
received the first presidential endorsement made by the organization in its
119-year history. He reciprocated with an appropriate campaign promise—a
pledge to support the creation of a separate cabinet-level Education
Department if elected president.

This book examines the creation and early implementation of a new
cabinet department. As an account of a reorganization effort, it provides a
glimpse into the reasons why reorganization efforts are ubiquitous and yet,
at the same time, so difficult to implement. As Harold Seidman and Robert
Gilmour have observed, "Reorganization has become almost a religion in
Washington."[1] Reorganization is an act of faith—and pronouncements of
belief are notoriously difficult to put into operation or, indeed, to evaluate.

We have attempted to interweave a number of themes through this
extremely complex case study of federal-level decision-making: the
importance of the stages of the policy process in shaping the nature of
political action; the internal tensions within the executive branch; the conflict
between the culture of analysis and the culture of politics; the role of interest
groups and issue networks in shaping public policy; and the continuing
uncertainty about the federal role in education. As the analysis unfolds,
these themes will provide the conceptual and theoretical underpinning for
the "tale". Although this case study deals systematically with these themes,
we have chosen to present the case in narrative form. We believe that the
momentum of a story has the power to place the reader in a context that most
closely approximates the perceived "reality" experienced by the participants
in the process. As Thomas J. Kaplan has noted, a narrative or story can often
present and explain a complex situation over time when other analytical
forms may not provide a sense of the richness of meaning and detail
involved.[2]

In our analysis of the process of policy development that led to the
creation of the Department of Education, we have examined the positions
and roles of the actors involved in the policy process; the functions that are
built into the institutional settings in which the decisions were made; the
bases of power and uses of political resources; the attributes and demands of
the policy environment; and the specific goals and objectives attached to the
issue.

STAGES OF THE POLICY PROCESS

There are, of course, many ways to think about the policy process.
Following Laswell, Charles O. Jones emphasizes the identification of "the
principal activities in the overall policy process which typically form patterns
as identifiable systems and processes. That is, these several activities

represent something rather consistent over time, to the point that we can identify definite patterns."[3] Others have focused on specific elements within the broad framework suggested by Jones. James Anderson has stressed the predictable elements of stages of the process: agenda setting, formulation, adoption, implementation, and evaluation.[4] Robert Nakamura and Frank Smallwood focus on three different functional environments in which different aspects of the process take place.[5] John Kingdon explains the agenda setting and alternative specification process through three elements: problems, policies, and politics;[6] while Roger Cobb and Charles Elder identify two kinds of political agendas: systemic (drawn largely from shared concerns and perceptions within the society) and institutional (formal elements before governmental bodies).[7] Even Michael Cohen, James March and Johan Olsen (who use the metaphor of a "garbage can" to describe the policy process) concentrate on three general properties of organizations: preferences, technologies, and participation.[8]

The conceptualization of the policy process in this study builds on this legacy. We describe a policy process that is continuous and open-ended. Each stage has its own functional demands and its own institutional setting. With the movement to subsequent stages, new opportunities are created and new sets of constraints are imposed. At the same time, the decisions are shaped by what has gone on before. As a policy issue moves through time and through various arenas where different actors have varying degrees of both authority and legitimacy, we see that issues are reopened that appeared to have been settled at an earlier point in the decision-making process.

In our treatment of the stages of the policy process, we build, especially, on the work of Jones and of Gary Brewer and Peter deLeon. Jones specifies problem identification, formulation, legitimation, application and evaluation as the systems which generate activities within the policy process.[9] Brewer and deLeon have disaggregated the various components of the process, noting that various phases (as they call the stages) of the policy process contain different characteristics and uses.[10] We describe a process in which the movement of an issue from one setting to another provides the opportunity for shifts in both process as well as substance. We have observed that the movement sometimes follows a chronological course but often begins a new stage before previous stages are viewed as completed.

As the context of policy development shifts from stage to stage so too do the key decision-makers change, reflecting the fragmentation of the American political process. This case study indicates the difficulty of finding an actor or set of actors who consistently influence the development of an issue over time. We have developed a new appreciation for the special need for the president not only to serve as the chief administrative officer as well as political leader but also, in Eugene Bardach's sense, to act as the "fixer" for a policy as it moves through its multiheaded decision arenas and shifts in key decision-makers.[11]

This case study also illustrates the way goals shift as an issue moves through the various stages of the policy process. As the arenas change and actors take on new responsibilities, roles or authorities, goals are redefined, newly articulated or reopened for debate. Because goals play an important role in defining the character of political action, the shifting goals reinforce the tendencies in the system to treat each decision arena as a new day in court. The process feeds itself—new actors ask new questions, the questions provoke a shift in the way that the goals and objectives of the issue are treated. In turn, the questions serve to stir up the configuration of interests, resources and issues that make up the environment of political action. As these changes occur, they create new relationships which, in turn, cause new actors to surface who ask new questions.

POLITICS OF THE EXECUTIVE BRANCH

The second of the themes that undergird this study deals with the politics of the executive branch of government. Observers of the federal government have spent much of their time during this century attempting to understand how the executive branch of the U.S. government works—the presidency itself, White House leadership, the federal bureaucracy, and the interrelationships between the various parts of the executive branch.

There are three aspects of this theme that can be examined through this study and each encompasses a separate set of dynamics. The first focuses on the White House itself. The debates and differences between various actors within the White House and the Executive Office of the President provide evidence, once again, that the presidency is not a monolithic and unified institution. The issue we study travels from the campaign trail, to the transition to the presidency, to the creation of a President's Reorganization Project within the Office of Management and Budget; and through the executive branch (including the Department of Health, Education and Welfare, the White House Domestic Policy Staff and other bureaucratic as well as political actors). The case study is, of course, bound to carry the idiosyncracies of a particular president and the personal as well as institutional baggage that he brought with him in organizing and running the presidency. This study adds to the commentaries that have been made by others (e.g. Lynn and Whitman)[12] about the particular strengths and weaknesses of President Jimmy Carter.

The second aspect of executive branch politics that is handled in this volume concerns bureaucratic responses to change. Charles Gilbert has commented that

> Bureaucratic resistance to change is probably common and presumably functional, reflecting rank-and-file commitments to established missions without which management would be much more difficult and less effective. Bureaucracy's logic—not its

formal top-down program, but its morphology as an assemblance of established functions and professions—militates in general against change.[13]

While one may agree with Gilbert's general proposition, there comes a time when it is counterproductive—from a number of perspectives—for bureaucrats to resist change. This study examines the responses of executive agency bureaucrats to a drive for change. For some of those career and program officials the proposal for a change of organizational status was welcome. For others, however, the creation of the Department of Education signalled a loss of program autonomy and disrupted relationships with other elements in the issue networks that supported budgets and new program development.

These issues are discussed within the context of the early development of the department proposal, its workings through the White House and the Congress, and in the early implementation stages when many of the old apprehensions about the change resurfaced in a more immediate and concrete fashion.

The third aspect of the theme dealing with the politics of the executive branch focuses on the strategy of reorganization itself. In her study of federal narcotics enforcement, Patricia Rachal has commented that administrative management of the federal bureaucracy has been an issue since the emergence of the "administrative state"—that is, the growth in number of administrative units within the federal government and the attendant growth in staff. Reorganization, she argues, is the technique applied by presidents to assume coordination and control of the federal bureaucracy.[14]

This study concentrates on a reorganization issue within the administration of a president who took reorganization seriously. At the same time, although attracted to structural tinkering, Jimmy Carter was also an individual who believed that people make a difference in the way that government operates. For some, it makes no difference how government is structured—the individuals who assume leadership roles within the organization determine how effective programs will be conceptualized and delivered. For others, the perception is exactly the opposite. Unless the organization is structured in a fashion that allows individuals to exercise their authority in an appropriate fashion, it makes no difference who is appointed to positions. The perceptions of whether people or structure make the difference influenced the way that individuals responded to the reorganization effort.

These different beliefs led to very different strategies of change. The relative importance of individuals as compared to organizational structure was particularly important in discussions involving interest group representatives and when the issue was debated in Congress. Organizational issues—and organizational analysis—are not as real to actors in the legislative arena as they may be to those within the executive branch.

THE CULTURE OF ANALYSIS VS.
THE CULTURE OF POLITICS

The third theme discussed in this volume concerns a variant of the conflict between C. P. Snow's two cultures.[15] Snow wrote about the gap between the humanities and the hard sciences; the dichotomy present in this case study is the conflict between the culture of politics and the culture of analysis. Nathan Caplan described this as a gap "due to differences in values, language, reward systems, and social and professional affiliations."[16] Others have written about the difficulties involved in assuring that policy analysis is used within the decision-making process.[17] Relationships to clients, methodologies employed, proximity to decision-making are but a few of the problems that have been associated with the often futile production of sophisticated policy analysis.

Analysis played an extremely important role in the formulation stages of the proposals for a Department of Education. Good analysis has as its goal the presentation of a thorough, comprehensive picture of all positions on the issue in order to facilitate an informed decision. Yet it is obvious that the concept of policy analysis as an endeavor based only on the rational paradigm of decision-making has very limited utility.[18] The culture of politics demands quick and concise information, based on guestimates and recognition of the implicit uncertainties involved in an urgent decision.

The analysts who participated in various elements of the Department of Education effort did attempt to break out of the narrow bounds of the rational paradigm. They did, to some degree, recognize that policy analysis is an activity that requires both technical as well as political analytic skills.[19] However, it is often difficult for individuals who are intentionally set apart as analysts to engage in the interactive elements of the political world. One of the consequences of opening the door to political analysis is that there are few ways to contain it.

The boundaries between the analyst and the political advisor are difficult to define when the analyst engages in the business of political prognostication. Others may make different political assessments of issues and, then, analysts are confronted by other analysts who make counter claims. Political analysis can contribute to inadequate substantive analysis of issues. Substantive concerns may become secondary as political costs of proposals become the major focus of attention.

The story of the Department of Education indicates how the cast of characters involved did not always behave in the manner that might be thought appropriate for their roles. Policy analysts are considered effective when they operate within, and in general sympathy with, the political commitments of the policy-maker. Thus, analysis that examines alternative options or outcomes not favored by the policy-maker is often discounted.

The model of the policy analyst as the technician appealed to those analysts who were uncomfortable making political judgments involving information about which they had little first-hand or expert knowledge. However, after several instances in which decisions were made without much consideration of the analysis, it appeared that analysts—if they wanted to have any influence at all—had to make assessments of political issues (particularly the relationship between a specific policy under consideration and other questions on the White House agenda). There was some confusion, however, among the policy analysts studying the education reorganization issue as to how much of a precommitment had already been made to create a separate education department.

The already difficult position of giving advice to a decision-maker was complicated by Jimmy Carter's own peculiarities as the client for the analysis. There were times when Carter appeared to believe that the best decision to emerge from the technical and comprehensive analysis should be the one that he carried forward to the Congress—even when he had strong political intelligence that the technical analytic decision was bound to encounter very strong opposition. At other times, Carter was willing to go along with the advice of his personal political staff who wanted to avoid rocking the boat and assuming new political risks. Much of the explanation for these differing approaches was contextual. Jimmy Carter did not like to think he had to make decisions on political grounds, but when the political heat intensified, he was pragmatic. These issues are traced throughout the design and development of the proposed department.

INTEREST GROUPS AND ISSUE NETWORKS

The fourth theme that informs this volume revolves around the tangled set of relationships between interest groups, executive-level career officials, and staff and committees in Congress. Interest group politics is, without doubt, an important component in the story of the creation of the Department of Education. Indeed, the most common interpretation of the reason for the passage of the ED bill centers around the role of the National Education Association and other powerful education interest groups and their ability to call in the political chits owed to them by Jimmy Carter in return for their support of his candidacy.

While we are not diminishing the importance of NEA's support to Carter, this interpretation misses an analysis of the dynamics of interest group maneuvering. Straightforward political analysis would suggest that an issue that was of great importance to an interest group with 1.8 million members spread across every state of the union, averaging four thousand members to every congressional district, was destined for success. NEA's special membership (articulate, well educated, experienced at working by rules and organizing) was able to use the revision of campaign finance laws to their advantage, organizing Political Action Committees to elect candidates who supported their education agenda.[20]

As the issue gained momentum, increasing numbers of groups became involved. Some of them were, in fact, mobilized by agencies affected by the proposed reorganization. These groups, in turn, began to raise issues with members of Congress. This process illustrates the so-called iron triangle theory. Control, according to this theory, is found in a series of relationships linking executive bureaus, congressional committees, and interest group clienteles. These triads, it is argued, make it difficult to change the way the nation's business is conducted. Iron triangles are considered to be the force most resistant to presidential attempts to exert control through reorganization. Indeed, congressional opponents to presidential reorganization attempts have based their opposition on the disruption that would follow a structural shift on the agency side of the triangular relationship.

However, the activity of interest groups around this issue suggests that the nature of interest group influence is much more complex than simple notions like iron triangle relationships would imply. Our analysis follows interest group activity throughout the process of creating the Department. The interest groups involved hold diverse views and have different priorities—despite the fact that many of them would be viewed as members of "the education establishment." As the ED proposal moved through its various arenas and types of consideration, it became obvious that something approximating Hugh Heclo's notion of issue networks was at play.[21] The issue network of education groups could be described, using Heclo's terminology, as a "web" of largely autonomous participants with variable degrees of mutual commitment or dependence on each other. The fluid nature of such an alliance, according to Heclo, results from the hybrid interests which are inevitably bred from the enactment of numerous and often less than compatible public policies:

> With more public policies, more groups are being mobilized and there are more complex relationships among them. Since very few policies ever seem to drop off the public agenda as more are added, congestion among those interested in various issues grows, the chances for accidental collisions increase, and the interaction tends to take on a distinctive group-life of its own in the Washington community.[22]

This study follows the activities of the education interest groups as well as other interest groups who demonstrated a concern about the creation of the Education Department while operating as the reorganization proposal's attentive public.

EDUCATION POLICY AND THE FEDERAL ROLE

The fifth theme that supports this study deals with the education policy arena. The reorganization issue was placed in the context of a broader policy environment which has historically been one characterized by controversy over the role of the federal government in education. This controversy is long-standing and we are no closer today to a political agreement on this issue that we were in 1954 with the historic *Brown v. Board of Education* Supreme Court decision. Since that decision, the federal role has broadened to promote equal opportunity on many fronts and to encourage change in education through the use of financial awards or incentives in what are essentially closed systems (local school systems). Most federal education programs were developed because states and localities were unwilling or unable to meet the requirements of students with special needs. Indeed, paradoxically, some federal programs provided funds to localities only because they had inadequately served the disadvantaged. Many state and local officials saw federal education programs as a necessary evil—at best—that represented a constant threat to the effective functioning of schools. They resented the imposition of explicit federal requirements that implied that federal officials knew better than the local officials how the needs of children could best be served. This built-in conflict between the levels of government meant that educational policy decisions almost always reflected a set of compromises about the appropriate federal role. Even the period of great federal activity in the 1960s did not produce a resolution of this basic problem. Adding further to the intergovernmental tension was the fact that the various federal programs were instituted piece by piece with little concern in the Congress or the bureaucracy about possible conflicts between the various pieces of legislation.

The controversy surrounding the appropriate role of the federal government[23] was never far from the debate about the creation of a federal department of education. This created both rhetorical and substantive problems for the Carter administration as it pushed the proposal through the policy process. Because it wanted to avoid charges that it was supporting national control of education (departing from the historical reliance on state and local control), the Carter administration attempted to straddle the line carefully. Carter's disposition was to play a leadership role in education through changes in organization structure without dictating education policies and avoiding proposals to increase expenditure on new or old federal programs.

These problems were particularly swampy for a president who was advocating the return of a number of responsibilities to the states and localities, arguing as a former governor that the Washington insider approach was ignoring the changes that had taken place around the country in the post Johnson period.

THE ORGANIZATION OF THIS BOOK

The themes that have been introduced provide the conceptual structure for a narrative, chronological account of the creation of the Department of Education. It concludes at the end of 1980, just before Ronald Reagan assumed the presidency. Because the account does move through time, we have attempted to use the calendar as the basic organizing principle for the book. Each time period that we discuss in the volume corresponds to a stage (often a hybrid stage) of the policy process. Thus the chapters provide the reader with an account of the agenda setting stage, the formulation stage, the adoption stage, a transition stage (the period after the legislation was signed but before the Department opened for business), and finally an implementation stage. While the specific events studied end with the final days of the Carter administration, the implementation chapter deals with some issues involving the Reagan administration.

Because of the complexiity of the activity that occurs within some of the time periods discussed, there is frequently a suborganization method employed that centers on specific actors and their issues. Activity, as was noted earlier, often took place in different arenas around different issues during the same time period. We have attempted to describe this activity in a fashion that makes it understandable to the reader. At the same time we try to give our readers a sense of the three-ring circus that characterized the real decision process.

NOTES

1. Harold Seidman and Robert Gilmour, *Politics, Position, and Power*, Fourth Edition (New York: Oxford University Press, 1986), p. 3.
2. Thomas J. Kaplan, "The Narrative Structure of Policy Analysis," *Journal of Policy Analysis and Management*, Vol. 5, No. 4 (1986): 761-778.
3. Charles O. Jones, *An Introduction to the Study of Public Policy* (Belmont, California: Wadsworth Publishing Company, Inc., 1970), p. 11.
4. James E. Anderson, *Public Policy-Making* (New York: Praeger, 1975).
5. Robert T. Nakamura and Frank Smallwood, *The Politics of Policy Implementation* (New York: St. Martin's Press, 1980).
6. John W. Kingdon, *Agendas, Alternatives, and Public Policies* (Boston: Little, Brown and Company, 1984), p. 17.
7. Roger W. Cobb and Charles D. Elder, *Participation in American Politics: The Dynamics of Agenda Building* (Boston: Allyn and Bacon, Inc., 1972), pp.85-86.
8. Michael Cohen, James March and Johan Olsen, "A Garbage Can Model of Organizational Choice," *Administrative Sciences Quarterly* 17 (March 1972): 1-25.
9. Jones, p. 149.
10. Gary D. Brewer and Peter deLeon, *The Foundations of Policy Analysis* (Homewood, Illinois: Dorsey Press, 1983).

11. Eugene Bardach, *The Implementation Game* (Cambridge, Mass.: The MIT Press, 1977).
12. Lawrence E. Lynn and David deF. Whitman, *The President as Policymaker: Jimmy Carter and Welfare Reform* (Philadelphia: Temple University Press, 1981).
13. Charles E. Gilbert, "Preface: Implementing Governmental Change," *The Annals of the American Academy of Political and Social Science*, Vol. 466 (March 1983), p. 15.
14. Patricia Rachal, *Federal Narcotics Enforcement: Reorganization and Reform* (Boston: Auburn House Publishing Co., 1982), p. 15.
15. C. P. Snow, *The Two Cultures and a Second Look* (Cambridge: Cambridge University Press, 1963).
16. Nathan Caplan, "A Minimal Set of Conditions Necessary for the Utilization of Social Science Knowledge in Policy Formulation at the National Level," in Carol H. Weiss, editor, *Using Social Research in Public Policy Making* (Lexington, Mass.: Lexington Books, 1977): 83-197.
17. See Carol H. Weiss, *Using Social Research*; Joseph A. Wholey, *Evaluation and Effective Public Management* (Boston and Toronto: Little, Brown and Company, 1983); Beryl A. Radin, "Evaluation on Demand: Two Congressionally Mandated Education Evaluations," in Ron Gilbert, editor, *Making and Managing Policy* (New York: Marcel Dekker, Inc., 1984); and Charles Lindblom and David K. Cohen, *Usable Knowledge* (New Haven and London: Yale University Press, 1979).
18. Graham Allison, *Essence of Decision* (Boston: Little, Brown and Company, 1971).
19. The dichotomy between political and technical skills is best discussed in Arnold Meltsner, *Policy Analysts in the Bureaucracy* (Berkeley, Ca.: University of California Press, 1976).
20. David Stephens, "President Carter, the Congress, and the NEA: Creating the Department of Education," *Political Science Quarterly*, Vol. 98, No. 4 (Winter 1983-84), p. 643.
21. Hugh Heclo, "Issue Networks and the Executive Establishment," in Anthony King, editor, *The New American Political System* (Washington, D.C.: American Enterprise Institute for Public Policy Research, 1979): 87-124.
22. Ibid.
23. See Rufus E. Miles Jr., *The Department of H.E.W.* (New York: Praeger Publishers, 1974); Norman C. Thomas, *Education in National Politics* (New York: David McKay Co., Inc., 1975); Stephen K. Bailey and Edith K. Mosher, *ESEA: The Office of Education Administers A Law* (Syracuse, New York: Syracuse University Press, 1968); and Beryl A. Radin, *Implementation, Change and the Federal Bureaucracy* (New York: Teachers College Press, Columbia University, 1977).

Chapter 2 THE CONTEXT FOR CHANGE

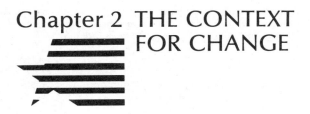

The efforts within the Carter Administration to create a new cabinet-level department of education took place within the context of past attempts at reorganization. Reorganization is often seen by public administrators at all levels to be one of their few tools for change. Hence, reorganization of the federal government has had a long and somewhat stormy history: since the earliest days of the country's political history, reorganization has been a continuing source of conflict between the Congress and the executive branch of government.

This chapter describes the historical background against which the effort to establish the Department of Education was played. This background is more than a set of past events that provide a perspective on the issue. The structure of federal educational programs inherited by President Carter reflected the cumulative results of past political victories and unresolved conflicts over a number of values and power relationships. These results were expressed in organizational arrangements that, to the outsider, appeared to be irrational or dysfunctional. To the policy participants, however, these structures were an expression of substantive policy decisions as well as the relative influence of different parts of the executive branch, the Congress and various interest groups.

FEDERAL EDUCATION POLICY AND ITS IMPLICATIONS FOR REORGANIZATION

Efforts to reorganize are often initiatives that seek to reorder priorities or power. Although issues of efficiency and program effectiveness frequently dominate the public discourse about reorganization, other questions may actually be more salient to the reorganization agenda. Underlying much of the debate about the establishment of the Department of Education was a concern about the appropriate role of the government in the education field and the relative importance of the Congress and the executive branch in defining that role.

For most of this nation's history, federal policies toward education have been incidental to the development of public education in the United States. Norman Thomas has commented that "It has often been asserted that 'education is a local responsibility, a state function, and a national concern'."[1] Until the 1960s, that "concern" was expressed in a rather oblique fashion. Through the early years of the nation's history, education support was limited to land grants; by the turn of the twentieth century, small grants for narrow educational objectives were made but were subject to very limited federal controls. Thomas has noted that attempts were made to obtain general federal aid to elementary and secondary education programs immediately after the Civil War. Clearly unsuccessful, the issue did not resurface until the mid 1940s.[2]

World War II did bring an increased interest in education efforts—funds were authorized for schools in communities affected by the war effort (the ancestor of impact aid) and the GI Bill of Rights was enacted following the war. During the period between 1945 and 1961, according to Thomas, efforts to enact general aid legislation were unsuccessful and controversial. However, Congress did pass a number of laws that were "expediential responses"[3] to specific problems and demands of specific interest groups.

The activity that occurred during the 1960s dramatically changed the context of the federal education role. Up to that period, American education policy was characterized as a complex but relatively stable policy system. Relationships were carved out between actors and policies implicit in the few federal education efforts to that time were respectful of those relationships.[4]

The multiple programs that were enacted in the 1960s and subsequently into the 1970s appeared to signal an end to those old relationships. The federal government, responsive to a wide array of criticisms about American education, was playing a more active role in this policy area. Activity, in this case, meant that the federal government itself was playing the part of a "change agent" or underwriting others to play that role. Perhaps the clearest illustration of that change status was found in the policies implicit in the Elementary and Secondary Act of 1965 (ESEA). This omnibus piece of legislation meant that federal policy could affect school financing, curriculum, classification of students and teachers, and placement of both students and teachers in classrooms.[5]

Bailey and Mosher noted that it was difficult to appraise the extent and meaning of this increased federal role. While school officials at both state and local levels wanted to claim the new federal funds, "they would like such aid without categorical strings—in their language without 'Federal Control'." According to Bailey and Mosher, "Whenever the Federal government (or any level of government for that matter) appropriates money for any purpose certain types of control are inevitable." Controls are necessary to ensure that money is spent according to legislative intent; controls must assure that funds are accounted for protecting against malfeasance and waste; administrative ground rules have to be established; and standards of performance are required to ensure attainment of results.[6]

Although the activity of the 1960s represented a quantum leap into an active federal role, Eidenberg and Morey, writing soon after the passage of the ESEA, were not sanguine that the issues had been resolved:

> There has been no resolution of the issue, only a series of temporary decisions made under changing circumstances. The forces of inertia and precedent give some permanence to a major federal role in elementary and secondary education. But the problems of administration, funding, and alteration persist.[7]

As the programs within the executive branch expanded, some observers of education policy argued that increased agency activity meant that the locus for policy change in this area shifted to the executive branch, away from the Congress. In this case, however, the executive branch was not the presidency or the White House. Thomas has commented:

> Although educational policy formulation centered in the Presidency, policy adoption was the manifest function of Congress, and implementation was the task of the bureaucracy, the agency's involvement extended deeply into the other two stages of the policy process. It was the only institutional participant actively involved in all stages. It was the central node in the communication network and the main locus for the interaction of the individuals and interests who made national educational policy. Its involvement extended to all substantive issues, and the ultimate achievement of policy goals was more dependent on the agency's performance than on any other component in the process.[8]

During the late 1960s and early 1970s, the number of interest groups in Washington concerned with education expanded significantly. The agendas of these groups ranged from broad program goals (such as compensatory eduation) to specific educational approaches (such as art education, legal education, conversion to the metric system).

While the Nixon administration appeared to argue against program proliferation (indeed, it proposed consolidation of programs into large block grants), it was not able or willing to resist the Democratic Congress's urge to respond to problems with specific, separate programs. The result of this expansion was a crazy quilt structure of multiple programs established by statute.

Thus the Office of Education, while a part of the Department of Health, Education and Welfare, had its own very separate relationships with the Congress and its interest groups. The formal organization chart, from the late 1960s on, showed a Commissioner of Education reporting to an Assistant Secretary for Education who, in turn, reported to the Secretary of HEW. In reality, however, Congress frequently ignored the organization chart and gave direct authority to the Commissioner of Education, delegating specific responsibilities not to the Secretary of HEW but to the Commissioner of Education.

As HEW's Office of the Secretary grew in both scope and size, various of the staff functions operating out of the Office of the Secretary began to take a central control responsibility more seriously. Budget decisions, legislative drafting, evaluations, regulation development, and other staff functions had been within the nearly exclusive purview of the Office of Education. By the mid 1970s, however, education policy was influenced—if not made—by a much larger array of bureaucratic actors within the Department.

A DEPARTMENT OF EDUCATION: A HISTORICAL LOOK

Herbert Emmerich has written that "the desire for autonomy characterizes the operating administrations and bureaus."[9] Programs—and their supporters both inside and outside government—appear to operate under the belief that the condition of being subsumed within a broader bureaucratic organization means that they are less than fully developed, almost a childlike condition that requires bureaucratic parental supervision. Emmerich notes that this desire for autonomy "is an apparently innate characteristic of administrative behavior."

For more than a century—even at a time when the federal responsibilities in education were extremely limited—calls for a separate cabinet-level department were heard. Some of these calls were in remembrance of things past—a time in 1867-68 when the few federal education efforts found a bureaucratic home in a tiny, sub-cabinet department. Soon, however, the department was downgraded to a bureau and that program eventually became the Office of Education (OE) (also known as the Education Division of the Department of Health, Education and Welfare (HEW)).

When the short lived Department of Education was moved in 1868, it was assigned to the Department of Interior and given the status of a small bureau. It stayed in this location for more than 60 years until President Harding attempted to raise its status in 1922. Harding requested the preparation of a bill creating a cabinet-level department of education, but his Commissioner of Education, Philander Claxton opposed this move. He prepared the bill to submit to Congress but spoke out against it. He was forced to resign even though the bill was never considered by the legislative body. Nearly ten years later, a commission appointed by President Herbert Hoover recommended the creation of a cabinet-level department of education, but Hoover did not request action on it.

In 1939 the Office of Education was taken out of the Department of Interior by President Franklin Roosevelt and was made a part of the Federal Security Agency, the predecessor of HEW. Roosevelt used his newly acquired reorganization authority in making this transfer. It has been argued that Roosevelt preferred the establishment of a separate education department but did not have the authority early in his administration to propose a new department under the reorganization authority given him by Congress. The move to create the Federal Security Agency followed the recommendation of Roosevelt's advisers on organization: Louis Brownlow, Charles Merriam and Luther Gulick. Although the President did have authority to create a new department later in his administration, he did not make such a recommendation.

After World War II a recommendation was made to establish a National Board of Education answerable to the President but without cabinet status. Ironically, the proposal was similar to that made by Philander Claxton some 30 years earlier.[10]

There continued to be advocates of a separate cabinet-level department over the years but serious attention to such a structure did not develop until the growth of federal education programs in the 1960s. Writing in 1968, Bailey and Mosher noted that "The recent emergence of education as a major national concern has raised insistent questions about the appropriate level and authority of USOE in the overall structure of the Federal government. The essential issue is this: is bureau status for OSOE commensurate with the importance of the functions it performs, and adequate to enable it to exert government-wide leadership in the field of education?"[11]

At that time, Bailey and Mosher described three alternative ways of dealing with that question. First, holding on to the present arrangement because raising the visibility of education in the federal structure would increase the fear of federal domination in education policy. Second, raising the Office of Education to a departmental status but keeping it within a superdepartment of HEW. This model would follow the design of the Department of Defense where a separate department would be subsumed under a broader cabinet-level umbrella. The third alternative would involve splitting HEW into two parts—health and welfare on the one hand and education on the other.[12]

Bailey and Mosher noted that there was some virtue in keeping boat-rocking to a minimum, but that a departmental status was warranted by the size and complexity of HEW as well as the need to give status to education.

> The shifting fortunes of departmental and agency status over the years in the Federal government have reflected a shifting consensus about national priorities. Education has now become a national priority, supported by an increasingly sophisticated and energetic constituency.[13]

While they acknowledged that traditional state, local and professional interests may find this difficult to accept, "Paradoxically, in spite of mistakes in judgment and execution, the Federal government's new role in education has surely had the effect of strengthening rather than weakening the authority and discretion of State and local educational agencies."[14]

Overall, wrote Bailey and Mosher, "creating a new department will not destroy ... myths overnight; but it can symbolize the need to make the Federal presence in education both highly visible and increasingly responsible."[15] For Bailey and Mosher—as well as for other analysts and advocates—it appeared that the creation of a separate federal department signified a final step in the evolution of a public policy issue. The process of public intervention began as a few individual programs were created. The programs increased and their constituencies also developed new political capacities and strengths. The next step was, inevitably, the creation of a cabinet-level department. Coming of age as a public policy issue meant that the constituency had its own full blown department. The momentum from the constituency for the creation of a cabinet-level department was aided by a tendency within Democratic administrations to look to the federal government as the locus of new social policy activity.

PAST REORGANIZATION ATTEMPTS

Redford and Blisset have written that "by the time of the Johnson administration, reorganization plans were an accepted mode of changing the structure of the executive branch."[16] The authority that had been granted by Congress under the Reorganization Act of 1949 (and its subsequent extensions) expired on the first of June 1963. When Johnson assumed the presidency that year he sought a permanent granting of presidential authority for reorganization. That permanent authority was not granted; indeed, the first renewal of the authority was provided only for an 11-month period. The Congress subsequently renewed the authority until the end of December 1968, providing Johnson with reorganization powers throughout his presidency.[17]

A useful summary of the reorganization authority contained in the 1949 Act is provided by Redford and Blisset:

> The legal bases are managerial. The purposes stated in the act include 'better execution of the laws,' 'more effective management,' 'expeditious administration,' to 'reduce expenditures,' 'increase the efficiency,' 'group, coordinate and consolidate ... according to major purpose,' 'reduce the number of agencies,' 'eliminate overlapping and duplication'; and the president is required to specify any probable reductions of expenditure. A finding of conformity with one or more of these purposes is included in the presidential message transmitting a plan.[18]

Although Johnson did send 17 plans to the Congress under the reorganization authority (and 16 became effective), a proposal for an education department was not one of the initiatives. But the absence of a proposal did not signal inattention to the issue during the Johnson years. In 1964, two parallel task forces were appointed by the President to examine organization issues relevant to the structure of federal education efforts.

A task force, headed by Don K. Price, the Dean of the Graduate School of Public Administration at Harvard, was appointed with the charge of studying the organization of the domestic functions of the executive branch. The report of the ten member group (known as the President's Task Force on Government Reorganization) included education as one of the 12 subjects under review. The November 1964 report of the group recommended the creation of a Department of Education, with a secretary in the cabinet. Included in the department, according to this task force, would be agencies with educational and research programs, including humanities and cultural affairs as well as the sciences.

The report noted:

> The advancement of education and of the basic research programs that are carried on primarily in educational institutions is the keystone of our future progress. The Federal Government has become a major supporter of these purposes, but without having a comprehensive organization that could help the President develop a policy for them. We believe that the President will wish to develop a policy calling for a sharp increase in Federal support for education and research and a better balance among various elements of the program. Our recommendation of a Department of Education is based on that assumption.
>
> Because the schools have been afraid of Federal domination, the Government has never had a comprehensive policy for the advancement of education and research. But it is unrealistic to think we can protect the freedom of education by pretending to ignore it.[19]

The Price report also recommended the creation of four other departments—Transportation, Housing and Community Development, Economic Development and Natural Resources. According to Rufus Miles, the President had instructed the task force to "allow him to determine the political feasibility of their recommendations, so they felt less constrained by such considerations than might otherwise have been the case."[20]

While the task force did not view the new department as the only federal agency involved in education, it did envisage the new agency as instrumental in redressing a perceived imbalance between higher education and elementary and secondary education, between the sciences and other areas of learning; and between research and teaching. All in all, the Price Task Force favored the development of comprehensive federal policy for the advancement of education.[21]

About the same time as he named the Price Task Force, Johnson also asked John Gardner, then President of the Carnegie Corporation, to chair a Task Force on Education. While the mission of this group was primarily substantive and programmatic, according to Miles, it did address the organizational structure question. A chapter on organization innovation was introduced with the statement: "The present Office of Education is incapable of meeting the requirements facing us."[22]

The report argued that:

> There should be at the highest level of the Federal government an agency adequately staffed to carry through penetrating analysis of current problems and needs, to lay down the broad objectives of government action, and to develop solid programs in

pursuit of those objectives. It would *not* be the purpose of such an agency to direct or control American education—no Federal agency ever could or should do that— but to introduce enough coherence into federal activities so that taxpayer dollars spent on education are well spent.[23]

Miles, who had served as the Director of Administration for HEW and was a long time student of HEW structure, found that the task force was split between creating an independent Office of Education at the presidential level (modelled after the Office of Economic Opportunity) or creating a new Department of Education. The majority of the group did favor the independent agency but commented that if a department were to be created "we do not believe that the new Department should be created by lifting the present Office of Education out of HEW and building around it. A completely new department should be organized, drawing functions from various parts of the government which now are carrying on significant educational missions."[24]

According to Redford and Blisset, both reports were submitted in November 1964 to a White House that had already considered the possibility of a separate department. As early as June 1964, write Redford and Blisset, the Bureau of the Budget had referred the subject to White House staffer Bill Moyers for consideration for inclusion in Johnson's legislative program.[25]

However, before the separate Department could be carefully considered, another problem involving federal education organization was forced on Johnson. Redford and Blisset comment: "A more urgent, almost a crisis, situation in educational administration confronted the President. The organizational structure of the Office of Education had been strained by the burdens of recently passed legislation."[26] A new deputy Commissioner of Education was appointed to focus on the internal administrative issues of the Office of Education. Bailey and Mosher report that this individual, Henry Loomis, "was appalled by what he found" when he assumed the new position in March 1965.[27]

The President himself became aware of the organizational problems found in OE and, at a reception for members of Congress, on the occasion of signing the Elementary and Secondary Education Act, Johnson said: "I am asking Secretary (Anthony) Celebrezze and Commissioner (Francis) Keppel to move immediately to prepare the Office of Education for the big job it has to do, just as soon as the funds are appropriated. Upon their recommendation, I am notifying the Secretary that I am going to appoint a task force to carry out his recommendations to assist him in the next 60 days on organization and personnel problems in this area to administer this bill."[28]

For the top officials in the Office of Education, the presidential move was extremely welcome. Bailey and Mosher noted that these officials were concerned about the "internal heat" that might be generated by a massive reorganization by managerial fiat. Johnson's appointment of an outside task force would, "in effect, pass the political burden of reorganization to the strong shoulders of the President and throw any adverse congressional or group interest reactions to reorganization into the complicated and forbidding arena of presidential relations."[29]

The task force was made up of three career civil servants, headed by Dwight Ink, then Assistant General Manager of the Atomic Energy Commission. The group worked quickly and within three months submitted a report detailing the personnel, financial, planning and evaluation, management, and organization structure components for the Office of Education.[30]

Although the report did not propose the creation of a separate department of education—indeed, its mandate precluded such a finding—it did move the Office of Education into a more generalist direction. A number of recommendations were made that had the effect of consolidating program units into functional rather than traditional program specialist categories.

Soon after the Ink Committee report was submitted, John Gardner was selected to be the next Secretary of HEW. Gardner's commitment to education signalled a heightened attention to education policy both in HEW and in the president's cabinet.[31] At the same time, the reorganization that was taking place within the Office of Education suggested that many of the concerns that had motivated both the Price and Gardner Task Forces might be addressed without the trauma of creating a new department.

When Gardner took office as Secretary of HEW, he asked management consultant John Corson and HEW Assistant Secretaries James Kelly and Donald Simpson to recommend the best way to structure the gargantuan department. The Corson study, as it was called, recommended a structure that would consist of three sub-cabinet level departments. At the same time, according to Miles, the major objectives of the plan were to

> strengthen the capacity of the Secretary to provide the needed policy and management leadership to the department without becoming overburdened himself, to improve the attractiveness of top-level positions to first-rate people, elevate the prestige and visibility of those primarily responsible for health, education and welfare programs, and focus responsibility on a single national spokesman in each of these fields.[32]

According to Miles, Gardner discussed the plan with Johnson and, following the conversation, made the proposal public at the President's request. Miles notes that the plan "had not received any review by the Bureau of the Budget, the organization that was responsible for making major reorganization recommendations to the President, and its revelation in advance of such review did not help its reception."[33] The proposal envisioned a Department of Education with three major components—the Office of Education, Educational Television, and Manpower Development and Training. Although this issue was not set to rest, the discussion of the form of the organization shifted from a separate department to a superdepartment including education as one of the major functions.[34]

About the same time that the Corson study group was making its recommendations to Secretary Gardner, President Johnson began another effort to examine the coordination and management of domestic social programs. The creation of a Task Force on Government Organization stemmed from a proposal from presidential assistant Joseph A. Califano for the establishment of an outside task force on government reorganization "to insure the coordination and effective implementation of federal programs, with particular emphasis on programs designed to meet the problems of the cities."[35]

Johnson named Benjamin Heineman, Chairman of the Board of Chicago and Northwestern Railway Company to head the task force. Redford and Blisset have commented that "the President's confidence in Heineman must have been comparable to that of previous presidents when they selected Brownlow and Hoover for reorganization studies."[36] Johnson had attempted to lure the Chicagoan to a cabinet position but had been unable to convince him to take a full time position. Califano worked closely with the task force which included a number of individuals who would return to the same issues during the Carter administration. Hale Champion was a member of the Heineman task force and Fred Bohen served as the staff director for the effort (both men were a part of the Califano HEW team during the Carter administration).

The Heineman task force has been described as Johnson's "secret" task force[37] because its study documents and recommendations were not released to the public. The study was commissioned as a way of anticipating future political battles; it appeared to many in the White House that a number of the Great Society programs were in trouble. Political sensitivity to criticisms of the programs seemed to the Johnson staff to justify the close-to-the-vest behavior. When Califano transmitted the final report to the President, he noted: "I urge you to read the report because it is one of the best I have seen." He commented that the report "finds weaknesses in the way we manage our domestic programs—an 'organization lag' as a result of over 50 more programs launched in three years."[38]

Because of interest in longer-range organization design considerations, a short six-page report was submitted by the task force that addressed the future administrative viability of the organization of American government. The report noted that the American public expects the President "will not merely propose but also deliver" the substance of programs. Two recommendations were made that directly affected the movement for a separate Department of Education:

> We urge resistance by Presidents to the persistent political pressure to create more executive departments and independent agencies. *Unchecked, these pressures to widen the President's span of control will emiminate the possibility of meaningful direction from, and contact between, the President and the major line officials of his administration.*

> To make the President's administrative job manageable, and to improve the coordination of related Federal programs, *we believe that the future line organization of the executive branch should be shaped over time to provide a small number (4-6) of line deputies to manage the full range of executive departments and agencies short of the President.*[39]

The Heineman Commission addressed the question of the creation of a new Department of Education specifically and, not surprisingly, argued that such a new department should not be created.[40] By the time that the Heineman reports were concluded, Johnson was preoccupied with other matters. The war in Vietnam and the political turmoil within the country did not appear to make it an opportune time to release the reports or to begin to devise strategies for putting those recommendations into action.

THE NIXON PRESIDENCY

Soon after he assumed office in 1969, President Richard Nixon asked Roy Ash, President of Litton Industries, to study the organization of the federal government. The report of this group was submitted in 1970 and its recommendations echoed many of the concerns voiced by the Heineman Commission. The report was used as the basis for a set of reorganization plans announced by the White House in early 1971.

The Nixon proposal called for a reorganization scheme keyed to the concept that "the executive branch should be organized around basic goals. Instead of grouping activities by narrow subjects or by limited constituencies, we should organize them around the great purposes of government."[41] The proposal sought to replace seven of the existing departments with four new ones: Natural Resources, Community Development, Economic Affairs, and Human Resources. Each department was to be given a mission broad enough to facilitate comprehensive policy decision-making.

Implicit in the Ash Council recommendations was an assumption that reorganizing the government structure would go a long way toward improving the efficiency of government operations and the delivery of services to the American people. According to Rufus Miles, the recommendations also coincided with the President's natural inclination to restrict his dealings with executive officials to the smallest feasible number of individuals.

The organization plan that was proposed for the Department of Human Resources had three line administrators—an administrator for health, an administrator for income security, and an administrator for human development. According to this scheme, education would be placed under the administrator for human development (along with programs in social services and manpower). Rufus Miles has commented that, in this proposal, education would be subordinated more explicitly to a line officer than it was within HEW. He noted:

The Ash Council was in many respects grounded upon the Heineman Commission report. Both task forces liked the idea of narrowing the President's broad span of control, creating large departments with management-minded Secretaries and closely-knit teams of planners and evaluators around the Secretary. Both were taken with the concept of delegating to powerful regional administrators the basic line responsibilities exercised—then and now—by program administrators located in Washington. Neither could see any reason to believe that the size or complexity of the Department of HEW might soon near the outer limits of manageability.[42]

Nixon's proposals had no support in Congress; indeed, the proposal for a Department of Human Resources was not even given the opportunity for congressional hearings. Its radical treatment of specialized program components was bound to engender the opposition of a wide array of organized groups. As such, the Ash Council approach—like the Heineman Commission before it—became an artifact of administrative history.

Although the question of governance continued to be of concern to Nixon's replacement, Gerald Ford, he did not focus on organizational structure as a method of improving the business of government. From 1971 until 1975, there was little attention to the question of government organization or the president's reorganization authority.

PAST CONGRESSIONAL ACTION

The reception that Nixon's proposals received in the Congress indicated strong skepticism on Capitol Hill to grand proposals for change. However, congressional interest in the creation of a department of education was a long-standing and rather persistent phenomenon. According to a report by the Legislative Reference Service of the Library of Congress (now the Congressional Research Service), from 1908 through 1951 more than 50 bills were introduced in the U.S. Congress to establish a separate cabinet-level department of education.[42a]

During that time period, nearly 20 days of hearings were held on various forms of the legislation and at least six bills were actually ordered reported to either the House or the Senate. However, no action was taken that brought the proposal beyond the Committee stage. In 1955, during the 84th Congress, Congressman Frank Thompson (D-N.J.) introduced legislation to establish an independent Office of Education. In 1962, during the 87th Congress, Congressman Herman Toll (D-Pa.) introduced a bill to establish a department. Another bill was introduced the following year by Congressman John Fogarty (D-R.I.).

By 1965, when the White House was beginning to show some interest in the creation of an education department, the momentum in the Congress also began to intensify. Senator Abraham Ribicoff (D-Conn.), former Secretary of HEW, was a strong advocate of a department in the Senate; Congressman John Fogarty carried the ball in the House. In December 1964, immediately following the issue of the Price and Gardner Task Force reports, Congressman Fogarty wrote to Johnson, asking him to make a department of education a part of his education program. According to Redford and Blisset, Johnson found the suggestion to be timely and promised that it would be considered during the White House review of the executive branch structure.[43]

The congressional intensity was clearly mounting. Five bills were introduced during the 89th Congress in 1965-66; three in the 90th Congress; and six pieces of legislation were introduced in the 91st Congress of 1969-70. Fifteen pieces of legislation were introduced during the 92nd Congress; eleven during the 93rd Congress and eight bills were introduced during the 94th Congress. All in all, during the decade between 1965 and 1975, 48 bills were proposed to Congress for the creation of a department of education.

During that period, a number of fairly predictable congressional advocates emerged as the champions of the idea. Congressman Fogarty's advocacy was strong; he was joined in the House by Congresswoman Edith Green (D-Ore.), Congressman Joshua Eilberg (D-Pa.), and Congressman Albert Quie (R-Minn.); Quie was the only Republican among the mainstays of the House effort. Senator Ribicoff carried the ball in the Senate, often joined by former Vice President Hubert Humphrey in supporting the idea.

It has been observed that the two branches of government—the legislative and the executive—have very different perspectives on the reorganization issue. Members of Congress tend to protect their own personal power stakes inside the elaborate power balance of the congressional committee system. This behavior is based on strong symbiotic relationships with interest groups and program bureaucracies. Members want to protect the policy goals of their supporters or, at the least, avoid disruption to successful political coalitions.[44]

The highly fragmented structure of the legislative branch sets up a system in which it is rational for members of Congress to be skeptical of schemes that concentrate power, programs or funds into a single department. Rufus Miles has noted that the Congress usually wants to break up large departments and resists efforts to increase the size of departments they consider already too large. He noted that "it is entirely possible that one of the principal reasons Lyndon Johnson did nothing with the Heineman Commission recommendations for the substantial enlargement of HEW was that he understood, intuitively, this difference of perspective and did not wish to risk a confrontation with Congress over it."[45]

The differences between the legislative and executive perspectives have their origin in the most basic structure of the U.S. political system. The Constitution provides the president with "executive power." But the authority to structure the executive branch is not clearly lodged in the presidency. Rather, it is a function of the American separation of powers doctrine; a president's attempt to behave as a chief executive officer in matters of organizational structure is thwarted at multiple points by congressional authority.

Congress has the ability to create administrative structures; it has the authority to define their powers and determine their processes. It shares authority with the president in administrative matters; congressional budget and oversight powers are balanced against presidential authority to name executive officers and assure the execution of the laws.

It has been difficult for both parties to acknowledge the interdependence required to make the federal government operate. From 1918 (when Congress enacted the Overman Act, legislation that gave President Woodrow Wilson the authority to reorganize war powers functions) through the New Deal, Congress broadened the authority of the president to create new executive departments. In all cases, however, it was clear that the presidential executive reorganization authority was the prerogative of Congress to give ... and to take away.

The tension between the perceived power of the president to effect reorganization and the unwillingness of the Congress to give such power has been a characteristic set of conflicts in all contemporary reorganization efforts. This dynamic was an important element in the development of a separate department of education.

PUTTING THE ISSUE ON THE CARTER AGENDA

When the issue of the creation of a separate department took on a new life in the mid 1970s, Rufus Miles, former Director of Administration for HEW and a long time student of HEW structure examined the topic for the American Council on Education. Miles had been known as a long time advocate of a separate department of education and wrote the report with four audiences in mind: the next President of the United States; the Congress; educators; and the public administration community.[45] The report concluded that American education is faced with more difficult challenges than is generally realized; that the relationships between the federal government and the educational systems in the country were not in good repair; and that strong leadership to address these issues is "virtually impossible" within HEW. Miles's analysis argued that it was difficult to give adequate consideration to resources for education in the HEW arrangement because so much of the non-education HEW budget was made up of uncontrollable programs.

The report called for the creation of a cabinet-level Department of Education, presided over by a skilled leader with a broad background. In addition, Miles argued that such a department should not merely upgrade the HEW Education Division but should include programs beyond those found in the traditional educational institutions. He concluded that the Secretary of the new Department should be the leading federal official concerned with the intergovernmental and interagency coordination of education programs. According to Miles, the Department should be the focal point of federal concern for improvement of services as well as institutional functioning of educational systems.[46]

Arguments that were specific to the education policy area were also reinforced by new assessments of the role of the president. As the federal presence grew in the post New Deal days, the ad hoc nature of White House organization was under increasing criticism. Despite well entrenched institutions (such as the Office of Management and Budget, the National Security Council staff, and the Domestic Policy Staff), turf battles were common.[47] The permanent institutions within the White House—the "institutional core" of the presidency[48]—were overshadowed by highly personalized relationships, resulting in piecemeal and reactive responses and a lack of organization strategy.

This concern about the institutions within the presidency was of special concern to the advocates of a separate cabinet-level department of education because, as Thomas has noted, "the most important force for change in the educational policy process was unquestionably the Presidency."[49] It was not clear whether a department of education would assist those who were searching for a more coherent presidential role. But it was clear that a president could not play a passive role in that debate if one desired a less reactive presidency.

As the political campaign of 1976 began to take shape, Miles's assessment of the receptivity of the idea of an education department included an observation about congressional interest:

> The bills (that have been introduced during the 94th congress) vary greatly in content. ... Informal interviews with various committee staff members indicate that the majority of members do not have any strong feelings one way or another about a new Department of Education. They would be influenced by the strength of the arguments, pro and con, by the reactions of their constituencies, and, if the plan were recommended by a President of their party, by their general disposition to go along with his recommendations. If a plan were submitted that created a great deal of opposition on the part of their constituencies, it would obviously affect their votes. On balance, at the present time, the disposition would be in favor of a separate Department of Education if it were designed in such a way as to avoid treading on too many toes.[50]

In summary, the arguments that were given to justify the creation of a separate department of education were remarkably similar over the years. Five main arguments were used to support the pro-department position:

1. A department would give education increased status and visibility. The United States is the only civilized nation in the world without an education ministry or department. Without a departmental status, education was

viewed as inferior to other sectors in the society, such as agriculture, labor or business. From this perspective, simply the creation of a department—no matter in what form—would bring the education policy sector to an increased status in the American society.

2. A department would provide better access to the president in matters of education policy. It was difficult for education interest groups to push the executive branch toward a coherent position on budget or programmatic matters when it had to compete with other HEW concerns. From this perspective, the creation of a separate cabinet department would give both a chief executive as well as the education interest groups increased political advantage—in opportunity and access if not always in substance.

3. A department would allow for coordination of education programs that were scattered across agencies of the federal government. Coordination would provide the mechanism to reduce overlap and duplication. It would also allow for programmatic reforms through a more integrated organizational structure. It was assumed that more efficient administrative practices would result from these opportunities for coordination.

4. A department of education would serve as the vehicle for a president to develop a coherent set of policies in education. The scattered authorities made it difficult to have more than a reactive presidency. A department would make it easier to develop proactive policy strategies. From this perspective, it would be possible for a president and the executive branch to devise programs and policies that were more effective than efforts that had been undertaken before.

5. Cabinet-level status for education would provide the vehicle for the federal government to induce change in the highly decentralized educational system. Those who advocated change—of any sort—saw the creation of a department as an opportunity to turn those proposals into reality.

The arguments that were used against the creation of a separate department also tended to be relatively consistent over the years:

1. Creation of a department of education would signal a dramatic increase in the federal role in education. This would counter the traditional American belief in education as a state and local matter.

2. Creation of a separate department of education would politicize an important national issue and force education policy to be dominated by special interest groups with narrow and self interests in maintaining the status quo.

3. Finally, the creation of a department of education would disrupt the precarious balance that had been struck in the U.S. between private and parochial schools. A separate department would create a new set of legal and political issues regarding the separation of church and state and other civil rights and civil liberties concerns.

Both sets of arguments about the impact of the creation of a separate department were speculative. Political as well as "intellectual" arguments could be mustered on both sides of the issue. The gurus of the public administration field were full of speculations about the conditions necessary to assure the successful drive for the creation of a department.

For some, there was a set of ideal conditions to be met before a department would be created. Herbert Emmerich has written that "a program must be thoroughly accepted to win departmental status, and its components must have some plausible relationship to begin with. No matter how diverse the components, they must form a visible image when combined or related, so that a department head can be chosen who can identify with them and in turn be identified as their spokesman by the public, the press, and by Congress."[51] Although this line of argument in favor of a department of education was somewhat persuasive, neither they, nor the arguments that were used to support the creation of HEW, HUD, and the Department of Transportation, were noncontroversial in nature.

THE EDUCATION BUREAUCRACY: AS CARTER FOUND IT

At the time Carter assumed office, education policy making took place at three distinct bureaucratic levels within HEW. The multiplicity of actors reflected the historical shifts that had taken place over the years as programs were developed. The Office of Education, headed by a Commissioner of Education, appeared on an organization chart at the "bottom" of the heap (see Figure 1). In reality, however, this office predated the 1953 creation of a Department of Health, Education and Welfare. Most of the programs that had been enacted by the Congress gave the Commissioner the crucial administrative and management authority to run the programs.

On paper, the HEW departmental structure implied that the Secretary of HEW held the formal authority over the agencies and the bureaus subsumed within it. Despite attempts by previous HEW Secretaries to exert such authority (and to develop a complex set of staff offices to assist in those attempts), up to the mid 1970s the balance of power between the Office of the Commissioner and the Secretary's office was weighted against the Secretary. Each actor had a distinct set of staff capacities in legislation, public affairs, management and budget, and planning and evaluation.

To make matters even more complicated, in the mid 1960s another layer had been inserted between the Commissioner and the Secretary: the Assistant Secretary for Education. This office was given the major responsibility for coordination of all of the education activities within the Department as well as the administration of the National Center for Education Statistics, the National Institute of Education, and the Fund for the Improvement of Secondary Education (FIPSE). However, the power of that office depended

DUPLICATION OF FUNCTIONS IN HEW EDUCATION OFFICES
(CURRENT ORGANIZATIONAL STRUCTURE)

DEPARTMENT OF HEALTH, EDUCATION, AND WELFARE

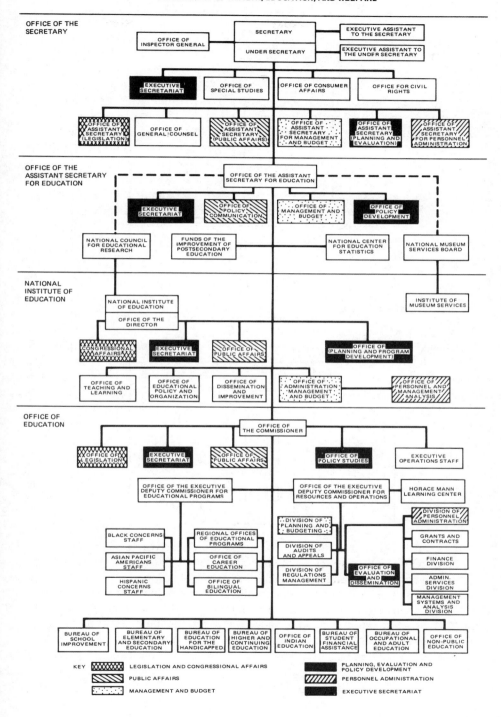

FIG 1   Duplication of Functions in HEW Education Offices (1977)

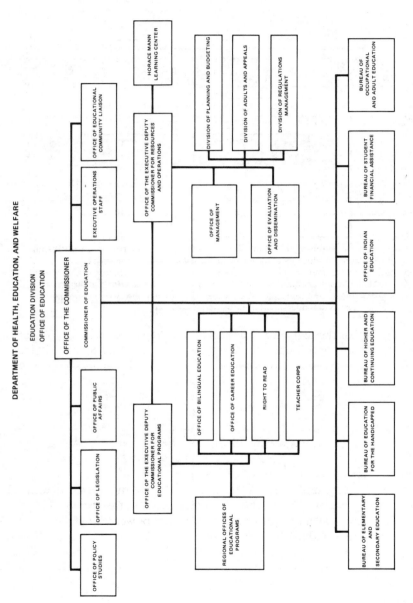

FIG 2   Education Division
Department of Health, Education, and Welfare, 1977

largely on the personal influence the particular Assistant Secretary had with the staff of the Secretary and Commissioner.

The Office of Education was able to play the internal bureaucratic game within HEW because of its ability to rely on its long time supporters on Capitol Hill and its strong array of interest groups that had a stake in the funding provided by programs administered by the Office. The major interest groups in the elementary and secondary education issue area were known as "the Big Six" (the National Education Association, the Council of Chief State School Officers, the American Association of School Administrators, the National Congress of Parents and Teachers, the National Association of State Boards of Education, and the National School Boards Association).

These groups played an important role in the development of federal education policy in the post World War II period. Students of education policy often characterize the array of groups and individuals involved in this area as highly elitist in composition. Thomas notes that

> although the system was not characterized by monolothic elite domination, it was highly elitist in composition and provided an inhospitable environment for substantial policy changes. This inhospitality occurred not because the proponents of radical change were excluded from participation—intellectual and academic critics were systematically sought out and consulted and unorganized interests received attention through surrogate representation—but because American politics affords a considerable advantage to defenders of the status quo.[52]

He argues that the sequence of approval steps required to move an idea to reality "affords a multiplicity of access points at which organized interests can modify or exercise a veto over policy change."[53] Thomas maintains that power, in this setting, is "exercised as much through the thwarting of initiatives and the frustration of action as through the positive mobilization of support from policy initiatives." Thus some of the more influential individuals in the policy process were "establishment groups—education professionals, state and local officials, and higher education administrators—who exercised power by virtue of the veto they shared with key individuals in Congress and the bureaucracy."[54]

Although many observers of federal policy-making acknowledge the importance of interest groups, they do not agree about the way in which one would measure, calculate, or characterize that power. Hugh Heclo has argued that our standard conceptions of power and control "are not very well-suited to the loose-jointed play of influence that is emerging in political administration." He believes that the concept of the iron triangle and subgovernments has pushed us to look for a few powerful individuals or interests who have developed autonomous relationships within the political environment. This search is misleading for it makes us "overlook the many whose webs of influence provoke and guide the exercise of power."[55]

Heclo calls these webs "issue networks." They

> comprise a large number of participants with quite variable degrees of mutual commitment or of dependence on others in their environment: in fact, it is almost impossible to say where a network leaves off and its environment begins. ... Participants move in and out of the networks constantly. Rather than groups united in dominance over a program, no one, as far as one can tell, is in control of the policies and issues. ... Network members reinforce each other's sense of issues as their interests, rather than (as standard political or economic models would have it) interests defining positions on issues.[56]

The fragmented nature of politics and the diversity of interest group demands are a major reason for the proliferation of federal education programs and the complexity of the organizational arrangements developed to implement them.

REORGANIZATION AND CHANGE

Change of all sorts has been a characteristic element in the American society of the twentieth century. Change affects all aspects of the society but is particularly problematic for the government. We are ambivalent as a nation about whether we want government to be involved at all in many areas of American life.

Reorganization—the restructuring of relationships between functions, individuals and organizations—has become one expression of the ambivalence of this society toward government. From time to time we decide that we want government to behave more like private business so we take the prescriptions for organizational change from the private sector and apply them to the business of government. At other times we decide that government should be responsive to values that make business-like processes inappropriate or that public organizations should have other—often symbolic—ways of communicating the importance of an issue or activity.

It has been observed that administrative reorganizations have become a characteristic feature of contemporary bureaucratic life.[57] Some of these changes in the structure of public organizations appear to be an organizational response to shifts—sometimes growth and sometimes decline—in the responsibilities of government. As the functions of government change, so too do its organizational forms. Agencies are added or subtracted. Agencies are merged or transferred. Relationships among or between agencies change. Whether by law, by executive decree, by legislative committee mandate, or by internal change, shifts occur in the structure of contemporary public agencies.

James March and Johan Olsen have commented that "the history of administrative reorganization in the twentieth century is a history of rhetoric."[58] They observe that reorganization rhetoric is of two types: the first is orthodox, administrative theory which values the efficiency and effectiveness of bureaucratic hierarchies. The second rhetoric is the rhetoric of *realpolitik* in which reorganization is viewed in terms of a political struggle among contending interests.

While reorganization is often tried, it is seldom successful in fully bringing about the intended changes. It is rare that either presidents or congresses (or, indeed, governors or state legislators) are able to meet their own objectives as they embark on major reorganization projects. Yet the ritual dance continues to occur. March and Olsen describe this dance as a "cycle of enthusiasm and disappointment."[59] Their review of major reorganization attempts in the federal government concludes that presidents begin reorganization studies at the beginning of their terms, "but by the time the studies are completed, they seem to have concluded that reorganization either will not solve their administrative problems or will not be worth the political costs." Why, then, do presidents and other key executives persist when the promise of successful reorganization is so limited?

Herbert Emmerich has argued that reorganization should be appreciated as far more than a process of streamlining. "Reorganization, I submit, ... affects the ability of heads of the executive branch to supervise and direct the manner in which the (executive) functions are exercised."[60]

Harold Seidman and Robert Gilmour suggest that this process continues to occur because "flawed and imperfect as they may be, the orthodox 'principles' remain the only simple, readily understood, and comprehensive set of guidelines available to the President and the Congress for resolving problems of executive branch structure."[61] These "principles", as Seidman and Gilmour call them, push a president to play the reorganization game— even if his political instincts tell him that the game cannot be won.

CONCLUSION

Past efforts to deal with the creation of a separate cabinet-level department of education caused a number of issues to surface that appeared to be a part of a "reality" of the proposed change. Reorganization decisions represent the outcome of political decisions about substantive policy as well as power relationships between the multiple actors with interests in education policy. While the Carter agenda was new, it was not played out on a clean slate; rather, the history of past reorganization and policy debates shaped the expectations held by various actors in the process about what should and could happen. If reorganization were to occur and become institutionalized, it had to challenge existing political relationships and replace them. The replacement process could not avoid a number of important, unresolved issues: What should be the federal role in education? How should the balance between the roles and powers of the executive and legislative branches be determined? How potent is reorganization as an instrument of change?

It was clear that one might anticipate different perceptions of these issues from various actors in the process. For example, elements within the Executive Office of the President—particularly the institutional role of the Office of Management and Budget (and its precursor the Bureau of the Budget) and the immediate office of the president—would see reorganization from different perspectives. Reorganization within the executive branch has been a key element in the struggle for presidential control. Both the Johnson and Nixon experiences indicated the complex interplay of bureaucratic and political battles around reorganization efforts. In addition, while presidents focus on their own reorganization agendas, they are sometimes preempted by the ongoing dynamic within the departments and agencies themselves; rarely do the agencies stand still waiting until the president's agenda for changes in organizational structure materializes.

Past efforts at reorganization also illustrate the ongoing conflict between the technical, analytical approach to the reorganization issue and those primarily motivated by political appraisals and calculations. Recent presidents had not had much luck in joining the two cultures—reorganization plans were either put on the shelf in the White House itself (for example, by Lyndon Johnson) or shelved by the Congress (for example, the Nixon Ash Council proposal). Politics, not analysis, seemed to be the predominant influence in the outcomes of those past efforts. Analysts had some difficulty determining what was "good management" and even more difficulty convincing anyone that their proposals would benefit those served by the programs affected.

Although there continued to be a significant element in the public administration community that was attracted to program decentralization, the weight of advice from the field of public administration emphasized the desirability of various forms of centralization and concentrated authority structures. The norms in the profession, thus, did not suggest that any of the major federal reorganization efforts of the past were totally inappropriate. Indeed, one could find a prestigious practitioner or student of public administration to defend any one of the approaches that came out of the very different White Houses in the period from 1964 to 1976.

The efforts at federal reorganization up to 1976 suggest several patterns of response within the White House. First, despite the initial concerns and pronouncements of a president, it is difficult for a reorganization effort to make strong demands on a president's time and attention. At least until the Carter administration, management was not viewed by recent presidents as the major business of the presidency. As March and Olsen noted, "while it is hard to predict what specific crisis, scandal, or war will divert presidents from the reorganization arena, it is easy to predict that something will."[62]

Second, most of the reorganization task forces or commissions operating during the post-1964 period were of the "blue ribbon" variety; that is, they drew on the status and expertise of individuals who were outside the day-to-day business of government. However, they attempted (not always successfully) to find a way to involve the permanent institutions of the presidency in their efforts.

Most of the actors in the education "establishment" did have a clear position about the creation of a department; however, they did not clearly focus on its impact on the federal role in education. Strong interest groups had been present in the program development of the 1960s and early 1970s. While they argued for an increased federal role in terms of the federal fiscal contribution, they did not define a meaning of such an increased federal role in terms of the substantive aspects of federal education policy. The creation of the department was an important program demand—but it was not easy to determine what would follow from such a decision.

NOTES

1. Norman C. Thomas, *Education in National Politics* (New York: David McKay Co., Inc., 1975), p. 19.
2. Ibid., p. 20.
3. Stephen K. Bailey and Edith K. Mosher, ESEA: *The Office of Education Administers A Law* (Syracuse, N.Y.: Syracuse University Press, 1968), p. 19.
4. Beryl A. Radin, *Implementation, Change and the Federal Bureaucracy* (New York: Teachers College Press, Columbia University, 1977).
5. Ibid.
6. Bailey and Mosher, pp. 210-211.
7. Eugene Eidenberg and Roy D. Morey, *An Act of Congress: The Legislative Process and the Making of Education Policy* (New York: W. W. Norton and Company, 1969), p. 215.
8. Thomas, p. 239.
9. Herbert Emmerich, *Federal Organization and Administrative Management* (Alabama: University of Alabama Press, 1971), p. 17.
10. Rufus E. Miles, Jr., *A Cabinet Department of Education: Analysis and Proposal* (Washington, D.C.: American Council on Education, 1976), pp. 39-40.
11. Bailey and Mosher, p. 227.
12. Ibid., pp. 227-228.
13. Ibid., p. 229.
14. Ibid.
15. Ibid.
16. Emmette S. Redford and Marlin Blissett, *Organizing the Executive Branch: The Johnson Presidency* (Chicago: The University of Chicago Press, 1981), p. 107.
17. Ibid.
18. Ibid., pp. 108-109.
19. Reported in Miles, p. 42.
20. Ibid.
21. Jane Stutsman, "Establishment of a Department of Education: A Current Policy Issue," Paper for Course in Policy Analysis, University of Southern California, Washington Public Affairs Center (December 1978).
22. Miles, p. 45.
23. Ibid.
24. Ibid.
25. Redford and Blisset, p. 160.
26. Ibid.

27. Bailey and Mosher, p. 78.
28. Reported in Redford and Blisset, pp. 160-161.
29. Bailey and Mosher, pp. 78-79.
30. Ibid., pp. 80-82.
31. Ibid., p. 90.
32. Miles, p. 47.
33. Ibid.
34. Redford and Blisset, p. 161.
35. Quoted in Redford and Blisset, p. 196.
36. Ibid.
37. Miles, p. 48.
38. Quoted in Redford and Blisset, p. 201.
39. Redford and Blisset, p. 203.
40. Miles, p. 49.
41. *Papers Relating to the President's Departmental Reorganization Program: A Reference Compilation* (Washington, D.C.: U.S. Government Printing Office, 1971).
42. Miles, p. 52.
42a. Education and Public Welfare Division, Congressional Research Service, *Proposals to the U.S. Congress for the Creation of a Department of Education and Related Bills Offering Similar Proposals* (Washington, D.C.: Library of Congress, June 1971).
43. Redford and Blisset, p. 160.
44. Patricia Rachal, *Federal Narcotics Enforcement: Reorganization and Reform* (Boston: Auburn House Publishing Co., 1982), p. 27.
45. Miles, p. 54.
46. Ibid., p. 6.
47. Roger B. Porter, *Presidential Decision Making: The Economic Policy Board* (Cambridge: Cambridge University Press, 1980), p. 25.
48. Redford and Blisset, p. 220.
49. Thomas, p. 234.
50. Miles, p. 137.
51. See Emmerich, p. 17.
52. Thomas, p. 232.
53. Ibid.
54. Ibid., p. 233.
55. Hugh Heclo, "Issue Networks and the Executive Establishment," in Anthony King, editor, *The New American Political System* (Washington, D.C.: American Enterprise Institute for Public Policy Research, 1979), p. 102.
56. Ibid.
57. James G. March and Johan P. Olsen, "Organizing Political Life: What Administrative Reorganization Tells Us About Government," *American Political Science Review* No. 77 (1983), p. 281.
58. Ibid., p. 282.
59. Ibid., p. 284.
60. Emmerich, p. 8.
61. Harold Seidman and Robert Gilmour, *Politics, Position, and Power,* Fourth Edition (New York: Oxford University Press, 1986), p. 9.
62. March and Olsen, p. 286.

Chapter 3 JIMMY CARTER: WHO WAS THAT MAN?

Most students of the presidency acknowledge that the unique characteristics of the individual in the White House make a great deal of difference in the way that policy—particularly reorganization policy—is conceptualized and constructed. Jimmy Carter's personal interests in both education policy and government management were essential ingredients in the development of the Education Department strategy.

Carter saw himself as an individual concerned about education. In his autobiography, *Keeping Faith*, he described his political evolution as a process driven by an interest in education. In both the County Board of Education and in the Georgia Senate, "I wanted to help shape government policy so that black and white children would not continue to suffer from it. ... As governor, my interest in education continued unabated."[1]

Education figured prominently in Carter's gubernatorial platform: he promised to give statewide kindergartens priority attention; he pushed for remedial reading courses; he advocated statewide testing of 11th grade students to all the school systems within the state; and he pledged to provide additional state funds to children with special needs within Georgia. Carter's efforts related to education met with significant success during his last two years as governor. Funds were increased in a number of education program areas. State responsibilities were expanded and efforts were made to reduce the burden on local communities for special needs. Carter served as an active member of a commission that studied long term educational needs for the state and the recommendations made by the group found their way into new legislative initiatives.

Despite his commitment to education, Carter's advocacy of programs did not always strike a responsive note within the state bureaucracy. The chief state school officer, Superintendent Jack Nix, already had a strong and independent view on these issues. Nix was also an elected official and reportedly objected to what he viewed as Carter's usurpation of his authority in the education field.[2] It was observed that Carter wanted decisions to be made through analysis and long-range planning while Nix felt that improvements would develop in the system if the quality of teachers improved.[3]

Carter found that it was frustrating to deal with the separate education authority base; Nix played up the separation, making it difficult for Carter staff to get information about education issues. He instituted a system by which any request for information by the governor's staff had to originate from the governor himself.

Although Carter's education record in Georgia is strong, it is ironic that he is known less for those issues than for an interest in government reorganization. The irony is particularly telling because Carter did not run on a platform that emphasized government reorganization. Indeed, Carter's Republican opponent, Hal Suit, ran on a platform that focused on government reorganization as a major issue. In his inaugural address, Carter advocated greater efficiency in state government.

Once in office, Carter did initiate a reorganization effort. He sought reorganization authority from the legislature, introducing a bill in the House on the first day of the General Assembly, even before his State of the State address was given. He tried to limit the legislative role in the reorganization to a reverse veto, placing the operative authority for the organizational changes in the office of the governor. With the assistance of some key legislative supporters, a reorganization authority bill was passed. However, it contained a number of compromises that Carter had initially opposed: the time limit for a legislative veto was extended and powers were given to elected constitutional officers to veto elements of reorganization plans.

The Carter reorganization team in Georgia was made up of more than 100 individuals, most of whom were bright, young executives and administrators from state agencies, business, and industry. The team was further subdivided into small working groups, one of which was dedicated to education. A Reorganization Executive Committee served as the coordinating body for the activity. According to some reports, Carter himself claimed to have spent more than 20% of his time during his first year in office on reorganization activities.

Interestingly, one of the recommendations made by the group was a call for the creation of a Department of Human Resources—a broad based umbrella agency that would include education as well as health and welfare programs. The effect of that proposal would be to abolish the elected office of the state school superintendent. Carter organized a grass roots public relations campaign to gain support for the proposal within the state. As would be expected, political opposition to the moves mounted as specific elements in the plan were unfolded.

Although much of the Carter proposal passed in the House, it had a much tougher ride through the Senate. All of the proposals to change functions and structure affecting constitutional offices—including the state superintendent of schools—were defeated. The result of the effort was a reduction of state budgeted agencies from 65 to 20. Students of the Carter presidency have speculated about the Georgian's pattern of behavior when he was in the state office and extrapolated to his predilections as president. In his study of the Carter term in Georgia, Gary Fink has observed:

> More than anything else, the combination of Jimmy Carter's reform psychology and, closely related, his fundamental abhorrence to the uniquely American practice of legislative logrolling produced his unorthodox legislative style and, in turn, provoked his volatile relationship with the more traditional politicians in the Georgia General Assembly. The planner-engineer mentality Carter brought into government bred an organic view of reform. He envisioned a major reform program as an interrelated, mutually dependent series of proposals. A significant alteration in one area would have repercussions in other areas that could ultimately convert a logically developed reform program into an irrational patchwork of unrelated or even contradictory changes. That is not to say that Carter lacked flexibility or a willingness to compromise but rather that his conception of the nature of reform restricted the areas in which he found it possible to compromise. When a proposed change threatened the logical construct of a program or violated established policy, his resistance to change grew along with his reputation for stubbornness and obstinacy.[4]

While the reorganization effort clearly changed the governor's control over executive departments, it was not clear whether the organizational changes led to substantive impacts on the delivery of state services. The drive to get the legislation passed was extremely acrimonious and created a number of political problems for the governor and his supporters. One analyst of the effort has commented:

> Ultimately, after five years of operation, the success and failure of the various aspects of Carter's reorganization seem to have depended not on the expertise of Carter's advisers, the abolition of bureaucratic red-tape, or even the soundness of the basic ideas behind reorganization. Instead, those areas and aspects of Georgia's state government which have operated effectively before reorganization, such as the natural resource agencies, have continued to operate well after reorganization.[5]

CARTER AS A CANDIDATE

Jimmy Carter had owed his success as a Georgia politician to his ability to read and respond to a changing political environment. Carter's victory in Georgia was possible because the state was changing; the old one-party control had been broken, making room for the new type of politician who was both pragmatic and ideologically moderate.

Changes, also, had occurred in the structure and organization of the national Democratic Party. The base for Carter's successful campaign for the presidency was not the traditional party machine but, rather, a widespread grass roots organization of politically active people. Carter's candidacy was made possible by the changes in the party's presidential nominating process— changes instituted after 1968 to meet complaints that the party failed to choose candidates who represented the rank and file Democratic activist. Because the reforms were still relatively new within the party, Carter was able to take advantage of the still malleable nature of the new structures and rules.

The reforms that were instituted under pressure from the liberal wing of the party made primary elections the major vehicle to the candidacy. The number of state primaries grew from 16 in the mid 1960s to 35 in 1976. The proportion of delegates to the national convention that were elected at state primaries increased from one third of the participants to almo t three-quarters of the delegates.[6]

Single-issue organizations and temporary organizations developed for individual candidates were established at the grass roots and provided the structure for a candidate to win the nomination. The system was based on proportional representation; therefore winning a majority of delegates at local conventions provided a candidate with a majority at each higher level.

Carter's campaign style in Georgia emphasized personal contact with ordinary citizens. His campaign for the presidency, it has been argued, began in 1971. He was in the running for the 1972 vice presidential nomination and was elected to be the chairman of the Democratic Campaign Committee for the 1974 congressional election.[7] That position gave him national exposure and provided him with personal contacts with grass roots party activists across the country.

One observer has commented that "Carter, the National Education Association, and the Democratic Party's new rules were well suited to one another."[8] As Carter became more visible in his candidacy, the NEA did appear to be a natural base of support. By the 1976 campaign, the NEA had nearly 2,000,000 members across the nation. Its activist and articulate membership was supported by more than 300 full time and over 1,000 part time organizers outside of Washington, a staff of 1,000 in Washington, good connections with other large unions, and long experience of legislative lobbying.[9] Unlike many other organizations which evaporated when an election was over, the NEA was not going to disappear after the first Tuesday in November.

The changes in the campaign finance laws allowing the organization of political action committees gave the NEA a pathway into electoral politics. The NEA Political Action Committee was formed in 1972 to work for candidates who would support education issues. NEA members were trained in political organizing workshops and the standard campaign organization cadre was established.

While the NEA worked on behalf of congressional candidates, it began to focus for the first time on the Democratic presidential race. In 1975, the NEA, the United Automobile Workers and several other trade unions formed a coalition to maximize the influence of its membership and programs. By the time that the 1976 Democratic convention was held, about 400 individuals (out of 3,000 delegates) were elected with the support of the coalition.

By the end of the primaries in June, the majority of the delegates in that coalition were committed to Carter; the bulk of those delegates were NEA members. When the convention met in July, NEA members provided Carter with a disciplined bloc of 172 votes.[10]

It was no secret to any candidate that the NEA's political agenda gave prominence to the creation of a department of education. In October 1975, the NEA issued a statement entitled "Needed: A Cabinet Department of Education." As he wooed the NEA, Carter acknowledged the importance of that issue. In a February 1976 statement, he noted:

> I will not hesitate to propose and support the following basic and controversial changes: The creation of a separate Department of Education. Generally, I am opposed to the proliferation of federal agencies ... But a Department of Education would consolidate the grant programs, job training, early childhood education, literacy training, and many other functions currently scattered throughout the government. The result would be a stronger voice for education at the federal level.[11]

Even earlier, in October 1975, Carter gave an interview to Iowa teachers after straw polls indicated that he had strength in that state: "The only department I would consider creating would be a separate Department of Education. I spelled out this position when I met with the leadership council of the NEA a year ago and I, just within the last two weeks, issued a press release that I would favor the establishment of a separate Department of Education."[12]

It is difficult to calculate the level of intensity aroused by this issue within the Carter campaign. Some have noted that the support for the issue was, from the beginning, a mile wide and an inch deep. Others have also noted that Carter's personal ambivalence about politics makes it difficult to comprehend a political promise such as this one—a promise that could be viewed as a deliberate ploy to obtain the support of the powerful NEA. Both Carter and the NEA were new to 'hardball' national politics; both can be seen to have used the other as the campaign developed.

The man who became Carter's running mate, Walter Mondale, was, however, no stranger to national politics or to the NEA. Mondale had close connections with the NEA; indeed, his brother was an NEA official in the midwest.[13] Addressing the national convention of the NEA before the Democratic Convention, Senator Mondale also sounded the clarion call for a department: "Now there is much more that we need to do. The present structure of education at the federal level is a disgrace and the NEA knows it. The time has long since past when we should create a new department called the Department of Education under a Secretary of Education."[14]

Mondale's selection as vice president was strongly supported by the NEA and other parts of organized labor. When he was named to be Carter's running mate, it appeared that the NEA was about to mount a strong campaign. And it did. The organization, for the first time in its 119-year history, endorsed a presidential candidate. The NEA's support is believed to have been crucial to Carter's election victory. Indeed, as estimated by NEA staff, the organization spent more than $400,000 on Carter's campaign.

After the election, it was reported that Carter made a personal thank-you call to John Ryor, the President of the NEA. He is alleged to have said that "the massive support from teachers was crucial to our winning. We turned to the NEA for help and it delivered nationwide." According to its detractors, the organization had moved from a "staid coffee and doughnuts professional association" to a militant organization taken over by a "Young Turk" faction among the membership, pushing the organization into a disruptive trade union posture.[15]

But whatever the cause, when Carter assumed the presidency it appeared that the NEA—and its political agenda—had to be taken seriously by the new administration. There was no doubt that Carter and his closest associates felt they owed a debt to the NEA.

TRANSITION PLANNING

At the same time that the Carter campaign staff was intensely involved in the political game of electioneering, a second team of Carter advisers was at work studying what President Carter should do after Inauguration Day the following January. A team of ten issues coordinators was named to parallel the subject areas of the campaign issue team. The effort was spearheaded by Atlanta attorney Jack Watson, a long time Carter supporter. Watson described the operation as an attempt "to take the most important policy issues and to do the more in-depth work on them which will enable (Carter) to move into the presidency with some bold initiatives."[16]

Operating out of an Atlanta office, rather than the traditional Washington base, a small transition staff was attempting to examine the immediate mechanics of a changeover and the quick staffing of key positions. The group was also conscious that 147 pieces of federal legislation were expiring in 1977 and that there was thus the need for a new administration to introduce some fresh perspective on these issues.

Working closely with the campaign issues staff, the transition group gave significant attention to the reorganization issues that were a part of the campaign. While cagey about specific Carter initiatives, Watson commented in October 1976 that he was convinced that Carter would move early on a "multi front basis" to reorganize, believing that the rigidly fixed operations of bureaucracy could be modified by executive directive. Only then, commented Watson, would Carter determine what kind of reorganization authority he would request of Congress.[17]

Despite Carter's clarion call for a new department of education in the campaign, some of the advisers to the transition were less sanguine than was the candidate about the appropriateness of the structural strategy for changing the federal education policy role. Hendrik D. Gideonese, Dean of the College of Education and Home Economics of the University of Cincinnati, detailed an alternative position to planners of a Carter presidency via a memorandum in September 1976. Gideonese argued that the "roots of the anger, anxiety, and disappointment in the federal Government lie deeper than organizational confusion and outmoded budgetary techniques."[18] He suggested an alternative way to think about the government, deemphasizing questions of structure and overlap and focusing instead on the more systemic nature of the responsibilities and role of the federal bureaucracy. Up to the point of the election, however, it appeared that arguments such as these fell on unreceptive ears.

The candidate, Carter, did give some indication of how he would function as a decision-maker:

> Exact procedure is derived to some degree from my scientific or engineering background—I like to study first all the efforts that have been made historically toward the same goal, to bring together advice or ideas from as wide or divergent points of view as possible, to assimilate them personally or with a small staff, to assess the quality of the points of view and identify the source of those proposals and, if I think the source is worthy, then to include that person or entity into a group I then call in to help me personally to discuss the matter in some depth. Then I make a general decision about what should be done involving time schedules, necessity for legislation, executive acts, publicity to be focused on the issue. Then I like to assign task forces to work on different aspects of the problem, and I like to be personally involved so that I can know the thought processes that go into the final decisions and also so that I can be a spokesman, without prompting, when I take my case to the people, the legislature or Congress.[19]

From these remarks, it appeared that Jimmy Carter, as president, was departing from traditional Washington behavior not only in the style of the campaign he had waged, but also in terms of the procedures and style of governance. In an article written just after Carter was elected, Jack Knott and Aaron Wildavsky commented that "if there is a danger for President Carter, it is not that he will support unpopular *policies*, but that he will persevere with inappropriate *procedures*."[20] They noted that in contrast to other candidates, Carter had articulated principles for making public policy that comprised a coherent philosophy of governance. Those principles, as they described them, involved simplicity, elimination of duplication, uniformity, and comprehensiveness.[21]

Knott and Wildavsky cautioned:

> We are concerned that President Carter will pursue procedures regardless of their efficacy, and that he will regard opposition to his procedural prescriptions as, if not exactly the work of the devil, at least irrational, a product of ignorance and special interests, not subject to the usual rules of evidence. The comprehensive, scientific approach, which is supposed to work to promote harmony, has as a basic assumption the lack of conflict. If agreement does not result from openness, if seeming support for long-range goals breaks down under short-range pressures, will President Carter be able to tolerate the frustration?
>
> His own recipe for controlling conflict is to make it boil over: comprehensive change, in his view, forces opposing interests into public debate where Presidents can confront and overcome them. But how often can this be done? Agitating some of the interests some of the time is not the same as upsetting most of them most of the time.

Interests are people, lots of people who depend on government. If he can space his appeals out so that he is not fighting on every front at once, he may have a chance; but if he has to fight simultaneously on many fronts, he (and the nation with him) may be in for a difficult time.[22]

This analysis turned out to be prophetic.

ASSUMING THE PRESIDENCY

The November election results meant that Jimmy Carter, the man who had campaigned for the presidency as the quintessential outsider, was now about to become the ultimate Washington insider—the President of the United States. Just a week after the election, the *National Journal* reported that "the relationship between Carter and Congress is much different now than most politicians had expected just a few months ago, when Democrats of all persuasions flocked to Jimmy Carter as their political messiah. There were few states and districts in which Carter did not appear to be an asset to congressional candidates, and his staff was besieged with requests for help. But, as his big lead disappeared, so did his coattails. ... As one House aide said, 'Congress doesn't owe Jimmy Carter anything.'"[23]

Carter himself acknowledged the importance of moving to forge good ties with Capitol Hill. In his memoirs, *Keeping Faith*, he notes that "except, perhaps, for a brief handshake at a reception, I did not know most of the ... members (of Congress) at all, and I was eager to meet them. They were even more curious about me."[24] Carter met with Democratic congressional leaders just two weeks after the election and, during the transition months, made a number of trips to Washington to meet with House and Senate members. "Some of the Democratic leaders," wrote Carter, "promised me full support in implementing my general platform, but as we began to discuss the hard details, the support often evaporated. I had to seek votes wherever they could be found."[25]

A major element of Carter's education to the Washington mode of operation took place around the reorganization issue. Carter's strategy was to repeat the agenda he had pursued in Georgia. As he noted, "it is well known that our first major test in Congress would come on a bill authorizing the President to address the problem of the federal bureaucracy—its complexity, its remoteness when people needed help, its intrusiveness when they wanted to be left alone, and its excessive regulation of the major industries to the detriment of consumers."[26] Carter viewed his Georgia reorganization effort as a major achievement and said that he was "eager to make similar changes in the federal government."[27]

Thus, one of the first things he sought was a law giving him the authority to submit reorganization plans to Congress and have them become effective automatically if they were not rejected by either the House or the Senate within a certain period of time.[28] As he later recalled, "on my first trip to Washington after the election, I met with both (Congressman Jack) Brooks and (Senator Abraham) Ribicoff to explain how important I considered the authorization." Carter was warned by his advisers that it would be politically costly—and perhaps not substantively worth it—to push for the reorganization effort. But he pursued the goal. In a post-election conversation with Jack Brooks, he emphasized that reorganization was an important campaign promise: "Mr Chairman, this is something I have promised the American people. I've got to have it, and I need your help."[29]

Carter's strategy was viewed as frontal and bold. The *National Journal* reported that Joe Mitchell, Carter's last executive assistant in Georgia, commented that the president-elect "learned in Georgia that because many times things you propose will step on special interests, you've got to move totally, boldly."[30] However, the *National Journal* noted that in his zeal to reorganize the federal government "he threatens to step on the toes of the very Members of Congress whose support he will need in other areas. Given his limited mandate, Carter may be forced to retreat a few steps on this plan, and there is already discussion among people in Congress that his first steps on government reorganization may not be as bold as he indicated during the campaign."[31]

As the Carter staff shifted its center from a campaign staff with a somewhat peripheral transition group to a full-blown transition effort, campaign promises took on new meaning. New staff and advice-givers appeared, now working to focus on very specific agencies and departments as Inauguration Day approached. In addition, names of prospective cabinet officials began to surface, and transition issues and executive agency agendas moved from abstract ideas to programs and policies to be implemented by a new team.

Transition groups were now organized around specific departments; the HEW team was headed by New York psychiatrist, Dr June Christmas. Among those who assisted with the HEW assignment was Dr Harry Weiner, of the Department of Urban and Policy Affairs at the State University of New York at Stony Brook. Weiner, an individual who was neither part of the political or education establishment, journeyed to Washington several days a week from election day to the inauguration and was given the assignment to draft a paper on the topic: "Should there be a department of education?" Although the campaign rhetoric suggested that the question had already been answered in the affirmative, there were some members of the campaign staff who had doubts about the desirability of creating such a structure. Weiner interviewed people, did research and wrote a paper that urged President-elect Carter NOT to establish a new department. The argument put forward in the paper focused on the probability that an Education Secretary could not command a president's attention. It argued that a powerful HEW secretary was more effective for education than a weak education secretary; that it was better to have a fraction of the HEW Secretary's time than a second-rank Secretary of Education.

Although the paper was circulated, little attention was paid to its argument. The campaign promise was taken seriously by the transition group. However, the presence of such a document was noted in the education press. Just three days before the inauguration, *The Chronicle of Higher Education* reported that the creation of a separate cabinet-level Department of Education "was not among the top priorities listed by his transition staff." But the Carter staff argued that "absolutely nothing has been decided. ... There is no time-table set for making any decision."[32]

The designation of former Johnson aide, Joseph A. Califano, Jr. to be the Secretary of HEW appeared to signal some doubt over the fulfillment of the Department of Education campaign promise. Califano was thought to be an advocate of the super-department idea of upgrading the position of education in the bureaucracy without going all the way to creating a separate cabinet-level department.

As Carter prepared to move to the White House, it appeared that there was momentum to make good the campaign promise. Some individuals within the public administration community voiced skepticism about a move to further fragment the federal bureaucracy. While education advocates were pushing hard for the structural reorganization, they did not lose sight of the policy problems facing the education sector as Carter began his presidency. There appeared to be six substantive problems that became a part of the Carter administration's rhetoric and reflected its assumptions about the condition of American education; these assumptions played a key role in the reorganization effort.

1. *Quality of Education*. Declining test scores, high illiteracy rates, persistent drop out rates, inadequate writing skills seemed, to many, to suggest that the performance of the American educational system fell far short of the desired levels of achievement.

2. *Equality of Education*. Large portions of the student population in the country were under-served or unserved, including the under-employed, unemployed, preschoolers, and others in special racial or ethnic groups. While social, economic, and cultural deprivation was pervasive in the society, it was the education sector that had to deal with the effects of various forms of segregation and discrimination.

3. *Pervasive Economic Changes*. There were signals that the public sector in general—including education—was beginning to have to confront the slowdown in the country's economic growth. Cutbacks were anticipated in all levels of educational institutions, in private as well as public schools.

4. *Youth Unemployment and Alienation*. The unemployment rate for 18- to 24-year olds was four times greater for those who dropped out of high school than for those who graduated. The issue was becoming more pervasive

particularly in large urban centers and was incurring both economic and social costs on those communities.

5. *Changing Public Feelings about Education.* The American people were beginning to express a sense of uncertainty about their public schools. A public opinion poll in 1976 reported that a clear majority of adults in this country believed that the quality of education received by children had declined. While school bond issues did continue to receive support, the willingness of voters to approve school bonds was decreasing dramatically.[33]

6. *Doubts about the Effectiveness of Federal Programs.* After a decade of increased funding through the federal government, there appeared to be a growing skepticism that increased dollars to state and local education agencies would improve the quality of schools.

All of these problems reflected the Carter administration's predilection for change in the federal role in education within the U.S.[34]

GOALS FOR CREATING A NEW DEPARTMENT

As Carter prepared to assume the presidency, five general concerns or goals appeared to be associated with the proposal for a new department, representing the range of actors and issues at hand at that time. These goals, which shaped the organizational alternatives considered and influenced the decisions to be made, were: *symbolic status, political advantage, efficiency, effectiveness,* and *change.* Each of these goals, it should be noted, reflected the arguments that had been made in favor of a new department for many years.

1. *Symbolic Status.* The problem which advocates of symbolic status addressed was simple: the United States is the only major nation in the world that does not have an education ministry or department. Perhaps more important to them was that failure to have a top-level agency for education issues indicated that education did not have a status equal to other service sectors in society, such as agriculture, labor, and business. Thus the goal for these advocates was clearcut: get a cabinet-level department. Many advocates of this goal believed that higher status, visibility, and a place at the cabinet table would translate into increased federal funding for education.

2. *Political Advantage.* Advocates of reorganization of the federal education enterprise frequently spoke in terms of partisan and personal political advantage. These advocates included the White House (as it prepared to deal with Congress and interest groups); Congress (as members dealt with interest groups); interest groups (as they dealt with both the White House and Congress); and career bureaucrats. The decision to create a department, the programs it would encompass, and its internal structure affected members of Congress whose support was needed on this, and even more important, on other issues on the president's agenda.

3. *Efficiency*. Arguments based on perceived administrative efficiency are the most common reasons given for administrative reorganization of any type. In the case of the federal education bureaucracy, the classic public administration diagnosis of problems was forthcoming—overlap and duplication were pervasive in the federal education enterprise. The product of a more efficient system was to be savings to the taxpayer or the delivery of more service for the same amount of money. Efficiency, it was argued, would also result in less delay in the preparation of regulations, legislation, budgets and other bureaucratic processes. This goal focused only on the process of the agencies—not on their substantive output.

4. *Effectiveness*. The effectiveness arguments used to support the creation of a separate Department of Education concentrated on the improvement of the quality of educational services within the existing distribution of responsibilities and structure of American education. The problem to be dealt with by such a department was fairly straightforward: federal programs have failed to solve the problems to which they were addressed, such as rectifying inequalities in educational opportunity and profiting from research and development resources to improve the quality of education. The effectiveness goal was concerned with using the new department as a way to take programs that were already in place and make them work "better". This focused attention on particular programmatic reforms that would be made possible by better and more integrated organizational structures. This approach stressed outcomes of bureaucratic processes but its advocates were concerned only about marginal and incremental changes.

5. *Change American Education*. The effectiveness and change goals overlap. But while the proponents of the effectiveness goal saw the problem in terms of program improvement, the proponents of the change goal argued for the need to alter fundamentally the way educational issues were perceived and the role of the federal government in inducing change. They saw the problem not only in programmatic deficiencies, but emphasized the professional monopoly in the field. This monopoly—characterized by school administrators and teachers—dominated education policies at all levels and resisted changes to the system. As a result, it was argued that coherent federal policies could not develop. A separate education department would provide the structure to allow these changes to be made.

CONCLUSION

The agenda setting stage of the department was, thus, a highly political stage in which a wide array of actors—constrained only by their resources and influence—alleged that the department was in the public interest and should, therefore, be created. In this case, the actors were found in the

Congress, in the interest group arena (particularly the NEA), and in the road to the presidency itself via the presidential campaign.

It was the campaign, however, that provided the venue for the movement of the issue from a perennially proposed idea to a serious policy issue. The changes that had occurred within the NEA, moving it to an active political role, merged with Carter's political ambitions. The large membership of the organization plus its financial resources was extremely important and appropriate to Carter's campaign strategy. In the campaign setting the differences that the NEA might have with other supporters in the Democratic Party (particularly the American Federation of Teachers) were not important. In addition, Carter was able to present the idea of a separate education department in the appropriate rhetoric of a campaign. As he described the proposal to a general public, it was tied to a concern within the American populace about children and the nation's future. Thus, though it could be viewed as a "special interest" promise to the NEA, Carter could present it as an effective "public interest" concern.

As Brewer and deLeon describe the first stage of the process (which they call policy initiation), the stage begins

> when a potential problem (which could just as well be an opportunity) is first sensed, i.e. problem recognition or identification. Once a problem is recognized, many possible means to alleviate, mitigate, or resolve it may be explored quickly and tentatively. In this early and most creative phase, one comes to expect numerous, ill-defined, and inappropriate formulations. Indeed, as much as casting about for answers, this phase emphasizes efforts to define (or redefine) the problem, to get a sense of it in terms of its possible importance and whether it merits further time, attention, and resources. Many problems will not or will languish in the initiation state awaiting additional and clarifying information. Initiation also refers to the innovative tasks of conceptualizing and sketching out the rough outlines of a problem, collecting the information necessary to lay out a range of possible responses, and then beginning to specify potential policy choices within that range.[35]

When Carter was sworn in as President on January 20, 1977, the process had begun. The campaign had provided the first answer to the question: should there be a department of education? Although others (including a few individuals in the transition staffs) remained skeptical about the answer given through the political campaign, once in office the campaign promise had its own momentum. The efforts on the outside—particularly the Rufus Miles report for the American Council on Education—indicated that the issue was being explored in other than campaign settings. Carter's personal interest in reorganization as a generic issue provided yet another form of support for the idea. And the substantive problems that faced the education field suggested that the issue could be viewed as more than a response to a political constituency. It did, indeed, appear to be an idea whose time had come.

At the same time, however, there were indications that the issue was not as simple as the campaign had suggested. The goals associated with the proposal were multiple and often conflicting once they were explicated beyond their rhetorical dimensions. Carter, himself, embodied somewhat problematic views about reorganization. While effective as a campaign strategy, his stance as an outsider posed problems when a president had to work out ways of influencing the bureaucracy as well as the relevant interest groups. Even the analysts within the transition group were not in agreement about the wisdom of the idea once the vote-getting strategy of the campaign was over.

The fragmentation of the presidency was indicated in the competition between the campaign staff and the transition group and, subsequently, by what seemed to be different perceptions about the issue involving the transition group and the newly appointed Secretary of the Department of Health, Education and Welfare. The vice president's role was important in terms of the campaign relationships with NEA; it was not clear how he might deal with this issue as the administration progressed.

NOTES

1. Jimmy Carter, *Keeping Faith: Memoirs of a President* (New York: Bantam Books, 1982), p. 75.
2. Gary M. Fink, *Prelude to the Presidency* (Westport, Conn.: Greenwood Press, 1980), p. 94.
3. Elizabeth Gray Bowden, *The Gubernatorial Administration of Jimmy Carter*, MA Thesis (University of Georgia, 1980), p. 57.
4. Fink, p. 166.
5. Bowden, pp. 92-93.
6. David Stephens, "President Carter, the Congress and the NEA: Creating the Department of Education," *Political Science Quarterly*, Vol. 98, No. 4 (Winter 1983-84), p. 642.
7. Ibid., p. 643.
8. Ibid.
9. Ibid.
10. Ibid., p. 644.
11. Jimmy Carter, "Statement to the National Education Association," (October 1975), from *Some Selected Statements by President Jimmy Carter Concerning the Creation of a Separate Cabinet-level Department of Education*, 1975-79.
12. Jimmy Carter, "Interview with the Iowa Teachers," (Waterloo, Iowa, November 1975).
13. Stephens, p. 644.
14. Walter Mondale, "Speech to the NEA Convention," (June 26, 1976).
15. Eugene H. Methvin, "The NEA: A Washington Lobby Run Rampant," *Readers Digest* (November 1978), p. 98.
16. *National Journal* (August 21, 1976), p. 1166.
17. Dom Bonafede, "Carter Staff is Getting Itchy to Make the Move to Washington," *National Journal* (October 30, 1976), p. 1547.
18. Hendrik D. Gideonese, Memorandum to Planners for a Carter Presidency, "Re: Executive Summary—Improving the Federal Establishment: Crucial Supplements to Reorganization," (September 22, 1976).
19. *National Journal*, quoted in Lawrence E. Lynn and David deF. Whitman, *The President as Policymaker: Jimmy Carter and Welfare Reform* (Philadelphia: Temple University Press, 1981), p. 262.
20. Jack Knott and Aaron Wildavsky, "Jimmy Carter's Theory of Governing," *Wilson Quarterly* (Winter 1977), p. 49.

21. Ibid., p. 51.
22. Ibid., pp. 62-63.
23. Daniel J. Balz, "Carter's Honeymoon on the Hill—How Long Can it Last?", *National Journal* (November 13, 1977), p. 1618.
24. Jimmy Carter, *Keeping Faith: Memoirs of a President*, p. 67.
25. Ibid., p. 69.
26. Ibid.
27. Ibid.
28. Ibid., p. 70.
29. Ibid.
30. Balz, p. 1620.
31. Ibid.
32. Karen J. Winkler, "Separate Department of Education Not Among Carter's Top Priorities," *Chronicle of Higher Education* (January 17, 1977), p. 13.
33. President's Reorganization Project, Office of Management and Budget, undated document.
34. President's Reorganization Project, Office of Management and Budget, "Memorandum to Patricia Gwaltney," (July 15, 1977).
35. Gary D. Brewer and Peter deLeon, *The Foundations of Policy Analysis* (Homewood, Illinois: Dorsey Press, 1983), p. 18.

Chapter 4   GETTING THE BALL ROLLING

As Jimmy Carter moved into the White House in January 1977, his campaign promise was subject to a new set of organizational and political realities. The proposal for the creation of a department was wrapped in a general reorganization strategy—a strategy that required that the president receive formal reorganization authority through congressional action and, following that, structure a reorganization activity within the executive branch. This chapter details those activities as well as the preliminary array of options through November 1977, when Carter made the first formal decision as president about what he would do about a new department.

AUTHORITY TO ACT

From 1949 to 1973, succeeding presidents were given the authority by Congress to reshuffle the federal bureaucracy within specific limitations. The authority applied below the level of cabinet departments and gave presidents the power to create independent agencies (such as the Environmental Protection Agency established in 1970) and to move bureaus in and out of departments (such as the creation of the National Oceanic and Atmospheric Administration, also in 1970). Unless vetoed by either the House or the Senate, reorganization plans devised by the president would become automatically effective within 60 days. By 1973, however, as Congress attempted to curb some of the powers that it associated with an "Imperial Presidency," this authority was allowed to expire.

In a December press conference, before he assumed the presidency, Jimmy Carter announced that he would request authority similar to that given to Richard Nixon. Like previous presidents, Carter's request for authority recognized the delicate balance between the Executive and the Congress on matters of reorganization. Within the legislation specifying the formal authority, a president would need congressional action every time even the smallest change was proposed in executive branch organization.

The legislation that was introduced on January 4, 1977—more than two weeks before Carter was sworn in as president—provided what had come to be viewed as relatively standard reorganization authority. Although it gave the president considerable latitude to make changes, it clearly specified that a reorganization plan could not be used to create a new executive department.

Carter's interest in reorganization was not surprising. As Joel Havemann of the *National Journal* reported on January 1, 1977:

> When Jimmy Carter moved into the Georgia governor's mansion in 1971, he quickly pushed through the state legislature a bill giving him broad powers to reorganize state agencies. He proceeded to use those powers to turn the Georgia bureaucracy upside down. Now Carter is about to move into a new home—the White House—and he is preparing to try to do to the federal bureaucracy what he did to Georgia's.[1]

Although Carter's authority in Georgia was broad enough to allow him to create and abolish cabinet departments, early conversations with leaders of Congress had indicated that there was reluctance to give him such powers at the federal level. Texas Democratic Congressman Jack Brooks, Chairman of the House Government Operations Committee, was particularly reluctant to extend such authority to the White House. Brooks was reflecting the traditional congressional skepticism about reorganization. Between 1949 and 1973, presidents had used reorganization authority 74 times to make changes in bureaucratic structures; Congress rejected these proposals 19 times. While Lyndon Johnson had been successful in getting two new departments created, he was stymied in his attempt to consolidate Commerce and Labor into a single department. Nixon's proposals for super-departments were completely rejected by the Congress.

Congressional reluctance to accept reorganization plans was also perceived to be related to the organization of Congress itself. Although congressional committee organization is independent of any changes in executive branch organization, a number of members believed that reorganization in the executive branch would be followed by reorganization of the congressional committee system—a shift that would potentially create changes in committee and subcommittee leadership positions. Interest groups also feared this kind of change, believing that it would undermine coalitions and their bases of support.

In Washington, as in Georgia, Carter's approach to reorganization centered on consolidation of governmental units with overlapping functions and reduction of the number of department and agency heads who report directly to the President. Carter's goal was to reduce the number of federal agencies to 200 from 1900,[2] a figure that included some 1400 federal advisory committees. Although the clear thrust of Carter's proposals went toward consolidation, there was a notable exception to that direction: his campaign promise to create a separate department of education, disaggregating the large Department of Health, Education and Welfare (HEW).

As Carter set about to begin his reorganization effort, there was no lack of advice from both academic as well as political quarters. Rufus E. Miles, long time HEW staff member, offered the new President 13 criteria by which to evaluate his reorganization activities:

1. Recognize that "organization is an important expression of social values" within the nation.
2. Place organizations "in a favorable environment for the performance of their central missions."
3. Remember that "organization affects the allocation of resources."
4. "Organization by reasonably broad purpose serves the President best." It should not be so narrow "as to be overly responsive to specific clientele groups, nor so broad as to be unmanageable."
5. "Wide span of control has significant advantages in improving administration and reducing unnecessary layers of bureaucracy."
6. "Organizational form and prestige are especially important at the federal level in attracting and retaining first-rate leader-managers."
7. Balance is important in government organization: "excessive concentration of important responsibilities in one agency diminishes the effective performance of most of them."
8. "When purposes overlap, one must be designated as dominant; otherwise responsibility is unclear."
9. A system of coordination must be established when purposes overlap.
10. "Programs should be grouped on the basis of their affinity or the potential for cross-fertilization."
11. "Reorganizations have traumatic effects which should be carefully weighed."
12. "Reorganizations that require congressional approval or acquiescence should be carefully weighed to make sure that they are worth the expenditure of political capital required and have a reasonable chance of approval."
13. "Economy as a ground for major reorganization is a will-o'-the-wisp."[3]

This advice did inform the reorganization staff (if not the President). But analysts disagreed about the operational implications of these views while acknowledging that they reflected the prevailing wisdom of the public administration field.

ORGANIZING THE PRP

Slightly more than a month after Carter took office, the new administration appeared before a House subcommittee with its supplemental budget request for money to support the reorganization effort. Harrison Wellford appeared on behalf of OMB Director Bert Lance before the House Appropriations Subcommittee responsible for the Department of Treasury, Postal Service and General Government on the 1977 Supplemental Request for the Office of Management and Budget.[4] The request submitted by Wellford was for an additional $1.6 million dollars and 62 additional full-time positions for the reorganization activities.

Wellford's statement noted that the reorganization staff would be located within OMB, with OMB Director Bert Lance as the leader of the effort. (Lance had been Carter's most essential strategist and ally in Georgia for that reorganization activity.) A new role of Executive Associate Director for

Reorganization and Management would be created in OMB with a full-time commitment to planning and directing the reorganization program, reporting to the Director and Deputy Director of OMB, and "accessible to the President and advisory Group as necessary on reorganization matters."[5]

Wellford, the individual named to the new Executive Associate Director role spelled out in the supplemental budget request, was a lawyer as well as a Ph.D. in American history who had worked previously in Congress and for consumer advocate Ralph Nader. He did not have previous experience in the executive branch. His background led him to emphasize the political nature of the reorganization issue.

In his testimony, Wellford noted that the new administration had studied the reorganization efforts of the last three administrations and identified three major problem areas:

> First, to a large degree, reorganization plans were developed in a political vacuum. Consultation with Congress, affected interest groups, agency personnel, State and local government officials and the public generally was either superficial or after the fact.
> Second, the scope of reorganization was too narrow and failed to address the problems at the program level where government meets the people. Recent reorganization attempts have focused primarily on box shuffling at the cabinet level and neglected improvements in administrative management and intergovernmental relations that determine the effectiveness of policy decisions within those boxes.
> Third, reorganization efforts have been conducted by study commissions, located in the Executive Office, without any ongoing institutional base of their own. There has been little connection between the formulators of reorganization policy and those who must implement it in the rest of the government.[6]

According to Wellford, Carter planned to prevent these problems from repeating themselves by taking the following steps:

> —He will consult Congress, the Cabinet and the public at every stage of the development of our reorganization plans and proposals. This consultation is already under way in a number of areas. The President will establish a reorganization advisory group to coordinate public hearings on his reorganization proposals before final submission to Congress. This outreach to the public may be expensive, but we feel it is essential to the integrity of the reorganization effort.
> —The President has defined the scope of reorganization to include a comprehensive effort to increase the competence and responsiveness of government in three broad areas.
> *Structural consolidation and streamlining* to reduce the waste, duplication, overlap, and complexity of government.
> *Implementation of "sunshine" and other openness initiatives and improvements in intergovernmental relations* to make government more responsive and compassionate in meeting public needs.
> *Development of an administrative management program for the President* to provide guidance for internal management reforms in the agencies and departments. Obviously, the President does not intend to manage the departments from the White House or OMB. He has emphasized managerial expertise in his cabinet selections and has made clear that the cabinet will be held accountable for the efficiency of their departments. The President, through management devices such as Zero Base Budgeting will provide guidance and encouragement to the cabinet effort but responsibility will remain with the agency heads.[7]

The purposes of the reorganization ("to make government work better—more efficiently, responsively, openly, and compassionately—through substantial improvements in the organization and management of the Executive Branch"[8]) would be met by a seven-point strategy. First, the effort would be a step-by-step incremental approach staged over a four-year period (rather than a one-step approach that would result in a single plan completed on a fixed date). Second, targets for reorganization analysis would be chosen from policy areas in which the President expected to make major initiatives during his first year in office. Third, reorganization would include coordination reforms in the areas of structural organization, cost control, productivity, budgetary control, personnel policies, and intergovernmental relations as well as changes in organization charts. Fourth, reorganization would emphasize a "bottom-up" approach (rather than a "top-down" approach) to program consolidation and realignment, with proposals developed out of program studies rather than by abstract management principles. Fifth, officials charged with implementation would be involved in the development of the plans, both during the study process and in the development of recommendations. Sixth, the effort would establish and maintain close working relationships with members of Congress, committees and staffs. Seventh, the program would include a strong public involvement effort to inform and win the support of important groups and the public generally.

The functions and responsibilities of the actors involved with the reorganization effort were detailed in the March 1977 document, beginning with the President himself. The President would have "a direct and continuing involvement in the reorganization effort" and would "make final decisions on all major policy questions." The Director and Deputy Director of OMB would "approve overall plans for managing and conducting studies; monitor the conduct and progress of the Reorganization Program on a continuing basis; assist in resolving study problems; and review final recommendations of the study teams."

A President's Reorganization Advisory Group would be established to provide independent advice on the project (to the president and to the OMB top officials) and to play an active role in the public awareness strategy. According to the March 1977 document, the group would be led by a full-time chairman who had "the confidence of the President, a working knowledge of reorganization, and prior experience in public awareness/involvement." Between 10 and 15 members were envisioned for the group, including senior members of the White House staff, individuals with experience in the federal government, the legislative branch, the business and labor communities, state or local governments, public interest groups, and research and academic institutions.

The full-time staff for the reorganization would include the Executive Associate Director (and a staff to that person); Congressional Relations and

Legal Affairs staff; a small Public Awareness staff; an Intergovernmental Relations and Regional Operations Group; an Administrative Management Division (concentrating on non-structural issues involving reorganization such as paperwork reduction, advisory committee reduction, civil service reform, and improved program evaluation); and the Organization Studies Division. That Division would be composed of six study teams, each led by a leader with agency personnel, OMB analysts and outside specialists brought in to collect and analyze information and develop a reorganization agenda.

In addition, Richard Pettigrew, a Floridian who had been involved in a reorganization effort within that state, was appointed as Assistant to the President for Reorganization "with primary responsibility for developing mechanisms to enlist public involvement in reorganization."[9] Pettigrew had two staff members assigned to him but it was never clear to the staff of the PRP what his role was to be in these activities.

According to the March 1977 plans, the reorganization staff would begin work on several priority items on which the President had promised immediate action. These included proposals to create a Department of Energy, to reduce the size of the White House staff and the Executive Office of the President, to eliminate unnecessary advisory committees, to consolidate civil rights and equal employment opportunity agencies, to reorganize oil spill pollution authorities, and to review the operation of the Federal Regional Councils. The campaign promise to create a Department of Education was not included in that list for immediate action. Indeed, the first reorganization plan (the reorganization of the Executive Office of the President) was submitted to Congress before a director for the education group was named.

WHITE HOUSE LOBBYING: THE REORGANIZATION AUTHORITY

It was not surprising that a Democratic House and Senate wanted to give a Democratic President some sense of a honeymoon period. While the momentum for support was strong, Texas Democrat Jack Brooks, chairman of the House Government Operations Committee, continued to voice opposition to the authority that Carter requested, for which there had been strong historical precedent. Carter attempted to convince Brooks of his position during the transition period. Brooks was concerned about the one-house legislative veto provision (a provision in which a committee of one house of Congress can stop a measure). Instead of giving the President the presumption of agreement—whereby a reorganization plan would become effective within 60 days unless vetoed by either house—he wanted the proposals to travel a normal legislative route.

Carter's inability to change Brooks' mind prompted an isolation strategy. Carter invited all of the House committee members to the White House in early and mid February—with the exception of Brooks.[10] While Brooks eventually acceded to the White House, emerging with a few refinements on Carter's proposal, there were those who believed that Carter's victory was somewhat hollow. A Brooks' aide was quoted as saying that "Carter showed disrespect for congressional tradition by 'going around the chairman' when he twice invited the committee members to the White House without Brooks."[11] The legislation that was finally enacted—the Reorganization Act of 1977—did give Carter essentially the authority he had requested.

THE EDUCATION STUDY TEAM

The staff assigned to work on the study and analysis of the possible options for a new Department of Education was located within the Human Resources Study team, one of the six study teams within the PRP's Organization Studies Division. The Human Resources group was headed by 31-year-old Patricia Gwaltney, who had been a career bureaucrat as well as a staff member on the Senate Budget Committee. She joined the PRP staff in April 1977. Although there were other projects undertaken by the Human Resources group during the course of the Carter presidency, the Department of Education effort almost always took precedence over other activities. This occurred despite efforts within the staff to spend time on health and safety regulatory programs and pension reforms.

The first staff members who joined Patricia Gwaltney in the spring of 1977 were almost entirely drawn from the career service—from OMB itself and from various parts of HEW. This reflected the general PRP strategy to rely on "detailees" to staff the effort. The discussion of possibilities for a separate education study director began in earnest in the early summer of 1977. Because the outcome of the education reorganization was viewed as somewhat risky, or at least unsure, it made sense for the appointee to come from the academic community, taking a leave without severing institutional bonds. The naming of Duke University political scientist, Willis D. Hawley, to the position in July 1977 also reflected an attempt to balance political advisers with academic analysts. This appointment of a study director required approval from HEW Secretary Califano as well as the top PRP staff.

While the PRP was organizing itself, all activity in Washington did not come to a halt, waiting for the White House to carry the burden on organizational issues. HEW Secretary Califano appointed a small, secret task force immediately after his confirmation to plan a reorganization that he announced as "the most far-reaching in the Department's 24-year history."[12]

The HEW reorganization effort was viewed as a controversial move. The cloak and dagger atmosphere that pervaded the planning had a Byzantine quality (the design group was kept to five people, sworn to secrecy, and met in the basement of the Pentagon). Failure to consult with individuals who were to be moved also appeared to violate civil service rules when those individuals affected were members of unions having bargaining agreements with the Department.

Califano announced that the purpose of the reorganization was "to make HEW a symbol of the manageability—not the unmanageability—of government."[13] Although grand in design and quite drastic in terms of the changes required in the health and welfare components of the Department, the Califano proposal just gently touched the education programs within HEW. His proposal consolidated all student financial assistance programs into a new Bureau of Student Financial Assistance—a proposal that, while important in terms of financial implications, did not signal a dramatic shift for the Education Division within HEW. It was not yet clear whether Califano's distance from the main education programs anticipated a separate education department. Califano's position on this issue, however, was soon to emerge.

GO OR NO GO: THE FIRST ROUND IN THE CARTER PRESIDENCY

As the March 1977 document suggested, the new Chief Executive was not about to plunge into a campaign to create a new department without some preliminary scrutiny of its political implications. That assignment was given to a high powered political task force, chaired by Vice President Mondale, with OMB Director Bert Lance, Domestic Policy Staff Director Stuart Eizenstat, and HEW Secretary Joseph Califano as members. That special task force would look at the politics of the organizational options at the same time that the inchoate Education Study team in PRP embarked on a substantive analysis of the idea.

The joint processes involving the Mondale task force and the PRP study team presented their first memorandum to Carter in June, 1977. While PRP staff were involved, they were "new kids on the block" and were not ready with substantive analysis of the potential of various options available to deal with the issue. The disagreements that would characterize the process for the next two years received their first presentation during that debate.[13a]

The Presidential Decision Memorandum that was submitted concluded that a thorough study of reorganization options for HEW was needed and that a relatively early decision on major structural questions was essential in view of congressional and constituency pressures. The task force recommended that a five-week study of organizational options be made; after that study was concluded, the determination would be made whether to proceed with a proposal for a separate department. If, after that point, the decision was made to proceed with the effort (to shift from the question of whether there *should* be a department to the question of *what* should be in it), a six-month study would follow.

The Presidential Decision Memorandum was accompanied by a cover memorandum from Vice President Mondale, reaffirming his inclination toward an immediate decision for a separate education department but noting that there were "reservations by Joe Califano and the OMB Reorganization Group." He argued that political realities demanded an immediate decision—NEA's political clout was important and the campaign promise loomed large. There was a real possibility that budget constraints might preclude other education initiatives. If the President did not act, there was a fear that Senator Ribicoff would move unilaterally.[13b]

HEW Secretary Califano did not agree. In an addendum to the memorandum, he opposed the department of education idea, arguing that education could not be viewed in a vacuum, independent of the government's health, cash payment, and social service programs. Indeed, he wrote, the decision to create a separate department "is certain to lead to pressure to create independent Cabinet-level departments of health and income security." He also stated his belief that the President needed fewer, not more people reporting directly to him; that he needed fewer, not more, constituency-oriented departments; that budgetary control problems would be greater in such a department where educators and NEA interests would dominate; and that "fragmented organizations will enhance Congressional control at the expense of Presidential control."[13c]

Califano argued for a quick study to assess the pros and cons of proceeding. Carter, however, disagreed, and decided to proceed with the six-month study. He called for a preliminary decision round in August, about half way through the six-month study, when the decision would be made whether to proceed with a separate department or maintain education as a part of HEW. While Carter's decision did not represent a clear go-ahead message, it tended to collapse the time schedule somewhat.

THE PRP BEGINS WORK

Carter's decision had the effect of throwing the ball to the PRP staff to begin its study process. Before it could begin to specify options for consideration by the President, the staff took the directives of the overall PRP to heart, working from a "bottom-up" analysis of the programs rather than from a "top-down" approach. The mission of the education group was detailed in a staff document.

> The President's Reorganization Project seeks to develop proposals that would increase the responsiveness and efficiency of the Executive Branch. The Project's Human Resources Staff has been directed by the President to coordinate a study of the organization of education and closely related programs. These programs will be examined carefully to determine the extent to which greater coordination or consolidation is desirable, and to develop a structure for education programs most appropriate to the Federal role and purposes in education and related areas. A

preliminary survey indicates that more than 250 education and related programs are scattered across 20 Federal departments and agencies. Further investigation will be undertaken to identify overlap, weaknesses, or inconsistencies which inhibit the effectiveness of the Federal investment in education.

In its conduct of the study, the Reorganization Project will draw heavily on the ideas and resources of the Congress and the White House Staff, Federal departments and agencies, State and local educators, and interested groups and individuals.

The components of the education reorganization study include an identification of the current and potential Federal role in education and perceived weaknesses and inadequacies of that role and the ways it is structured, the specification of new and improved program directions, and analyses of the relative effectiveness of alternative ways of reorganizing the Federal capacity to achieve existing program objectives and to successfully undertake new initiatives.[14]

Although the commissioning of a study gave the White House an opportunity to deal with Califano's opposition, it also had some negative aspects. It was hard to know whether the study acted as a smokescreen, as a delaying tactic, as a ritual dance, or as a way of backing out of the campaign promise.

The study team began its work by developing a typology of education programs, generating laundry lists of every conceivable education-related program to be considered. Programs were analyzed by function, by purpose, by budget, by organization setting as well as by beneficiaries. In one document, the PRP education staff noted that the two major thrusts of federal education policies were to promote opportunities and access, and to foster improvements in the quality of education. These goals would be addressed in three ways—schooling (activities that take place in schools); skill development and knowledge building taking place outside of educational institutions; and increasing linkages between education and other social programs.[15] As the PRP staff began its analytical work scrutinizing program candidates for inclusion in a department, it attempted to classify programs balancing three types of considerations:

1. The benefits that consolidation would have for the recipients of the programs involved.
2. The contribution that bringing these programs together would make to the quality of American education.
3. Political opposition or support for transferring programs to a new department.[16]

The initial array of organizational options that emerged for discussion clustered around three possibilities. Maintaining the status quo (keeping the present Education Division within HEW as it was); reorganizing and elevating education within HEW, (this was usually known as the sub-cabinet option); and creating a new department that would be broader in scope than the programs embodied as the Education Division of HEW.

There were a number of organizational possibilities that were discussed around the sub-cabinet option. These varied in the way that responsibility and power were allocated between the Office of the Secretary and the operational components of HEW, ranging from a design in which the Secretary continued current power to one in which a sub-cabinet department of education would enjoy virtual autonomy. Four sub-cabinet options were considered by the PRP group: 1) a strong Secretary of HEW with a new Under Secretary for Education (raising the education responsibilities from an Assistant Secretary and Commissioner of Education to an Under Secretary); 2) Staff Under Secretaries and a Sub-cabinet Secretary of Education (limiting the Office of the Secretary of HEW to policy and management roles only until concerns which cut across the Department's divisional boundaries arose); 3) a small HEW staff with a strong Secretary of Education (a situation where HEW would be very decentralized and a Department of Education, under a secretary, would virtually run itself. The HEW Secretary would again be involved only in cross-cutting concerns); and 4) an organization resembling the Department of Defense where HEW would have a secretary (as well as separate secretaries for each of the functional components.)

At least five configurations were considered for a separate department: (1) a cabinet department that included the Education Division and related HEW and outside programs; (2) a Department of Labor and Education, adding the Education Division, Head Start, and School Nutrition programs to the existing Department of Labor programs; (3) a Department of Health, Education and Science, bringing together health research and education programs of HEW, the science programs of NSF, and the Endowment for the Humanities; (4) a Department of Science and Education, an outgrowth of a Carnegie Council on Policy Studies in Higher Education Report that attempted to bring together science and education functions and gain more federal support for education and basic research; and (5) a Department of Education and Human Development, bringing together some of the HEW programs from the Office of Aging and the Children's Bureau, some Department of Labor programs and ACTION (the national volunteer agency). In addition, an independent agency configuration was also considered, to operate like the National Science Foundation, with a separate board of advisers and the power to operate more autonomously from the White House in budget review processes.[17]

The arguments that were used to support the various options were as diverse as the possibilities considered. The analysis of the internal reorganization options suggested that it could be based on several political and symbolic grounds. For example, it was argued that elevation of the federal education function to a cabinet level would violate the American belief that education was primarily a state and local responsiblity; the federal contribution to elementary and secondary education was the smallest of any of the three levels of government and it was therefore fitting that the highest federal education post be no higher than an assistant secretary level.

It was also suggested that the sub-cabinet options generated fewer organizational and political costs than would a larger scale reorganization; that better coordination could be achieved both within the Education Division and with other human services programs through an internal reorganization option; and that a sub-cabinet option would be perceived to create fewer disruptions in congressional committee operations.

The arguments that were developed for the creation of a cabinet-level department during this early stage of policy formulation indicate that the PRP staff found the new department option to be much more compelling. Arguments to maintain the status quo were few and far between, except for those advanced by HEW Secretary Califano and his key staff. Although on the surface it appeared that the political costs and logistical difficulties of maintaining the status quo would be fewer than making any sort of change, the set of expectations surrounding Carter's election and the momentum generated by the PRP itself made it quite difficult to argue for no change whatsoever. After all, reorganizers want to reorganize.

THE ANALYSTS PROCEED

Through the summer and early fall of 1977, the education group within PRP grappled with difficult substantive and political issues. The substantive choices that became clearer as the months progressed involved two issues: first, should education have a cabinet or non-cabinet status? Second, should the education function (however located) be viewed as a narrow or a broad set of programs, relationships and issues?

These two questions were posed within a political environment in which there were a number of conflicting signals. First, the momentum to create a cabinet-level department was not only driven by Carter's campaign promise but was also being pushed by activity within the Congress. Ribicoff had reintroduced legislation to establish such a department in March 1977 that ultimately had more than 70 co-sponsors. That bill, S210, included the education division within HEW as well as other education-related programs. Ribicoff had already scheduled hearings in the Senate for the fall of 1977.

Second, as the PRP education study group began its analytic activity, it attempted to place its effort within a broader context. Many of the PRP staff were individuals who had strong views on education issues and were aware of the increasing national concern about declining enrollments, declining test scores, school violence, parental perception that schools were not responsive to them, and substantial teenage unemployment. As the staff attempted to place its concern about organizational options within this context, it became increasingly attracted to the options displaying a broad, comprehensive character. The movement toward broader and more inclusive organizational units was also reinforced by the reorganization efforts of the past decade at both state and federal levels of government.

TESTING THE WATERS

The outreach strategy used by the PRP education group echoed the approach established for the PRP as a whole. As PRP chief Wellford had promised, the staff invested considerable time and energy in contacts with Capitol Hill and the interest group community. As it tested the political waters of Congress, the PRP education staff discussed potential or possible linkages between education and human services programs. While they found general and abstract support for the concept of a broad department, there were few substantive suggestions for bringing that idea to specific organizational form. Because the reorganization proposal would go to the government operations committees, the PRP did spend considerable time meeting with members of those committees as well as their staff. Ribicoff's staff, in particular, was supportive of these efforts. At the same time, however, staff met with members and staff specifically involved in education programs (both authorizing as well as appropriations committees).

The meetings with interest group representatives were essential to the PRP strategy; the education staff met with over 200 interest groups, representing elementary, secondary, higher, and vocational education interests, as well as labor unions and civil rights groups. At this point in the process, the discussions with the groups were very general. Most of the elementary and secondary education sector—with the exception of the American Federation of Teachers—supported the idea of a department, while the higher education community was more ambivalent about the desirability of a separate department of any construct.

The PRP conversations with interest groups centered around two separate issues—should there be a department and, if so, what should be included in it? Although the issues were logically separate, politically one could not answer the first without also answering the second. The consultation process appeared to jump quickly to the second question. To some degree this occurred because few groups were opposed to the theoretical idea of a separate department; it did seem to be an idea in good standing.

The marching orders given to the PRP by Carter had provided that there would be an opportunity for the President to review the progress of the study at the end of the summer. In the middle of August 1977, the PRP staff was told (through White House aide Hamilton Jordan) to go ahead with its efforts. At that point, the staff was clearly intrigued by the potential of the broad department, cited the campaign promise language (which moved toward a broad department), and viewed Carter's response as support for that direction.

Just before Carter reviewed the PRP progress, an article appeared in the Sunday *Washington Post* Outlook Section entitled "Promises to Keep: Will Carter Really Create An Education Department?" by Mark A. Shiffrin, a Washington freelance writer.[18] Shiffrin's opening captured Carter's dilemma:

Remember candidate Carter's campaign promise to create a new cabinet-level department of education? Well, President Carter might prefer that you had a shorter memory.

It's listed right there in the 'Promises Book' prepared by the Carter transition team and released by the White House last February. It ranks three separate mentions and is the first promise listed under "Reorganization". But, as presidential aide Mark A. Siegel remarks, Carter is 'reevaluating' his promise. "The President is dealing with a clean slate. He will make a decision based on merit ... not on the needs of separate constituent groups."

The article proceeded to detail the political questions and interests involved in the decision. "The public arguments most often heard about an education department deal with management. Some even speculate that management efficiencies eventually would help the classroom by improving the quality and coordination of federal education programs. But it's really less a question of the merits of the arguments than of commitments made by President Carter and Vice President Mondale during the campaign."

Shiffrin's analysis emphasized HEW Secretary Califano's opposition to "carving the E out of HEW" and alternative proposals to upgrade the education function within the overall HEW structure, attempting to give new attention to the issue of coordination. "Nobody knows whether creation of an education department would clarify or alter the federal role in education. Education programs throughout the government theoretically are coordinated already by HEW's assistant secretary for education through what is called the Federal Interagency Committee on Education (FICE). But FICE has been troubled since its creation in the 1960s." Califano's proposal to the President, according to Shiffrin, was to issue an executive order strengthening FICE—but the writer wasn't convinced that it could accomplish the coordination goal.

The article concluded with the specification of a number of options available to Carter. "Jimmy Carter will not have to make his decision on these or other options immediately. The OMB study allows him to put that off at least until the end of the year and possibly longer. But ultimately, he will not be able to avoid making a choice, and the evidence indicates that the decision may well turn out to be rooted more in the politics of keeping a presidential promise than in educational logic."

OTHER EXECUTIVE BRANCH ACTIVITY

The relationships that the PRP staff attempted to cultivate with the myriad of interest groups at least potentially affected by the emerging options were not developed in a vacuum. Most of the interest groups had long and intense relationships with the career bureaucrats in their area of interest (as well as with the relevant congressional committee staff and members). The conversations with the PRP staff members (who were both energetic and earnest about these contacts) did not replace the regular contacts that were part of the standard operating procedure of both the bureaucrats as well as the interest group representatives.

As the Washington information mill churned out both rumor and fact, a sense of apprehensiveness began to develop in some executive branch agencies. If programs and organizational units were to be moved out of other departments, on what grounds would these decisions be made? The prospect of change along the lines of a broad department appeared to signal concern for at least a few agencies and their constituents.

The Indian education programs, located within the Bureau of Indian Affairs (BIA) in the Department of Interior, were among the education-related programs considered for inclusion in a separate department. Although the Native American community for years had complained about the education programs in BIA, and there were two Indian programs already in the Office of Education, some shifts had occurred that tempered the past perceptions. The Carter appointees within the Bureau of Indian Affairs were believed to be more responsive to the demands and concerns of the Native American community. New legislation reauthorizing the program had established a community involvement and advisory process that promised a less paternalistic treatment than the community had experienced with BIA in the past.

In addition, the idea of change of any sort was threatening both to the BIA as well as to the Native American groups; the relationship between the two was a fragile one and both feared that the trust which had been developed would be eroded with an organizational shift. They feared that a department of education would de-emphasize the Indian part of Indian education and would, rather, push the program to comply with other education efforts. In sum, as one Native American representative attempted to explain the attitude of his constituency toward BIA, he commented, "They may be bastards, but they're our bastards."

Other groups, such as the advocates of the child nutrition and feeding programs within the Food and Nutrition Service in the Department of Agriculture, began to develop arguments that could be used to avoid inclusion in the PRP proposals. Although there had been arguments in the past that suggested that these programs were marginal to the Department of Agriculture's concerns (and some proposals had been made in the past to transfer at least components of the programs to HEW), the Carter appointees within the Department began to emphasize the unique elements of the programs—their consumer orientation and the advocacy concept that was built into them. The argument clearly implied that a shift in the organizational location would dramatically curtail the improvement in quality and administration of these programs that had been (or was about to be) attained. As long as the programs were surrounded by the support of the agriculture

agriculture lobby, it was also believed that they were in a better position to protect their resources in Congress.

Because it was still not clear whether Carter would, indeed, proceed with a separate education department, the debate within the executive branch indicated that the issue was still up for grabs. HEW Secretary Califano's opposition to the department was well known and quite clear. Other Carter loyalists believed that without clear marching orders from the President their attempt to make a case to exclude specific progams and units from a new department was appropriate. In addition, the consultative process encouraged interest groups and their bureaucratic allies to believe that the issues were still dangling.

The education bureaucracy within HEW, however, did not seem clear about what it should do as the issue was taking shape within OMB. It did appear that the Commissioner of Education and the Assistant Secretary for Education were not opposed to the idea but were not prepared to make their views public at this point. Both individuals were a part of Califano's leadership team and were not ready to risk consequences that might have resulted from public opposition to his view. And that might have been pointless if Carter was, indeed, still open to the possibility of "chucking out" the campaign promise.

While attentive to an outreach and involvement strategy outside the executive branch, the PRP was instructed to ignore the largely career education bureaucracy within the Education Division, not to "muck around" in Califano's territory. The education bureaucracy also knew that there was a conflict between Assistant Secretary for Education Mary Barry and Secretary Califano on this issue. If the PRP staff thought about it at all, they tended to assume that the silence from the education bureaucracy signalled acquiescence and support for the reorganization concepts. PRP had little interest in developing information about the way that education programs actually worked.

EVEN THE BEST LAID PLANS ...

With a staff in place and a sense that they had been told to go ahead with their analysis activity, the PRP education study anticipated submitting a proposal to the President at the end of November. As they prepared to complete the first phase of the study, however, some dramatic shifts were occurring within the White House.

Carter's plans to proceed with a reorganization had been constructed on an assumption that one of his closest and most trusted associates—Bert Lance—would be the key figure involved. The location of the reorganization activity within OMB could be justified on a number of compelling grounds—but probably none was as compelling as the presence of Lance at its helm. Carter himself noted that "it is difficult for me to explain how close Bert was to me or how much I depended on him. ... I did not hesitate in making Bert Lance the first person I asked to serve at the top level within my administration after the election. He was the only one of the Cabinet-level members with whom I had ever worked before, and I planned for him to be the leader on matters dealing with the budget and government organization."[19]

On September 21, 1977, OMB Director Bert Lance resigned, responding to allegations about his financial dealings involving an Atlanta bank. Lance was replaced as OMB Director by James McIntyre, his deputy, who also came with Carter from Georgia. Although McIntyre was trusted by Carter (indeed, he was named Deputy to Lance at Carter's personal insistence), he had neither Lance's personal relationship to the President nor his status in dealing with other actors inside the White House and on the Hill. Within OMB itself, the shift of top leadership affected the plans to integrate reorganization, management improvement efforts, and the traditional budget role of the agency. Because of the short period of time that Lance served in the position, it was not clear whether he would have been able to juggle the various agendas subsumed within OMB's mission statements.

In his book on OMB, Larry Berman has commented that "While the Bert Lance episode did little to improve OMB's *public* image, insiders never charged Lance with incompetence as OMB Director."[20] During his confirmation hearings, Berman reports that Lance assured everyone that "OMB should not be trying to run the government through the Executive Office, but should provide constructive coordination where required, and where the President wishes." Berman commented that "Lance, in fact, was probably the most influential in a long line of BOB/OMB Directors qua Special Assistants. His critics argued that Lance did not pay enough attention to OMB's internal organization and was not familiar with budgetary details. Nevertheless, during budget presentations to President Carter, Lance gave senior careerists the opportunity to explain decisions directly to the President (while Lance sat at the President's side of the table)."

McIntyre was less able to deal with the complexity of the agency. Although the original plans for the PRP conceived of the effort as a regular operating arm of OMB, as the months progressed it appeared that McIntyre was preoccupied with the budget side of OMB and that budget concerns were driving both his interests and his time. Because the budget process had its own momentum and schedule, it almost always pushed out competing claims for time. A budget had to be submitted to the Congress and the budget process itself required rapid timing and quick turnaround time for response.

As a result, the day-to-day leadership given to the PRP was provided by Harrison Wellford. Wellford (and the other top PRP staffers) were dependent on McIntyre to present proposals and to represent their views. The Executive Committee on Reorganization (conceived to be an essential component of the reorganization strategy) seemed to evaporate after Lance's departure. And the PRP was confronted with a pervasive sense of skepticism about reorganization in general among the White House staff, particularly in the Domestic Policy Staff.

LEAVING THE POLITICS TO OTHERS ... RELUCTANTLY

While the PRP education staff was told to proceed with the analysis of possible options for a new department and to "leave the politics" to others in the White House, the reorganization team was aware that their task was fundamentally political and that political implications would have to be taken into account before a final determination could be made on how to proceed. The consultation process undertaken by the team was an attempt to understand the political forces that would shape the feasibility of alternative proposals. However, the very character of the PRP staffers made such a political feasibility assessment quite difficult. Most of the staff members were very young; both Wellford and McIntyre were under 40; three of the five Deputy Associate Directors responsible for substantive policy areas were in their early 30s; a substantial number of the staff of the PRP were under 30. While not lacking in intelligence or energy, this team found it quite difficult to make a quick assessment of the political forces at play. While "whizz kids" may hold their own in a world of weapon systems assessment or other areas where quantitative analysis is both appropriate and influential, the circumstances surrounding reorganization were significantly changed from that of the Kennedy era.

In addition, the PRP staffers knew that they would not be a match for other White House staffers whose expertise did lie in the political assessment area. Those individuals were in a better position to assess the impact of a reorganization recommendation on other initiatives undertaken by the Carter administration. This did not stop the PRP from attempting— unsuccessfully—to undertake regular soundings of the depth of political sentiments in the Congress and among the more influential interest groups.

The operating rule of thumb for the reorganization effort was the motto, "if it's not broke, don't fix it." This meant that intellectual principles of organizational design which had traditionally served for previous reorganization efforts would not be used here as the principal arguments for change. The PRP staffers did, of course, justify their proposals on grounds of rationality, efficiency, and economy. But they were much more concerned about outcomes for children and families as the basis for change.

But focusing on outcomes is not easy. The state of evaluation and information on social programs is problematic; it is difficult to prove past or current effects of many of the education programs that were being considered by the PRP group. It was even more difficult to "prove" what outcomes would be in the future if a program were organized differently. The political process looks at outcomes in symbolic, impressionistic and highly personal ways; analysts are rarely comfortable with those sources of information. Members of Congress, if they look at quantitative information at all, tend to look at how many people are served and the various resources that are used (commonly known as input measures), rather than the benefits that might accrue to the participants. They assume the benefits will follow from the allocation of resources or the regulations involved. Representatives of constituency groups understood the difficulty of focusing on outcome measures and had learned to justify their programs in terms that were amenable to the political actors.

At this point in the process, the interest groups, led by the NEA, concentrated their energies on the most general strategy to unify supporters of a new department. Through the creation of a Citizen's Committee for a Cabinet Department of Education (an organization that included a broad array of groups and acted to broaden the support for the Department beyond the perceived parochial interest of the NEA), efforts were made to keep arguments for the department as general as possible, avoiding any specific proposals that had the potential to undermine the broad base of support.

The PRP staffers were, thus, entering the debate in a way that made their arguments difficult to integrate into the process. The seemingly simple approach to "fix broken programs" was illusory. It turned out to be difficult to determine whether a program with multiple objectives was, indeed, "broken." It was difficult to develop information in a way that seemed to make a compelling case for change. As analysts, the PRP staffers wanted to develop specific analyses that focused on details of particular configurations of programs. And it was an uphill battle to argue that programs supported by strong political allies were not working effectively, particularly if some of those allies were the most vehement supporters of the drive for a new department.

THE NOVEMBER PROPOSAL
TO THE PRESIDENT

The proposal that was submitted by PRP to the President in late November 1977 emphasized alternatives that moved toward a broad department of education, maximizing the potential for coordination of services at the delivery level. The PRP had come to the conclusion that a department of education and human development, cutting broadly across education and human resource development activities, but excluding the large cash transfer programs in the social welfare and health areas, would be the appropriate path for Carter to take. This approach, it was believed, would introduce a diverse array of actors into the policy environment of the department who would bring different and needed perspectives on the problems of education. A broad department would avoid the pitfalls of narrow constituency control.

The PRP developed an even more ambitious plan than the one it submitted as alternatives to the President. This plan called for a fundamental realignment of federal domestic programs dealing with human services. All programs involving financial security would be grouped in a department of labor and income maintenance (this would include unemployment compensation, food stamps, health benefits, and Social Security). All programs that supported the delivery of state and local services would be included in a department of human development and education.

The sorting out of responsibilities in the two departments was extremely attractive to the PRP staff who justified its exploration of the possibility by citing Carter's interest in a broad department. However, the PRP staff did recognize that such a proposal would go beyond Carter's initial concept and did not submit this grand scheme to the President.

The PRP presented three alternative structures: a narrow department of education; a broad based department including education and other human development activities; and a strengthened Education Division within HEW. Each of the three alternatives was evaluated against three standards: its ability to improve the federal government's capacity to develop and implement effective education policies; consistency with overall reorganization of government; and assessment of political feasibility and responsiveness to campaign positions.

As it presented its overall conclusions, the PRP noted that "in terms of most of the criteria employed in this analysis, a narrowly based Department of Education is the least attractive alternative,"[21] while "a broadly based department including education and other human development activities seems promising as the alternative best suited for developing comprehensive approaches to the challenges associated with education." The memo argued that the education division should be restructured whether or not it remained in HEW. This restructuring option, it should be noted, reflected the work of the HEW Secretary who had been developing options for elevating the status of education within HEW. His options revolved around the creation of an Under Secretary/Commissioner for Education and an internal restructuring of the education division.[22]

The PRP proposal included the transfer of a large array of education programs from HEW as well as from other agencies. The arguments used to support the proposal were rooted in the rhetorical principles of "good government", more effective coordination of programs and delivery of services, and an expansion of the constituency base. Among the programs that were targeted by the PRP for inclusion in the broad department were Head Start, Child Nutrition, Science Education, and Indian Education (programs which became extremely controversial in the saga of the Department's creation). The proposal to include Head Start in the broad department rested on a somewhat different argument than did other programs. The PRP acknowledged that the Head Start program was not "broke" but believed that other programs were not operating effectively because they were isolated from Head Start. In a sense, the PRP stood its "if it's not broke" argument on its head: it argued that Head Start (a program whose design integrated education goals with health, nutrition, and other community development objectives) ought to be used as a model within a new department to show other programs how linkages could be developed between education and other human development programs. The PRP was so intrigued by what it viewed as the potential for this approach that it did not accurately take account of the vehement opposition to such a move from Head Start advocates.

As it recommended the inclusion of the Child Nutrition programs into the broad department, the PRP believed that it was giving the program the ability to strengthen its service delivery success. As long as these programs were located in the Department of Agriculture, the PRP argued that they would necessarily be geared to goals related to farm income maintenance rather than to feeding children in school. If all of the child nutrition programs were moved to the new department, according to the PRP, the programs would be delivered more effectively. As in the case of Head Start, the PRP did not calculate the effects on political support of keeping the programs within Agriculture.

The PRP proposed that the Science Education programs be moved from the National Science Foundation because they had been receiving little attention from the agency. These programs were focused on efforts in elementary and secondary education settings and, the PRP argued, were not a high priority for an agency that otherwise concentrated on programs in universities and colleges. The PRP assumed that moving the Science Education programs to a new department would give them more attention and provide them with an organizational opportunity to influence other education efforts.

Despite the opposition to such a move voiced by the Native American community, the proposal to the President also included a recommendation that the Indian Education programs be transferred to a new department, out of the Bureau of Indian Affairs in the Department of Interior. The PRP argued that moving these programs into the new department would bring them into the education mainstream and give them a higher priority. Data was presented to show that Indians were among the nation's lowest achievers and the gap was not narrowing.

At the same time that this analytical work was being developed, the PRP was having some internal difficulty deciding on the jurisdictional location of specific programs within the entire PRP enterprise. The broader the education staff perceived the possibilities for inclusion of programs into the education department, the more likely it was to be viewed as "invading" the jurisdiction of other PRP groups, especially the Economic Development team. Since the analyses undertaken by all of the PRP teams were to be done from the "bottom-up", it was almost inevitable that the PRP's sub-units would develop conflicting reorganization strategies. Such conflict, based as it was on different analyses, not only diverted the energy of PRP leaders and slowed the decision process, but also provided ammunition to the critics of reorganization who could assert that the PRP was on a "shopping spree", unconstrained by a clear view of what was really needed.

WHAT DID CARTER SAY?

The proposal for a broad department wsa submitted to the President by the PRP in late November with the endorsement of the OMB Director, James McIntyre. The report marked the end of the six-month exploratory effort, viewed as the first of a two-phase study of the organization and delivery of education-related programs.

The report presented a range of options to the President, from announcing support for a narrowly based department of education to explicitly rejecting such a department and announcing steps to strengthen the education division within HEW.

As the PRP memorandum laid out the options, it offered Carter two choices within the option of "Indicate Preference for a new Department Including Education and Other Human Development Activities." The announcement by the President of such a position could either:

(A) Reaffirm your campaign pledge to a broad department and direct the Reorganization staff, together with DHEW and the Domestic Policy Staff, to develop a full proposal after extensive consultation with interested groups and Members of Congress, or

(B) Defer a final decision on the three structural options but note that the broad department seems very promising in view of the challenges associated with education, and direct the fuller development of the options with the benefits of a full public and congressional debate.

In either case you would authorize Secretary Califano, working closely with the Reorganization staff, to take some immediate steps to strengthen the Education Division in DHEW.[23]

The memorandum concluded that the PRP staff was in favor of (B), the deferral option on a final decision. "We believe that the potential benefits of a new department in which education and related services are effectively joined are large. Our reservation about announcing such a department now is based on our judgment that more time is needed both for further development of the programmatic details and more extensive public consultation."[24]

All of the major actors were present at the November 28th meeting—the Advisory Committee members (Campbell, Shultz, and Mondale); HEW Secretary Califano; members of the Domestic Policy Staff, and OMB and PRP officials and staff. As one participant described it, "the grandeur of the cabinet room, with its portraits, silver tea service and flags, added to the sense that this was a moment when the PRP was finally on center stage."

The President entered the room cheerily congratulating everyone for the good work they had done and announcing, with a grin, that on no other issue had he received so many staff memos recommending so many different courses of action. As the meeting progressed, it was clear that the President had read all of these memos and knew the issues well. The President then invited various people to present their cases in summary fashion. Campbell and Shultz made a tepid argument for maintaining education programs within HEW and maintaining its status. The Domestic Policy Staff argued for a narrow Department of Education. The PRP presented cases for both a broad department and the option II—further study of the major realignment. When Califano endorsed the option for further study, the PRP was surprised and cynically surmised that delay would reduce the likelihood of change.

President Carter interrupted presentations with questions that demonstrated his awareness of the weaknesses in the various positions being taken. Some questions seemed to be his way of showing the participants that he had done his homework on the issue.

The meeting went on for about 90 minutes with the President actually directing an interchange between the key participants. Somewhat abruptly, the President announced that he was late for a meeting of the National Security Council and that he wanted "the broadest possible Department of Education we can get." Vice President Mondale left with him without elaborating on the statement or adjourning the meeting.

This meeting between Carter and his top aides was open to a myriad of interpretations and definitional disputes. There was agreement on some aspects of that meeting—first, that the President would reaffirm his commitment to establish a new education department. Within the administration, HEW Secretary Califano was the only major figure resisting this position. Second, that cabinet-level status would increase the visibility and strength of the national government's role as a leader in education. The establishment of a new department would be viewed as evidence of Carter's commitment to making education a high priority.

From that point on, however, the agreement about the meeting dissolved. The President did agree with the recommendation that the new department should be as broad as possible. But the definition of "broad" appeared to be open to dispute, and perspectives on what was "possible" differed greatly. After Carter left the room, Domestic Policy Chief Stuart Eizenstat stood up and said, "what the President said was that he wants the broadest department possible. What he means is ... " And then Eizenstat went on to describe a narrow department. All participants in the meeting acknowledged that a narrow department, based on the contours of the current Education Division within HEW, would probably pass the Senate and the House if it had the President's support; the broader the proposal for a department, the more difficult it would be politically. And the more difficult politically it would be to create a department of education, the more difficult it would be to pursue successfully the legislative priorities seen by most in the room (perhaps with the exception of the PRP staff) to be of much greater importance.

While the PRP did not get its first preference endorsed by the President, it came away from this stage of the process relatively pleased with itself. Its general position had been sustained against the opposition of the powerful and effective Secretary of HEW and some of the President's closest advisers.

The PRP expected this decision to be publicly acknowledged. The next day, during the President's press conference, they waited for the decision to be announced. But the press conference was focused on other issues— nuclear disarmament and the oil crisis among them.

CONCLUSIONS

During the first months of the Carter presidency, the activities that took place in the executive branch represented the new administration's attempt to devise a strategy for the formulation stage of the education department issue. As the activity during the pre-inaugural period suggested (when staff started to reexamine the idea of a department altogether), campaign promises serve to put an issue on the agenda but do not assure that it will proceed.

The development of this stage reopened the question of whether there should be a department at all. The PRP staff was there to develop analytic work and to provide advice to the President on this issue. The unfolding of this stage of the policy process created new opportunities for input and added new actors to the decision setting.

When the formulation stage began—a time when analysts set up a series of questions and attempt to disentangle the various components of a policy issue—the idea of a department was no longer placed in a context of urgency and the momentum of political dealing. Time was counted in years, rather than in weeks (or even days). In this environment, it was appropriate to go back to basics and ask the first question: should there be a separate department of education? While that question was still directed to the education interest groups, it now had a broader array of interested parties: the executive agencies and departments affected by the proposals and OMB itself. These were actors who were irrelevant in the campaign context.

As the PRP education study group was organized and began its analytic tasks, it found itself operating in a turbulent sea full of unknown and unforeseen political and bureaucratic creatures. It did not appear that anyone in the PRP was prepared for the uncertainty and chaos which characterized the environment in which it was operating. Relationships within OMB were complex enough; members of the PRP group were largely outsiders to the institutionalized patterns of OMB, especially on the budget side of the agency. The impact of the shift from Lance to McIntyre does not appear to have been completely appreciated by the PRP staff. Was reorganization dependent on the personal relationship between Lance and Carter rather than on the analytic abilities of the hardworking and extremely loyal staff?

Dependent as it was on others to make its case, the education group had difficulty calculating the level of support it could assume from the President himself. Who did, indeed, speak for the President? Similarly, the PRP group found it difficult to assess the degree of opposition that was beginning to surface from other executive-level departments, particularly the efforts of HEW Secretary Califano.

Although the PRP group regarded Jimmy Carter as its "client" (despite the difficulties that it had dealing directly with him), it was also quite clear to them that Congress—not Carter—had the authority to decide whether a Department would come into existence.

As the reorganization effort was carried on within the Executive Office of the President, the political and analytical perspectives on the issue were structured in a way that reinforced different world views. Analysts were found in many locations within OMB but most of those analysts were attached to the budget side of the agency. The analytic perspective that was found in PRP was largely that of the evaluator of program effectiveness, concerned much less with cost than with program design. It was difficult to find anyone in OMB who actually worried about the implementation of programs; if implementation analysis was done at all, it was found in the program agencies.

The bureaucratic location of the PRP staff clearly separated them from the political operators who were found on the Domestic Policy Staff (and other offices in the White House proper). The policy analysts were placed in a separate unit within OMB, ostensibly connected to the decision process through the OMB institutional link, but rarely had either the time or the influence to have impact on other decisions being made in the White House. The analytic perspective was characterized by the "bottom-up" approach and an attraction to a comprehensive, holistic view of the issue. Although the PRP staff were told to "leave the politics to others", they were damned if they did ... and damned if they did not. Few of the analysts were comfortable with political feasibility assessments, both because they did not have the information or expertise to make such assessments and because they were uncomfortable with the non-specific, symbolic, and intuitive judgments necessary in those circumstances.

The difficulties of dealing with the political system were illustrated as the PRP education group attempted to carry out its mandate of broad consultation and participation. Although the staff consulted with more than 200 interest groups during the first months of its operations, it found it very difficult to evaluate the importance of those consultations. The PRP found that the interest groups were largely defending the status quo arrangements and did not want to disturb their relationships with the existing organizational structure within HEW (or other agencies). Similarly, the visits to Capitol Hill did indicate that the PRP staff was stumbling into a complex web of relationships that extended far beyond the reorganization issue. But it was not clear to them how to deal with those relationships.

The PRP and the political actors had very different approaches and modes of operation. The PRP pushed itself to be very specific, to refrain from talking about issues in the abstract. The motto "if it's not broke, don't fix it," was really a call for analytic specificity. At the same time, the interest groups supporting the department were at a stage when they were attempting to broaden their base of support and, hence, were driven to be as general as they could be to bring in as many organizations as possible into their coalition. The formation of this coalition was not simple; most of the organizations had very strong ties with existing program units in the executive branch and clearly did not want to join in a coalition that might disrupt those cozy relationships.

As the PRP analysis progressed, it became more and more attracted to the arguments which indicated that a separate department of education would provide the organizational framework that would make current federal education programs more effective or, indeed, to change the direction of federal education programs. But while the PRP had equated reorganization and substantive education policy, it had failed to look at the most difficult problem in federal education policy: the question of the extent of the federal role. Federal-state relationships, the crucial issue in federal education policy, appears to have been ignored at this point of the policy development, both by the PRP and by the Domestic Policy Staff. "Potomac myopia" appeared to be rampant.

By the time that the first stage of the PRP study was completed at the end of November, the education study group found itself increasingly attracted to a broad department, encompassing more than the traditional education programs, as a way of setting the scene for significant change.

NOTES

1. Joel Havemann, "Reorganization—How Clean Can Carter's Broom Sweep?" *National Journal* (January 1, 1977), p. 4.

2. Ibid., p. 6.
3. Rufus E. Miles, "Considerations for a President Bent on Reorganization," *Public Administration Review* (March/April 1977), pp. 156-162.
4. Harrison Wellford, Testimony to House Appropriations Subcommittee on Department of Treasury, Postal Service and General Government, "Supplemental Request for OMB," (February 24, 1977).
5. President's Reorganization Project, "Plan for Conducting Federal Government Reorganization and Management Improvement Program, Discussion Outline," (March 1977).
6. Wellford Testimony, pp. 2-3.
7. Ibid., pp. 3-5.
8. President's Reorganization Project, March 1977 Plan.
9. Jimmy Carter, *Presidential Papers: Executive Committee on Reorganization* (June 2, 1977), p. 1052.
10. Dom Bonafede, "Carter's Relationship with Congress—Making a Mountain Out of a 'Moorehill'," *National Journal*, (March 26, 1977), p. 456.
11. Ibid., p. 462.
12. Joseph A. Califano, "Statement" *HEW News* (March 8, 1977).
13. Ibid., p. 7.
13a. "Presidential Decision Memorandum to President Jimmy Carter," (June 1977).
13b. Walter Mondale, "Cover Memorandum to Presidential Decision Memo to President Jimmy Carter," (June 1977).
13c. Joseph A. Califano, "Memorandum to the President," (June 1977).
14. President's Reorganization Project, Education Study Staff Document (undated).
15. President's Reorganization Project, "The Purposes and Program Content of a New Department of Education," (July 18, 1977).
16. Ibid., p. 2.
17. Patricia Gwaltney, President's Reorganization Project, "Note to Ben Heinemann and Fred Bohen, HEW" (May 20, 1977).
18. Mark A. Shiffrin, "Promises to Keep: Will Carter Really Create an Education Department?" *Washington Post* (August 14, 1977), p. B-3.
19. Jimmy Carter, *Keeping Faith: Memoirs of a President* (New York: Bantam Books, 1982), p. 128.
20. Larry Berman, *The Office of Management and Budget and the Presidency—1921-79* (Princeton, N.J.: Princeton University Press, 1979), pp. 128-129.
21. President's Reorganization Project, "Memorandum to the President," (November 1977), p. 15.
22. Joseph A. Califano, "Memorandum to the President," (July 11, 1977).
23. President's Reorganization Project, "Memorandum to the President," p. 17.
24. Ibid., p. 18.

Chapter 5 THE PLOT THICKENS

It was clear after President Jimmy Carter left the cabinet room that there would, indeed, be a proposal for a new department of education. But the substantive thrust of the proposal was hardly clear. Carter had instructed his staff to devise a department that was "as broad as was politically feasible." But the definition of political feasibility was clearly in the eye of the beholder.

This chapter is the account of the administration's position as the specifics of the proposed department were defined. The position which finally emerged during the testimony of OMB Director James McIntyre on April 14, 1978 was the result of a period of conflict between groups within the Executive Office of the President, influenced by a number of pressures and events emanating from Capitol Hill as well as many interest groups and other federal agencies.

The conflict was largely played out by two forces: the PRP staff within OMB and the Domestic Policy Staff in the White House itself. The two groups represented the classic tension in policy development between the imperatives of analysis and the demands of politics. The culture of analysis calls for the presentation of a thorough, comprehensive picture of an issue as well as the development of extensive alternatives before an informed decision can be taken. The culture of politics, on the other hand, pushes for quick, concise information that assures consolidation of power and maintains political survival.

As events unfolded in the period from November 1977 to mid-spring of 1978, the controversy between the two cultures revolved around the scope of the new department. The actors within the Domestic Policy Staff quickly moved toward the idea of a narrow department whose creation would cause minimal disruption of past political and bureaucratic relationships. The PRP, on the other hand, was developing its proposals for a broad depart-ment. Both groups believed that they had received the go-ahead from the President himself. DPS Chief Stuart Eizenstat heard Carter's instructions to devise a department that was as broad as was "politically feasible" as an expression of support for a minimal disruption strategy. The PRP, having been admonished by the President earlier to stay out of politics, took the position that all of the goals of reorganization sought by Carter (except for the political goals) could be best served by a broader department.

Carter himself probably contributed to the conflict through his own ambivalence toward the two views. There was evidence that Carter was attracted to the highly rational, analytical approach; his personal style and his training as an engineer reinforced the belief by the PRP staff that he wanted them to behave as a high quality analytical group. At the same time, the President had chosen close personal advisers whose expertise and commitments were focused on the political strategy approach. For some, the President seemed to be giving conflicting signals. For others, the President's message was clear but he failed to put right those who did not interpret that message with similar clarity.

As the account develops, the position of the Domestic Policy Staff was reinforced by the actions of interest groups who opposed the broader approach and, as well, by administrative agencies affected by the more inclusive proposals. The representatives of the agencies were caught in a double bind. On the one hand they did not want to oppose the general idea of the creation of a department; on the other hand, they argued that the PRP did not understand how their programs really worked and that the proposals for a broad department would engender interest group antagonism that the President did not need. For the education bureaucracies, however, the point was moot. Whether or not the department proposed would be broad or narrow, they would leave HEW. Hence the education bureaucracies were largely passive during this entire period.

CONFLICT AMONG EOP FACTIONS: A CLOSER LOOK

The conflict that arose between the DSP and PRP actors was, as has been described, a culture conflict between perceptions. While the conflict revolved around specific personalities and approaches that were idiosyncratic to the education department issue, it also reflected a more systemic set of forces within the White House. Even among the President's closest advisers, there is a continuing struggle for influence that reflects—at its best—the diversity of deeply held commitments to roles and to policies. In such an environment, the key actors guard their issues and are reluctant to share their authority and access with persons who are viewed as more "expert" on those issues.

"Expertise" on the construct of the education department was not unanimous. The budget side of OMB contained critics of a broad department of education and human development. Other analysts within the Executive Office of the President came up with different conclusions than did the PRP staff.

For some of the political opponents of the broad department, the opposition had little to do with the substantive merits of the issue. The White House staff and legislative liaison team were opposed to the broad proposal because it would result in the need for extensive political bargaining when other domestic administrative initiatives—such as welfare reform—were in trouble. At the same time, in the international arena, SALT negotiations, the Panama Canal treaty, and the energy crisis were preempting the limited time and resources of the presidency. Some White House staffers believed that HEW Secretary Califano had not been given an adequate chance to improve the management of education programs at HEW.

Except for the PRP, the political advantage goal for reorganization was the dominant approach within the Executive Office of the President. Carter's personal staff believed that a department was acceptable because it met the administration's campaign commitments. The best way of meeting the campaign promise and causing minimal problems was to devise a narrow department. The education interest groups were letting the White House know, in no uncertain terms, that cabinet status for education was absolutely essential. At the same time, Senator Ribicoff made it clear that the existence of a plan to strengthen the education programs within HEW, endorsed by Califano, would not deter him from pursuing the bill already endorsed by more than two-thirds of the members of the Senate.

The November 28th meeting reflected a level of consensus among the President's advisers that the administration should go forward with its commitment to a new education department. But the conflict that existed within the EOP also indicated that it would not be easy to proceed with the initiative.

The difficulties that were facing the education group within PRP were not unique. In a November 22, 1977 memorandum to PRP Assistant Director Peter Szanton, staffer Keith M. Miles attempted to evaluate the status of the entire reorganization effort. He wrote:

> Recently, it seems that we have spent much of our time on the defensive, responding on an ad hoc basis to agency criticism and confusion about whether the kind of reorganization we are tending toward will be sufficiently "bold" and simplified to be judged a success in the eyes of the President, the public, and ourselves. ... I think a major part of the problem stems from one fact: *To date we have not done an adequate job of establishing firmly in our own minds, and communicating to the outside world, the goals of the reorganization, the rationale for our approach, and the significance of this effort in contrast to others.* The result is some embarrassment and frustration about the vagueness and generality of our goals (and our inability thus far to operationally define our projects in terms of these goals), some doubts about the wisdom of our approach, and a hesitancy to engage our critics and aggressively sell our effort to the public.[1]

Miles' memorandum called for nine action steps to address the problems he detailed. Most of those recommendations, however, called for more attention to the reorganization processes and goals on the part of the President himself.

A JANUARY DECISION

From the November 28th meeting through the holiday season, the PRP was hard at work, attempting to build support for its broad design for the department. On the same day that Carter met with top White House staff, PRP staffers also met with Senator Abraham Ribicoff, the most powerful political ally for the broad department. According to a memorandum written by PRP Assistant Director Patricia Gwaltney to OMB Chief McIntyre, Ribicoff, "after hearing our description of the rationale for the broad department (he) enthusiastically agreed. He said that the creation of a department which is too narrow would not be worth the effort. He also agreed that it would be difficult to broaden such a department later. He said that he would postpone hearings until April to give us time to consult with the groups and continue our analysis."[2]

Ribicoff's support for the PRP approach, according to Brian McGovern, another PRP staff member who was present at the meeting, was very strong. McGovern reported that Ribicoff made the following comments:

—While I don't favor a narrow based Department of Education, I don't want the department bogged down by non-educational programs. Any program placed in the new department must have an education factor.

—The NEA is wrong in wanting a narrow Department ... I will talk to them and tell them so ... without my support there won't be any new department ... I will talk to them.

—Don't include National Endowments for the Arts or the Humanities in the new Department.

—If you face up to the interest groups that want to leave the Head Start program in HEW, you will win.

—We're thinking along the same lines about the Department ... we will coordinate the hearings with you ... The Administration will testify ... the hearings should take place just after Easter, before mid-April ... not beyond 1st of May ... we don't want to lose the present momentum.[3]

At the same time that McGovern noted Ribicoff's support, he commented that "there are 'mines' that will have to be avoided. For example, the Committee staff appears to have a different perspective than the Senator does as to what programs the department should have. Therefore, coordination with the Senator's staff will require large amounts of tact, PRP staff time and negotiation if the common ground the Senator, Harrison and Pat stood on is to be preserved."

Ribicoff's support was extremely important to the PRP study team—a group that was not privy to the political deliberations in the White House across Pennsylvania Avenue. Ribicoff represented the study group's trump card as they battled with the Domestic Policy Staff over the issue of breadth of the proposed department. To ignore the PRP staff was one thing. To ignore Ribicoff was quite another. When Harrison Wellford and Patricia Gwaltney met with Ribicoff and his staff to review the three options that would be presented to Carter later in the day, the meeting was not only to inform Ribicoff. His support for the broader option was viewed as essential to the strategy.

Gwaltney and the study group had hoped that the November 28th meeting would bring a clear decision by the President as to the basic programmatic structure of the department. Gwaltney had been asked by OMB Director McIntyre to make a list of steps that should be taken after the President made a decision. She responded in two ways: first, by describing in some detail the steps that would be taken if the broad department should be pursued; and second, by describing in very sketchy fashion what should be done if the narrow department option were chosen.[4] Under a broad option, Gwaltney called on the President to "direct Secretary Califano and Stu Eizenstat to work with us" on the proposal for the new department as well as on the proposal for internal restructuring of HEW. She also requested that the President meet with interest group and congressional leadership and make a public announcement on his preference for a broad structure. The narrow department was assumed to require much less: meetings with NEA and Hill leadership and quick preparation of a noncontroversial bill.

Carter's comment at the November 28th meeting was interpreted by the PRP study group as a go-ahead for the broad department strategy. By mid-December, PRP staffers were busy preparing analyses of various program pieces that were candidates for inclusion in the proposal. It appeared that the PRP took Ribicoff seriously when he agreed with them; although he had clearly noted that the Endowments should not be included in the proposals, analyses did include those programs as possibilities (although "not likely") for the bill.[5]

Despite the PRP activity, there were three issues that remained unresolved from the November meeting. These issues dramatically illustrated the continuing conflict between the advocates of analysis and those who worried about political "realities." Clarification of Carter's position was sought via a memorandum to the President from OMB Chief McIntyre.[6]

McIntyre began the memo by noting that the November 28th meeting to discuss options for reorganization of education programs produced agreement that:

> Your commitment to a new Cabinet-level department encompassing education and related programs should be reaffirmed publicly.
>
> The new department should be as broad in scope as possible, and should not be dominated by a single constituency group.
>
> We should work with Senator Ribicoff in developing a legislative proposal.
>
> The Education Division of DHEW should be restructured internally as an interim step toward and consistent with movement toward a new department.

However, noted McIntyre, several issues were still to be resolved: what should be the forum for a public reaffirmation of the department; how to characterize the breadth of the new department publicly; and how to restructure the Education Division of HEW in the interim.

Issue 1: The forum for public reaffirmation of Carter's commitment to the department.

Carter was given the choice of a number of formal announcements (the State of the Union address; a special Presidential message on education policy and reorganization; or a statement of speech by the Vice President) or less formal ways such as a response to a question in a press conference. Carter agreed with McIntyre's suggestion that he make an "informal response to a press question, while we proceed to work with Senator Ribicoff and other Members of Congress, and the interest groups." Carter also noted that a vice presidential statement on this issue was "also OK."

Issue 2: How to characterize the breadth of the new department publicly.

In the memorandum to Carter, McIntyre noted that

> there was some disagreement on this issue at our November 28 meeting. Joe Califano, Charlie Schultz and Jack Watson advised that you make no statement of preference for a "broad" department but that you should rule out a "narrow" department. Stu and Hamilton advised that you should reaffirm your campaign commitment to a new department without stating a preference that it be broad. Stu thinks that social services should not be included because of their strong relationship to welfare, social security and medicaid.
>
> We advised that you should state your preference for a broad department including education and related human development programs. I understand Stu's argument about social services. We will have to evaluate these programs carefully to determine which ones are most closely related to education and should be included. I do, however, advise that you indicate that you favor a department which views education in the context of the family and related community institutions. This would give us the leeway we need to work out the substantive and political details. Senators Ribicoff and Williams, and Congressman Brademas have said they would like to pursue this broad concept.

Carter noted that he agreed with the recommendation but included a marginal comment on the memo: "be general not specific".

Issue 3: Restructuring the Education Division.

McIntyre was concerned that the changes that Califano proposed (such as consolidating the offices of the Commissioner and the Assistant Secretary for Legislation under a single point of leadership) would require a formal reorganization plan. He noted: "Though this change is desirable, the submission of a reorganization plan to the Ribicoff committee may be confusing and burdensome in light of the legislative proposal for a new department. I suggest that Secretary Califano be authorized to include changes that cannot be accomplished administratively and are compatible with movement toward a new department in the education legislation that we will submit to the authorizing committees." Carter also agreed with this recommendation.

Carter's decisions on the McIntyre memorandum were circulated to McIntyre, the Vice President, Stu Eizenstat and Hamilton Jordan on January 9, 1978. That same day, Eizenstat sent a memo to Jordan and McIntyre on the cabinet-level Department of Education.[7] Jordan and Eizenstat noted that Carter had made a comment on the most recent draft of the Vice President's Agenda: "Endorse Ribicoff approach—broad Department— initial reorganization plan RP (Richard Pettigrew) to consolidate." The DSP Director commented that "It is the Vice President's impression, based on his conversation with the President, that the President wants to 'step back' after the initial endorsement and not become too deeply involved in thrashing out the details of the Department in Congress."

Eizenstat reported his own positions on the three issues that had not been resolved during the November meeting. He argued that the "education groups would be most pleased with a brief announcement in the State of the Union (together with a reference to our major education budget increases and new legislation). We are doing so much for education this year that we should make a special effort to claim credit. If earlier announcement is desired at this week's press conference, I think it should be in response to a question rather than in the opening remarks. There is so much current news in the President's trip, the Mideast situation, the state of the dollar, and our efforts to focus on energy that an opening statement on education would appear out of place." Eizenstat's position on the "narrow"/"broad" issue was that "While both HEW and OMB argue for a 'broad' department, my own view has been that the President should not address this question in his endorsement. While HEW and OMB may want to work with Congress to achieve the best possible organization, we do not want the education groups to say we are trying to insist on a new department so controversial that it cannot pass."

Finally, Eizenstat called for action on the interim reorganization question. "Califano (his former boss in the Johnson administration) should be allowed to proceed *if* he can obtain the concern of the NEA and other key education groups. They may be willing to go along, since in any event adoption of legislation to create a new department is likely to take a year or more. If the Secretary can obtain Congressional and interest groups support, I would favor granting a slot for a reorganization plan. We should not waste a reorganization slot on a proposal which is not broadly acceptable."

Eizenstat's positions on specific outcomes were clearly consistent with the President's responses to the McIntyre memo. However, his interpretation of the issues cast Carter's terse decision points and marginal notes into a more political and less analytical framework.

Just a week after the Carter decision memorandum was circulated to the inner reaches of the White House, the *New York Times* published an editorial that was extremely critical of the PRP approach. The editorial, entitled "The High Price of Cheapening the Cabinet,"[8] was a strong defense of the Califano position. The editorial began: "The President is reported ready to propose creation of a Cabinet-level Department of Education. We hope the report is wrong; or that the Administration can be persuaded to change course. It is an empty, even harmful idea, bad for the President, bad for the Cabinet, bad for education." The piece noted that education had fared badly in competition with other parts of HEW and that many education programs were found outside of the HEW education bureaucracy. It continued:

> Still, it is one thing to seek order and efficiency, another to pay the political price. To achieve a broadly restructured department, the Administration would have to pay a high price indeed. In the face of such a reorganization, the Veterans Administration, for instance—and its interest groups and Congressional supporters—would be just as tenacious in protecting their turf as, say, the National Education Association would be pleased to raid it. And that is only one of a number of foreseeable conflicts. Even if the Administration is willing to spend political capital generously, the legislative bargaining process is quite likely to erode the scope of a broad new department, perhaps leaving no more than a new label for the old Office of Education.

The *Times* went on to criticize the symbolism of power (arguing that a title does not change power relationships) and to view this as a step toward further fragmentation of an already fragmented system.

The editorial concluded: "If the President is in fact persuaded that the Commissioner of Education needs more respect, then he can pay that respect now, whatever the incumbent's title. If the President thinks education spending should be increased, he has abundant authority now to ask Congress to agree with him. The issue should be education, not bureaucratic trappings. As Robert Frost once wrote of tennis courts: 'We are on them not to see if the lines are straight, but to play tennis.'"

On January 19, as he delivered his second State of the Union address, Carter did make mention of the department of education proposal. "We've made a good start on turning the gobbledegook of federal regulations into plain English that people can understand. But we know that we still have a long way to go. We've brought together parts of 11 different government agencies to create a new Department of Energy. And now it's time to take another major step by creating a separate Department of Education." Carter's statement in the address was not specific; PRP staff were disappointed in the language. While Carter's words did not preclude a preference for a broad department, the language he used was hardly explicit.

Carter's announcement—however murky—meant that the PRP study team was now engaged in a public political struggle. The new department was no longer an abstract idea examined within the White House. It had evolved into a political football to be tossed and thrown about by a myriad of actors. As the arena changed and the issue became more public, it was obvious to the PRP team that political realities and forces had to be incorporated into its proposals if the department would come to life.

In early February, the Education Study group within PRP undertook a "very speculative and tentative discussion of what a new Department of Education would look like given what we know now about the desirability and feasibility of bringing a host of programs within the new department."[9] Three "measures" were used to assist in the formulation:

1. The benefits that consolidation would have for the recipients of the programs involved.
2. The contribution that bringing these programs together would make to the quality of American education.
3. The balance of political opposition and support relating to inclusion of the programs within the new department.

The discussion grouped program clusters in a number of categories: "Programs that Almost Certainly Should and Could be Within a New Department"; "Programs that are Strong Candidates for inclusion"; "Programs Whose Inclusion is a 'Close Call' and about which no Direction Should be Indicated"; "Programs that are Unlikely Candidates"; "Programs Sometimes Named as Candidates that Should not be Included"; and "Programs About which we Know too Little to Speculate."

The "should and could" category included all programs within the Division of Education, Vocational Rehabilitation programs in HEW, education related aspects of the Office of Civil Rights, the College Housing Loan program in HUD, the National Commission on Libraries and Information Science, the USDA Graduate School, and some parts of the Indian Education programs within the Department of Interior.

The "strong candidates" category included the education directorate of NSF, the National Endowment for the Humanities, the Indian schools, Juvenile Justice and Delinquency Prevention from Justice, the Educational Broadcasting and Telecommunications Programs, the Commission on Presidential Scholars, the Runaway Youth Programs in HEW, the Service Learning Program in ACTION, the summer youth Program in CSA, the summer youth employment program in DOL and the Youth Employment Demonstration Project Act in DOL.

The "close call" category included the child nutrition programs; Head Start, DOD dependent schools; the International Communications Agency, parts of the Comprehensive Employment and Training Act (CETA) within

DOL; student assistance programs administered by the VA research and development programs within the Administration for Children, Youth and Families within HEW, the Smithsonian Institution, the Job Corps, and student assistance programs dealing with health manpower.

The "unlikely candidates" named were NSF, the Library of Congress, on-the-job training programs within CETA and the Employment Service within the Department of Labor. The "should not be included" list included the Harry S. Truman Scholarship Foundation, the National Endowment for the Arts, the Public Service Employment Program, and the National Institutes of Health. The final category included two progams about which too little was known to speculate: the National Sea Grant Foundation and the National Oceanic and Atmospheric Administration.

A POLITICAL STRATEGY

Within this framework, a political strategy was established within the PRP group. A February 6, 1978 paper outlined a "broad strategy for managing the politics of establishing the proposed Department of Education."[10] The strategy outlined was viewed as a three-part, sequential process, beginning with interest group conversations, moving to highly focused congressional consultations, and finally to "timely presidential leadership." Three "action-forcing" events were seen as providing "opportunities for momentum and substantive guidance"—a message by the President on education in late February; a possible Mondale-McIntyre-Califano news conference, tentatively set for February; and the Ribicoff hearings in mid-March.

The analysis regarding the political strategy was based on a number of assumptions outlined in the paper:

1. The President's and Vice President's strong personal convictions on this initiative assure that it can receive top-level leadership.
2. The Administration's position in favor of the department may be seen by many as a political response to the NEA for its campaign support, and not as an initiative advanced primarily because of its merits.
3. Some will think that Administration support for the department is divided.
4. Legislation creating a department should be enacted this year, but reluctance to deal with controversy before elections, this year's short session, and other major issues before the Congress (e.g. Panama, energy, taxes) compound possible congressional reluctance to move that fast.
5. Most congressional interest in establishing a new department is centered in the Senate, and little enthusiasm now exists in the House.
6. Congressional momentum, particularly in the House, to create a new department will be prompted primarily by the activity and support of organized interest groups.
7. The education interest groups will not oppose including most programs which could become part of the department, as long as they feel a proposal is not too controversial, and will thereby endanger the entire initiative. Higher education groups will continue to remain aloof from the issue.[11]

The strategy that was devised was oriented toward Congress and the constituent groups, and was "designed to cascade carefully developed support from the interest groups into a proposal key Members of Congress will feel comfortable in supporting."[12] The "snow ball" approach toward interest groups was one in which "we carefully nurture various clusters of interest groups so that they will support the inclusion of 'their' programs in the new department."[13] The first wave of interest groups to be contacted would include groups concerned with youth, handicapped, Indians, child nutrition, children, science, arts and humanities, and labor. The second round of consultations would be held with organizations representing state and local officials, the civil rights community, and education groups that had expressed reservations about a new department. This round would be held "to determine whether they support transfers of programs clustered around themes the first round of consultees preferred." Themes and a roster of programs would emerge from these two sets of consultations; at that point, a third round of conversations would be held with other education interest groups as discussions about the "consensus on the outlines of a new department."[14]

The congressional consultation strategy outlined for PRP action concentrated on three distinct sets of members of Congress: key congressional leaders (Senators Ribicoff, Pell, Williams and Byrd and Representatives Perkins, Brademas, Ford, Brooks and O'Neill); subcommittee chairmen and ranking minority members who had jurisdiction over programs included in the agreed-upon transfer clusters; and members of the Governmental Affairs and Government Operations committees who were viewed as "likely to have an interest and to support this initiative."[15]

The final step in the three-pronged strategy involved "timely Presidential Leadership." "After this 'snowball' consultation process, the President should become involved publicly. He would be able to enunciate the broad theme(s) that should characterize the education department and announce his support for a detailed proposal."[16] This could be a part of the education message that was set to be delivered in late February, followed by a "possible" Mondale-McIntyre-Califano news conference. According to the paper, "This approach would provide an opportunity for the President to take a public leadership role in the issue before the Ribicoff hearings. It would become *his* initiative. At the same time, the consultations process outlined above will protect him from supporting a proposal that cannot pass and demonstrate good management of the issue. If this approach is followed, the President could refer positively in a public forum to the congressional leaders who are supporting the proposal. This would enhance efforts to motivate them to obtain enactment of the legislation this year."[17]

The paper concluded with a recitation of three "tactical objectives" for the strategy: increasing the House's involvement; utilizing "good government" spokespeople (who would emphasize the responsiveness, coordination, priority-setting, and foresight abilities of a new department); and by calling for the early and continued involvement of affected cabinet officers.[18]

The strategy outlined by the PRP rested on yet another—but unarticulated—assumption. The PRP group proceeded as if the decisions coming out of the Executive Office of the President were unilateral and settled. For this group, the battle was over; the President had decided that there would be a Department of Education and the force of the executive branch would be united to assure that this presidential decision became a legislative reality.

If one needed public evidence of the lack of solidarity within the administration on this issue, HEW Secretary Califano gave it. During hearings on the Labor-HEW budgets before the Senate Appropriations Committee on February 2, 1978, Califano was reminded of his opposition to the creation of a department by Massachusetts Republican, Edward Brooke.[19] Califano acknowledged that he had opposed the department in a book published earlier: "I can't change the words," he admitted. While the HEW Secretary did note that support for a department was "the Administration position and we are supporting that position," he used the opportunity of the hearing to throw ammunition to the opponents of the department.

Asked by Senator Brooke whether he was planning to recommend any major changes in the education provisions, Califano retorted: "It depends, Senator Brooke. Now when you talk about the Department of Education, you are—the biggest aid program in the Federal government is the Veterans Adminstration. So, for it to make sense, you put that program into the Department of Education. The Ribicoff bill, as you know, since you are a cosponsor, it would put Head Start in there, the arts and humanities program in there. ... Now there is a lot of objection to some of that going in. Take the Office of Civil Rights. Do you put them in the Office of Education or leave them somewhere else? When it started, it was Education. You may recall in the '60s it was moved out, because there was no enforcement in Education." Califano concluded his conversation with Senator Brooke by noting that "It would make sense, in my judgment, speaking personally, if the fight over the Department of Education dragged on for an extended period of time, to make some administrative changes in that office. ... If we didn't pass it this year, I think some administrative changes ought to be made."

Califano's message was clear. He was, in the eyes of the PRP, throwing a red herring to those who were apprehensive about the development of a broad department; VA and Head Start were both programs with strong and vocal constituencies who did not want to be placed in a new department. The reminder about civil rights enforcement was of great concern to civil rights advocates who had fought long and hard for enforcement. And his comment about the time delay suggested that Califano—one of the few real "pols" within the administration—didn't expect action on the measure.

Several weeks later, testifying before the House Labor-HEW Appropriations Subcommittee, Califano made another pitch for his strategy—preempting the creation of a department by devising a dramatic reorganization within

HEW, giving the education programs an under secretary at their helm. The *Education Daily*, an important Washington education newsletter, reported Califano's testimony with a headline, "Califano Suggests Under Secretary as Alternative to Education Department."[20] When questioned by Representative David Obey (D-Wis.) about the makeup of the new department, Califano was reported to have replied that "veterans' programs, Labor Department jobs programs, the National Science Foundation, Indian schools, arts and humanities, Defense Department schools, child nutrition programs in the Department of Agriculture, Head Start, college housing loans, some programs from the Community Services Administration and institutional training under CETA Title II are Office of Management and Budget 'candidates for inclusion in a department of education.'" Again the HEW secretary was providing ammunition for those who feared they would be swallowed up by a new department.

The Califano testimony evoked an official retort from OMB Director McIntyre in the form of a memorandum to the Vice President, Hamilton Jordan, Stuart Eizenstat, and Frank Moore on "Secretary Califano's List of Agencies Considered for New Education Department."[21] McIntyre responded to a report in the *Washington Post* on Califano's testimony in which a number of candidates were listed for inclusion in the new department. "The following were listed in the article as candidates for inclusion but are not, in fact, now being considered: Veterans' Educational Programs (with the exception of educational loans), National Science Foundation (except for the Education Directorate), Job Training Programs (except for new education-related programs), Community Services Administration, and Day Care."

McIntyre noted: "To be sure, the PRP has been studying a wide array of potential candidates for inclusion in the new department. This activity has been carried out in keeping with the President's desire to create as broad a department as possible. Because a program is being studied for inclusion, of course, does not imply that it will be recommended for inclusion."

The congressional strategy outlined by the PRP, however, did not operate within a problem-free environment. A few short weeks after taking office, Carter found himself on less than cordial terms with a number of members of Congress. Frank Moore, Carter's Assistant for Congressional Relations, had come under heavy criticism and was accused of being "insensitive to the unwritten laws of protocol that help determine the relationship between the executive and legislative branches."[22]

Carter himself was viewed as a single-minded advocate opposed to compromise. By the time that the education strategy was being developed, press reports found Carter less than effective. His first-year initiatives were generally characterized as overly ambitious, due to a lack of experience. The administration was described as lacking a clear course of action. As the Congress prepared to reconvene in 1978, the legislative priorities on the agenda reflected a sizeable number of items that were "unfinished business." These included the completion of Carter's comprehensive energy bill which had been tied up in a House-Senate conference for three months. Carter sought prompt action on a plan to pump more money into the economy by a $25 billion tax cut and the creation of new jobs. A comprehensive welfare reform program had been submitted by the President in September 1977. The administration was looking toward early Senate action on the Panama Canal treaties and a new arms treaty with the Soviet Union. And the President hoped to resolve the hospital cost containment issue which had been stalled in committee in both chambers of the Congress.

There were also reports that the administration's relationship with Senator Ribicoff (and especially his staff) was strained. The PRP had gone further than the Ribicoff committee in proposing a number of programs for the new department: the transfer of child feeding programs in addition to nutrition education from the Agriculture Department as well as at least one of the Endowments. Tension was also present in the strategy that would be adopted. It was not clear whether the administration would accept Ribicoff's bill (S. 991) or would propose its own measure. The good relationship that had been struck early on between the PRP and the Ribicoff staff appeared to be eroding somewhat. The Ribicoff staff argued that anything less than the full and forceful support of the President would undermine the Committee's confidence in Carter's commitment to a department.

The PRP team concentrated its efforts, at this point, on key congressional leaders, many of whom were in general support of the creation of a department, but who—as committee or subcommittee chairmen or ranking minority members—had jurisdiction over programs proposed for transfer. The decentralized nature of committee jurisdiction meant that there were nine committees or subcommittees in the House and nine committees or subcommittees in the Senate with jurisdiction over the programs that were viewed as "strong candidates for inclusion" in the proposed department.[23]

The consultation with these committees and subcommittees was an extremely delicate matter. Not only were the congressional members protective of their programs and interest groups, but they were also apprehensive about reorganization in general. Attempts had been made over the years to "rationalize" the committee structure of the House (especially by Rules Committee Chairman Richard Bolling, Democrat of Missouri). For some— especially members of the House Education and Labor Committee—the reorganization of the executive branch was viewed as a pivotal move to force the reorganization of the Congress itself, not only changing the jurisdictional structure of the committee but also disturbing the balance of power between the agencies, their interest groups and their congressional advocates.

The meetings with congressional leaders in the House revealed what had been anticipated: there was less enthusiasm for the legislation in the House than there was in the Senate. There was no House member who was playing a leadership role on the legislation whose position was comparable to that of Ribicoff. Although several bills proposing a department had been introduced in the House during the session (by Democrat Carl Perkins and by Republican Margaret Heckler) it had been difficult to get the support of Ribicoff's counterpart in the House—Texas Democrat Jack Brooks, chairman of the House Government Operations Committee.

Brooks was not a fan of reorganization attempts. He had expressed deep reservations about Carter's reorganization plans early in the administration. In his autobiography, Carter commented, "In fact, because of Jack Brooks's opposition, as the new Congress prepared to convene, I could not get any Democratic member to introduce my proposed reorganization legislation!"[24] Brooks was finally convinced by President Carter to introduce a companion to S. 991—but his support for the measure was never enthusiastic.

INTEREST GROUP MEETINGS

The strategy that had been outlined by the PRP was based on an assumption that support from essential interest groups was both obtainable and controllable. But the meetings with interest groups did not produce what had been hoped for. The PRP strategy had assumed that the groups contacted would be fairly forthcoming with their positions on program transfers. It was thought that the meetings with the various organizations affected by the potential proposal would give staff an opportunity to test the political waters and, thus, to devise a plan that was responsive to these positions.

The PRP hopes were hardly fulfilled. The education groups that were backing the creation of the department showed very little interest in engaging in discussions on the specifics of program transfers. For groups such as the NEA, the issue was not about the specific elements within the department— it was about the department itself. The specific interest groups (such as groups representing labor, youth, handicapped, Indians, child nutrition, children, science, and arts and humanities) were much more comfortable being given the opportunity to react to PRP proposals than in generating them. For a number of these groups, it was a case in which they asked the PRP to show its hand before the group took its own position.

The proposals dealing with Indian Education illustrate the complexity of the consultation route. It was clear that a majority of tribes and Native American groups found the Ribicoff proposal to move all Native American education into the new department unacceptable. At the same time, the proposal to move the Indian schools out of the Bureau of Indian Affairs was made because Indian leaders had spent years criticizing the quality of Indian schools and the unresponsiveness of the BIA. Yet when these groups met with the PRP, they were extremely noncommital about their position on this issue. It appeared that these groups were using the threat of removing the Indian schools from BIA to shake up the BIA and scare that organization into more responsive action.

For some issues, it was much easier to get a reading of interest group views from the executive branch agencies that embodied their concerns than from the groups themselves. However, it was not always easy to ascertain whether these agency views reflected interest group perspectives or actually molded those views. The community of concern around some programmatic areas was so strong and united that it was meaningless to try to differentiate between the views of the interest groups, the executive agencies, or the congressional committee and subcommittee staffs.

The debates over the transfer of the Education Directorate of the National Science Foundation to the new department illustrate the interchangeability of these perspectives. The PRP had targeted the science education programs within NSF for possible movement to the new department. Those programs were largely grants to local school districts for curricular and teacher-training efforts. Approximately 9% of the NSF budget was targeted to the improvement of science teaching and science curriculum—a relatively small part of the total NSF program. Early conversations held with the President's Science Adviser, Frank Press, and with representatives of the Congressional Office of Technology Assessment reinforced the PRP staff view that these components within NSF could be moved into a new department with very little disruption to the ongoing operations of the science agency.

However, the PRP staff and its advisers had failed to see the other functions that the science education program played within the NSF. Science education was the only program within the agency that had a broad geographical distribution around the country; most of the other NSF funds found their way to the prestigious universities (which were largely concentrated on the two coasts). The science education program allowed the agency to show many members of Congress that their districts were benefiting from its program. That "political cover" was perceived by some NSF officials (and other science advocates) to be an important element of its base of support.

In addition, individuals within the science education community perceived a loss of status if they were moved from the prestigious mission of NSF. They believed that by being severed from this independent and quasi-autonomous agency (and being identified with education interests), the science education community would have its status immediately reduced. As PRP staff met with representatives of the science community, it also became clear that the NSF constituency believed that the education department would be dominated by elementary and secondary school interests—and that the representatives of higher education would find themselves to be the "odd man out."

In a sense, the exchange of views between the PRP and the NSF constituency was a futile act. The PRP was focusing on program effectiveness. It tried to show that the transfer of science education programs would not affect the overall mission of the NSF. Indeed, divested of the science education programs, the PRP argued that the NSF would be in a better position to do what it did best—focus on innovation.

A PRP staff paper detailed the argument: "The respective roles, policies and procedures of NSF and HEW education programs need clarification. A degree of overlap and duplication of effort exists due to the fact that programs in NSF and OE attempt to meet similar institutional and student needs. More serious, however, is the lack of policy and program coordination, particularly with respect to curricula development projects, support for major educational technology demonstration projects, educational needs of special interest groups and more general areas relating to research, innovation, and dissemination strategies."[25]

While the PRP paper acknowledged that "the science and academic communities will find more disadvantages than advantages to any program transfers of NSF science education programs,"[26] the document strongly suggested a move toward the clear separation of the new agencies.

The PRP argued that there was no evidence that the science education programs were particularly effective; test scores in science and mathematics had deteriorated; fewer students were choosing to take science electives in high schools; about half of the public high schools in the country did not offer physics courses.

The PRP staff also did not buy the argument of the higher education community that it was inevitable that a new department would be dominated by elementary and secondary education interests. They attempted to argue the reverse: movement of programs like science education into a highly visible and strong new department would increase the commitment and involvement of the university and scholarly communities in educational issues.

PRP's arguments, however, did not change many minds. A meeting was held in early February 1978 with the President of the National Academy of Sciences, the Executive Officer of the AAAS, the Vice President of the Carnegie Council, the President of Johns Hopkins University, a faculty member from Harvard, representatives of the Office of Science and Technology Programs, the President's Science Adviser, and PRP staff. The meeting was held to discuss general concepts that might justify a department of education and science, specific arguments for and against a department of education, and the desirability of including particular science and research-related programs in the new department. PRP staffer Arthur Sheekey summarized the meeting in a memo to Willis Hawley: "The general summary of this meeting is that a strong or weak Department of Education could negatively affect Federal support for science and research. Basic research is always vulnerable to attacks and competition and a representative in the Cabinet would be able to lobby for more funding of 'school programs'; the university community could suffer."[27] The participants in the meeting were less concerned about organizational configurations and more concerned about the mission and purpose of the department.

Sheekey's summary continued: "Research and science play a very different role. They are components of a national policy relating to 'national survival,' 'national security' and the general health of the nation. Any attempt to build organizational bridges between science and education could have very negative and even explosive consequences. Science and research have everything to lose and nothing to gain in such a marriage."[28]

INTEREST GROUP ACTIVITY

At the same time that the PRP was engaged in its own political strategy to determine the specific composition of the department, there were a number of activities undertaken by interest groups themselves around the same issues. In some instances, the interest group activity was independent of the actions within the Executive Office of the President. In other cases, the interest group activity was provoked by the administration's activity.

Many education and other related organizations orchestrated their activity around the basic argument for the creation of a department, echoing the themes that had been struck for years by these same groups. They alleged, again, that a separate department would foster more effective, capable and visible leadership of education at the highest level of government. This leadership role would eventually command greater resources for education programs. The NEA continued its pivotal role on this issue; it was highly effective in persuading a vastly divergent contingent of groups, representing a broad range on the spectrum of education interests, by focusing almost exclusively on general principles rather than by highlighting specifics of the proposed legislation.

The NEA strategies were reminiscent of its presidential campaign organization. The NEA sent thousands of press releases and editorials into the hometowns of its local affiliates, along with pictures of NEA leaders at the White House and with the President. This activity was coordinated with the White House; even before the administration presented its formal proposal to the Ribicoff committee, White House representatives met regularly with the NEA and the other top education groups to plan a strategy for their campaign. However, the NEA's strategy was to focus on general, abstract support for the department while the PRP and other White House strategists were concentrating on the specifics of the programs to be included within the department.

While NEA wanted to mobilize its significant resources to ensure the passage of a department, it was sensitive to the perception by opponents to the move that a new department would be entirely controlled by NEA. To assure that it was not alone in its support for the proposal, NEA helped organize a coalition of groups in support of the department. While NEA clearly played a dominant role, other groups were also involved. The coalition took two forms: a broad Citizen's Committee for a Cabinet Department of Education, and a small coordinating group made up of Washington representatives of major education organizations.[29]

At this point in the evolution of the proposal, the opposition to the idea of the department was much less developed than was the support for it. The American Federation of Teachers—the NEA's competitor in the effort to organize and represent teachers—struck out against the idea. Most press commentary on the AFT characterized its opposition as simply an antagonistic stance to the NEA. Ted Fiske, education editor of the *New York Times*, was quoted as saying that AFT "would consider coming out against the use of lunch boxes if the association came out for it."[30]

However, in addition to the AFT, there were other opponents of the idea of the department: a number of labor unions, some anti-union groups, the U.S. Catholic Conference, private school interests, and a batch of individuals who represented both liberal and conservative political ideologies. The task of building a coalition representing this diversity of interests was formidable. Some argued against the department because it violated the constitutional precept that education was a local and state affair. Others argued that a department would not ensure a strong enforcement role involving equal educational opportunity, that it would capitulate to state and local education agencies. Although the AFT and the rest of the labor movement felt strongly about a department, it was difficult for them (as well as many civil rights advocates) to stake out a position directly in conflict with a sitting Democratic president.

THE HEAD START CONTROVERSY

Although a movement of general opposition to the department did not materialize during this period, specific activities were undertaken against the anticipated recommendations from the PRP. No mobilization activity was as well-organized—and as effective—as that waged on behalf of the Head Start program. Head Start—a preschool program with parental and community control, a diverse delivery system, and comprehensive services—was established as a part of the Johnson War on Poverty. Despite both research and political attacks on the program, Head Start survived—indeed thrived—during the Nixon years. As the Carter administration took office, the program was viewed by many community and civil rights advocates as the only remaining Great Society program in which many of the poorest Black communities still had a major stake: 65% of the Head Start children were from minority groups in 1977 and approximately 80,000 individuals from poor communities had paid jobs in the programs.

The most vocal spokesperson for the Head Start program had become Marian Wright Edelman, the founder and president of the Children's Defense Fund, an organization that grew out of civil rights activities in the South and represented a broadening base of support for children's issues. During the 1976 campaign, Edelman was a Carter adviser and supporter. Her work on education issues was respected by many in Washington; she had been a close adviser to Vice President Mondale when he chaired the Senate subcommittee on Equal Education Opportunity.

Marian Edelman's concerns about the direction of the reorganization activity were expressed in December 1977 in a letter to Vice President Mondale.[31] She began her communication with the Vice President by noting that they had spoken some months earlier to "discuss CDF's concern that the Administration create a coherent policy process to support the President's commitment to families and children. ... This memorandum is provoked by what we have heard and read about the current reorganization alternatives now being considered for education and social services."[32] Edelman expressed her view that "reorganization is not a goal in itself" and argued that while organization does matter, it is the "combination of indirect yet potentially pervasive (and perverse) consequences that makes the most careful analysis of reorganization proposals necessary. Premature action could divert energy that would be better spent in making existing programs work, degenerate into empty exercises of shuffling boxes on organization charts, or, most important, produce unintended but destructive results for program beneficiaries."[33]

We fear, argued Edelman, that the President's commitment to strengthen the family in a revitalized community "may be lost in the rush to political decision on the question of establishing an independent Department of Education."[34] She detailed CDF's concerns and criteria for assessing any reorganization of HEW:

1. Will the organizational change increase the quality and quantity of services that can strengthen the family and foster the healthy development of all children?
2. Will it improve the access, comprehensiveness, and responsiveness of services at the point where they are delivered to parents and children in their communities?
3. Do proposed structural changes enhance the power of the family unit to participate in decisions on the public programs that affect them *and* hold the professional bureaucrats charged with providing services accountable for their actions, or inaction?
4. Will reorganization improve the federal capacity for enforcement and evaluation to insure local compliance with national purposes and a constructive redefinition of the programs designed to achieve those purposes?
5. Does the executive (and possible legislative) restructuring encourage the development of a stable, public constituency able to sustain adequate program support in the future?[35]

Edelman noted that the two options now being considered by the President (the "narrow" department of education and the "broad" department of education and human services) both raised serious problems for CDF in terms of meeting the organization's criteria. An "unproductive professional parochialism", a "single minded emphasis on specialization" raised serious concerns for Edelman.[36] Conversely, she remained skeptical that there were indeed opportunities for a comprehensive, pluralistic, and coordinated service system even under a broader department.

By March 1978, Edelman and the Head Start advocates were becoming increasingly concerned about the possibility of Head Start being moved into the education department. Another communication was sent to Vice President Mondale, this time called "Reasons Why Head Start Should Not Be Included in a Department of Education or Placed Under Educational Auspices in the Absence of Such a Department."[37] The paper sent to the Vice President was a carefully argued document that focused only on the Head Start program. Edelman noted that the Head Start community was not taking a position on the department of education per se but was, rather, concentrating on one program "that we strongly feel should remain outside of any separate education department if created, and independent of educational auspices in the absence of such a department." She argued: "We are convinced that such an organizational change, *regardless of any assurances to the contrary*, would be a forerunner to public school control of the program—an eventuality perceived quite unfavorably by many child development experts, minority parents and civil rights groups."[38]

Six reasons were detailed in the paper for opposition to transfer of Head Start to a new department. First, it was not an education program; second, parents played a central role in Head Start; third, minority communities had a major stake in Head Start and lacked equal alternatives; fourth, Head Start offered children a constructive, flexible environment which had been conducive to their healthy development; fifth, Head Start was a success; and sixth, Head Start in its present form was cost effective.

The opposition to the Head Start move was growing and becoming more adamant. Mississippi civil rights activist Aaron Henry met with PRP staff in early March in two different meetings; PRP staff picked up mixed signals from the meetings and did not appear to understand the political sensitivities around the issue.

On March 21, 1978, Marian Edelman wrote to Harrison Wellford, head of the PRP, expressing her "deepest possible concern" about the proposal to include Head Start in a separate Department of Education. Her arguments were strong:

> From the early, volatile confrontations in Mississippi after the establishment of the Child Development Group of Mississippi (CDGM), we have struggled against segregationists who wanted to destroy these poor community centers and the machinations

of two Republican administrations designed to assert control over the independence of these local efforts. What an irony to now face a Carter Administration proposal to deliver the program into the hands of the educational establishment, whose rigidities and parochialism Head Start was designed to overcome. If you do this, I and those thousands of poor people in the 1,200 Head Start communities who have sacrificed all these years to keep going, and with whom CDF works, will view your action as a betrayal. We will fight you in every way we can.[39]

Copies of the letter were sent to 42 individuals, including Mondale, the top White House staff, key members of Congress, all of the major civil rights leaders, and the HEW officials with responsibilities for Head Start.

A day later, members of Congress and Harrison Wellford received a telegram from 12 key civil rights leaders, calling for the rejection of Head Start in the administration proposal. The telegram concluded with the sentence: "To threaten the integrity of Head Start at this time could only be viewed as a betrayal by many of the poor who have found hope in its reality and faith in the promise of this administration."

THE VOCATIONAL REHABILITATION COALITION

While the Head Start constituency was striving to keep its program from being included in the new department, another constituency group, by contrast, was attempting to ensure its inclusion in the new organization. The vocational rehabilitation programs—designed to provide vocational training and sheltered workshops for disabled individuals—were programs with a long and proud history. For many years, in the tradition of other HEW efforts, the programs had operated as an independent, autonomous unit within the large department. From the mid-1960s on, secretaries of HEW had attempted to devise schemes to place some accountability checks on a number of specialized programs that had their own powerful constituencies and strong ties to Congress. The vocational rehabilitation professionals and the traditional advocates for those who received program benefits were not happy about the reins that were being pulled, limiting their autonomy. HEW secretaries, on the other hand, were concerned about the independent fiefdoms that existed and which precluded efforts to coordinate similar social services programs.

A good deal of the past strategy to control the program had taken organizational form. Over the years the vocational rehabilitation programs moved from autonomous organizational structures within the Department to positions in which they were subsumed by larger structures. At the time of the education department development, the vocational rehabilitation programs were one of several program components within the HEW Office of Human Development Services—an umbrella-like unit that included programs for children, families, the elderly, Native Americans, and other specialized populations. Many of the programs within this unit were targeted toward individuals who had both economic and other problems similar to the traditional welfare population. The vocational rehabilitation community feared that it was losing the prestige and high status that had been associated with its programs as it competed with other programs that were viewed by them as less prestigious.

In addition to the dynamics occurring within the federal government, since the early 1970s there had been attempts in a number of states to place all social services programs under consolidated or umbrella structures. The most dramatic attempt to consolidate programs occurred in Florida and was violently opposed by the vocational rehabilitation constituency (which finally went to federal court to pull itself out of the umbrella structure). Although it had won that battle, these groups were not assured that the problems would be avoided in the future, particularly if the program were viewed as another social services program.

Because of these problems, the vocational rehabilitation interest groups saw the potential—very early on—for improvement of their lot through the creation of an education department. Led by a few strong special interest groups (the Council for Exceptional Children, the American Coalition of Citizens with Disabilities, the Council of State Administrators of Vocational Rehabilitation, and the National Association for Retarded Citizens), the vocational rehabilitation constituency used the department proposal to further its own agenda. As one interest group member put it, "If they were creating a department of peanuts, we would have tried to get the idea of an Assistant Secretary for the disabled in somewhere." Although the groups sought status and visibility through this reorganization scheme, they argued their case on efficiency and effectiveness grounds, noting that the consolidation of the programs for the handicapped in the Education Division and the programs within HEW would bring these improvements. Although the PRP staff had never studied the move in any great detail, they had found that the majority of vocational rehabilitation funds were spent in educational institutions and that the proportion of those expenditures had increased over recent years.

The vocational rehabilitation lobby was characterized by one of its members as an "unholy coalition," made up of people who could agree on the move but for very different reasons. The coalition attempted to push the idea of the transfer to the new department within the Executive Office of the President; it was quickly shot down by OMB Chief McIntyre (the Domestic Policy Staff and reorganization adviser Richard Pettigrew were also opposed—Pettigrew had battled with the vocational rehabilitation community in Florida). When it became clear that the reception for its proposals was less than enthusiastic in the administration, the interest groups proceeded to make their case in the Congress, drawing on powerful and

time-tested allies such as Congressmen Brademas and Horton and Senators
Randolph and Humphrey (Senator Muriel Humphrey eventually became the
major advocate for the cause in the Senate).

In all of these cases, the PRP's attempts to involve the interest groups in
substantive analysis of the department's content and structure failed. Failure
came, however, for a number of different reasons. In some cases, the PRP
efforts were simply ignored because the staff was not viewed as politically
powerful in the Washington scheme of things. In other instances, the PRP
staff was not trusted and so groups would not express their real views on
issues. In yet other cases, the PRP was ignored because it was working in an
official capacity to develop an administration proposal. By the time that the
administration was ready to go to the Hill with its official proposal, most of
the interest groups had already decided that the action was to be found down
Pennsylvania Avenue in the Congress. The AFT had strong ties with
members of the House Education and Labor Committee. The vocational
rehabilitation groups were cultivating their friends on the Hill and won the
support of Senator Muriel Humphrey. The Head Start coalition appealed to
Senators Cranston and Nelson, members of the Head Start authorizing
committee, as well as Senator John Glenn, a member of the Government
Operations Committee. Although the official arena had not yet changed
(Ribicoff was still "waiting" for the administration position), the interest
groups actors—including the NEA and the other supporters of the
measure—were focused on Capitol Hill.

THE BUREAUCRACY RESPONDS

In early April, a memorandum was circulated to members of the cabinet
and heads of agencies affected by the new department asking for their views
and comment on the administration proposal to be unveiled before the
Senate on April 14, 1978. Secretary of Labor, Ray Marshall, commented
that a transfer of several Department of Labor youth training and employment programs was "based on a misunderstanding of employment and
training programs in general and little understanding of the specific programs
targeted for transfer."[40]

Marshall argued that the employment and training programs had very
separate missions from those of the education sector; that there were other
Labor Department programs which would be affected if such a transfer were
made; and that moving these programs to a new education department
would mean that federal influence in the training programs would be limited.

Similar arguments were heard from Assistant Attorney General Patricia
Wald, who noted that while the Department of Justice was generally supportive

of the proposal, "we strongly object to the tentative recommendation to transfer the programs, personnel and the entire $100,000,000 budget of the Office of Juvenile Justice and Delinquency Prevention to the proposed Department of Education," pointing to "compelling programmatic and administrative reasons for retaining this program in the Department of Justice."[41]

Livingstone Biddle, Chairman of the Endowment for the Arts, noted that the Endowment and its Council were in agreement with the tentative recommendation that neither endowment be included in the department, but also used the opportunity to restate the reasons why it was inappropriate to think of moving these programs to a new education department, either at that time or in the future. A similar theme was expressed in a communication from the National Endowment for the Humanities which reminded McIntyre of the legislative mandate for the Humanities Endowment—a mandate that seemed to preclude even a casual consideration of those program components.

NSF Director Richard Atkinson's response reiterated his well-known opposition to the transfer of the science education programs. He wrote to the President: "Given a well-conceived plan for a Department of Education, an argument can be made for transferring the National Science Foundation's (NSF) Science Education programs to that department. However, the new department, as proposed by the Reorganization Committee, does not have a discernible rationale and does little more than add the science education programs of NSF to the general education programs of HEW."[42] Atkinson concluded his letter: "For these reasons, the National Science Board joins me in strongly opposing the transfer of the NSF Science Education programs to the proposed Department of Education."

HEW Secretary Joseph Califano also used the opportunity of commenting on the draft administration proposal to make an argument against the general thrust of the effort. He noted: "As I indicated earlier, the Department of Education concept rests almost wholly on issues of organizational visibility and status, and the significance attached to such organizational symbols by well-organized education interests, especially teachers."[43] Califano made specific comments about three decision choice areas—the Head Start and handicapped programs should not be moved to the new structure; the education related enforcement responsibilities of HEW's Office for Civil Rights should not be moved; and the youth service programs should also remain where they were found (in HEW, Labor, Justice and ACTION).

As the White House prepared to make its position ready for the Ribicoff hearings on April 14, 1978, it was greeted by less than enthusiastic support from the mass media. Although the campaign in support of the department had elicited a slew of editorials in favor of the new structure, there were also opposing editorials in roughly equivalent numbers. The large and opinion-setting newspapers of the country, however, sharply criticized the plan. Criticisms came from the *New York Times*, the *Washington Post*, and the *Wall Street Journal*, characterizing the measure as a constituent-based reorganization— a payoff to the NEA in return for its 1976 endorsement of Carter.

THE PRESIDENT DECIDES

Because of its promise to make its position known before hearings of the Ribicoff Governmental Affairs Committee on Friday, April 14, 1978 the administration faced a real deadline. For about a week before this date, the multiple actors within the Executive Office of the President attempted to hammer out a position that would be acceptable to Carter and would reflect the information that had been received during the consultation process from interest groups, members of Congress, and executive branch agencies.

Two meetings were held during that time in the Roosevelt Room in the White House to discuss the recommendation that would be forwarded to the President. The first, held on April 6th, was attended by Vice President Mondale, Jordan, Watson, Eizenstat, Pettigrew, Carp, and key PRP staff; its agenda was to discuss the program components that would be included in the new department. Mondale and Jordan left the meeting early and Eizenstat took over the session. The primary concern in the discussion was what to do with the vocational rehabilitation programs. Most of the group in attendance were doubtful about including those programs, believing that vocational rehabilitation was not an educational program and, while appropriate for a broad department of education and human development, did not belong in a narrowly conceived structure focused on education. Other program components were discussed during the meeting—Head Start, DOD schools, Indian education. One participant in the meeting described the session as indicating a lack of enthusiasm for the entire idea of the department. Participants were mindful that the President's own views might be different from those that were emerging from the group consensus. Stuart Eizenstat was quoted as saying, "The President may turn against too narrow a department. He wants a broad department."

A few days later another meeting was held with many of the same cast of characters (and again Mondale left the session early). At this point, the White House staff had received the comments from cabinet officials and agency chiefs—most of which suggested that it would be difficult to portray a picture of a unified administration if the proposal for the department went much beyond the traditional education programs. It was during this meeting that it became clear that the political "realism" of the Domestic Policy Staff would prevail. The specific programmatic suggestions were discussed, one by one. Although there was serious consideration of the PRP staff's approach on many of the points (one observer noted that there close calls on many of the issues), the decisions that emerged from the session pushed the recommendation to the "narrow" rather than "broad" formulation for the department. There appear to be a number of reasons for this outcome. First, the top OMB representatives, Wellford and McIntyre, did not perceive themselves to be in good political stead with the President and his close advisers; they were beginning to feel that the whole issue itself was a "turkey." Most of the PRP officials were mindful of the past track record of other reorganization proposals—recommendations that were quickly shot down for being politically unfeasible. The Carter reorganization effort, they pledged to themselves, would be different and would be characterized as a realistic—though not expedient—attempt.

In addition, the decision process itself had the effect of excluding the views of individual participants who did not go along with the prevailing substantive thrust. The drive for consensus was spurred on by the urge to protect the President from political problems. Whether "groupthink" (as described by psychologist Irving Janis[44]) or simply the result of pressured political processes, those who held dissenting views were not able to convince the other participants of the wisdom of their views.

The memorandum that reached Carter's desk in the days just before April 14th was sent by OMB Director James McIntyre and Domestic Policy Staff Chief Stuart Eizenstat.[45] The memorandum requested the President's decisions on the "scope and specific programmatic content of a Cabinet Department of Education." It noted that McIntyre would be testifying before Ribicoff's committee on Friday and that "We plan to testify on Senator Ribicoff's bill, S. 991, rather than introduce new legislation in the Senate." The document reviewed the process that had been undertaken since the meeting with Carter the previous November, noting that "you instructed us to undertake a cooperative effort with the Congress to establish a Department of Education. You also indicated your preference for a department that is as broad as possible and not dominated by a single constituency."

The memo also reviewed the political situation:

> Senator Ribicoff's proposal now has 58 cosponsors, and we anticipate Senate passage of a bill to create the department this year. Action by the House this year is uncertain, however. Many Members of Congress support the concept of establishing a Department of Education but little consensus exists on what programs should be included in it. Most Members with whom we consulted including Perkins, Brademas, Ford and Thompson, favor a broad department but disagree on what its components should be. Some Members of Congress who support the idea of a department do not favor action now to establish it because of the controversy that may be aroused, uncertainty about its specific goals or fear that it will be dominated by a tradition-bound "education establishment." The House leadership is especially concerned about any controversy that will lead to disputes among Democrats in this election year.[46]

The remainder of the document was organized in four sections: a description of the general purposes and themes of the department; a presentation of two options for the administration's position on the scope of the department; specific program description, discussion and recommendations; and an identification of next steps for the effort.

The document argued that the basic purposes of the new department should be 1) to continue and strengthen the federal commitment to ensuring access to equal educational opportunities; 2) to promote improvements in the quality of American education by emphasizing both basic skill development and educational excellence; 3) to broaden the approaches to meeting educational needs by strengthening linkages among schools, community services, training, work and the home; and 4) to strengthen the capacity of states and localities to meet educational needs.[47] Two criteria were presented to the President as the basis for evaluating options for the scope and programmatic content of the department: "1. Transferring programs should not undermine the effectiveness or integrity of the program itself and should minimize the negative effects on the agency of which the program is now a part. 2. The decision to recommend transferring programs should take into account political support of Members of Congress, interest groups, executive agencies and the public."[48]

The President was presented with two options:

1. Establish this year a department which includes a narrow range of education programs with a view toward transferring additional programs by reorganization plan later.
2. Establish this year a department which encompasses a broader range of education-related programs to set in place a structure which might also facilitate even further program transfers later.[49]

The first option would transfer the 130 programs currently in the Education Division of HEW as well as the NSF science education programs; the HUD college housing program; the USDA graduate school; the HEW Office for Civil Rights; the HEW instructional telecommunications demonstration program; the HEW budget oversight of special institutions; the USDA school-based nutrition education programs; the HEW and Justice Department student loan programs; and the Department of Interior education programs for American Indians.[50] This combination would give the new department 164 programs, a budget of approximately $13.3 billion, and a staff of almost 6,000 individuals.

The document analyzed both the advantages and disadvantages of this option. The advantages of Option 1 were given as follows:

Increases the visibility and attention given to educational needs.

Attracts high caliber leadership to top level Federal positions in education.

Increases the capacity of Federal education leaders to develop effective mechanisms for interagency coordination.

Enhances the responsiveness of Federal policymaking to the needs of State, local and private educational agencies.

Allows time for more extensive public debate and information about effective program linkages and approaches before expanding the programmatic content of the department.

Avoids divisive political opposition from constituent groups (e.g., Labor and the Head Start constituency) which oppose inclusion of these programs in a department which they "fear" would be dominated by the "narrow and traditional" interests of teachers and school administrators.[51]

The disadvantages of Option 1 were also detailed:

Continues the isolation of traditional education programs and institutions from related training and social services programs provided in the communities.

Diminishes the prospects for eventually broadening the types of programs and constituent groups that a new department might encompass, once the "narrow" structure is in place.

May be viewed as politically expedient, particularly by some Members of Congress who favor a broader and more diverse group of programs and competing interests. (There is, however, little agreement on the specific elements of that broad construction.)

Does not respond effectively to the problem of fragmentation of education programs across the Federal Government.[52]

The configuration that was proposed in Option 2—establishment of a more broadly based department—would include all of the programs detailed in Option 1 as well as youth services programs in Justice, CSA, HEW and ACTION; youth training and employment programs in Labor; and Project Head Start in HEW. The department, in this option, would have 199 programs, a budget of approximately $15.9 billion, and a staff of nearly 8,000.

Again the advantages and disadvantages of the option were detailed. The advantages of Option 2 included all of the advantages listed for Option 1 as well as these additional points:

Fosters policies which recognize that learning is a process that transcends the classroom.

Increases the possibilities for better coordination among education programs and related activities.

Fosters a diverse range of approaches to education involving parents, communities and employers.

Responds to your campaign statement favoring a department which "would consolidate the grant programs, job training, early childhood education, literacy training and many other functions scattered throughout the government."[53]

The disadvantages of Option 2 were also presented:

Generates substantial political opposition from constituent groups (e.g. Head Start advocates, labor unions) that fear that the department will be dominated by professional educators whom they see as unsympathetic to their programs.

Fragments the administration of human services programs by separating certain training and other services for children, youth and the handicapped from related labor, welfare and health programs.

May not encompass a sufficiently diverse and balanced set of programs to accomplish its broad mission (although Option 2 is substantially broader than Option 1).

Increases the transition costs because a greater number of programs would be relocated.[54]

The recommendation that was given to the President by these advisers was for Option 1; the memo noted that "After extensive consultations and analysis, we have concluded that such a broad scope (as would be accomplished through option 2) is impractical at this time on both substantive and political grounds."[55] Two major reasons were given for this determination: "Unlike the programs included in the Department of Energy, many of the education and education-related functions outside the education division are not discrete units that can be transferred easily. ... Also, our extensive consultations with interested groups and Members of Congress have led us to conclude that a proposal to create a broadly based department could not pass the Congress in this election year."[56]

A number of specific program options were then presented to the President via the memo. In each case, the recommendations of OMB and DPS were compared to the provisions of the Ribicoff bill. OMB and DPS recommended inclusion of the science education programs in the new department (the Ribicoff bill included the entire NSF education directorate). The administration recommendation was for inclusion of student-oriented parts of nutrition education from Agriculture in the department; this program was not included in the Ribicoff bill. Both parties agreed that education-related civil rights responsibilities be included in the department. The Ribicoff bill did not include the Indian education programs within its provisions; however, the OMB/DPS recommendation was to include these programs. Both Ribicoff and the administration twosome did not include youth services programs or youth training and employment programs as candidates for inclusion.

OMB and DPS recommended that Head Start be excluded from the administration proposal; the Ribicoff bill did include Head Start. Similarly, the recommendation from Eizenstat and McIntyre was to exclude DOD schools from the measure even though the DOD schools were a part of the Ribicoff proposal. In several other cases, the OMB/DPS recommendation was more limited than the Ribicoff bill. Carter was asked to exclude the National Foundation on the Arts and Humanities as well as the Bureau of Indian Affairs Schools; both were in the Ribicoff proposal.

The memorandum to the President did not really make a convincing argument for the preferred option. It reflected, in many ways, the PRP study team's own view that a broader department was the way to go. The arguments for the narrow department were presented to Carter as what they were—a calculation that political realism dictated a less expansive approach. There was no attempt in the memorandum to present the arguments for Option 1 in a less political matter; the drafters of the document had forgotten their client—an individual who might make politically motivated decisions but who liked to think that he was making those determinations on other grounds. Carter—both as Governor and as President—was not the sort of individual who liked to acknowledge that he was constrained by limited political reasons that limited the potential of "good ideas".

Although the memorandum was written several days before the deadline of the 14th and forwarded to Carter on April 11th, it did not reach the President until the evening of April 13th. The President had a busy calendar during that period: he announced his program to combat inflation on the 11th; he met with Romanian President Nicolae Ceausescu on the 12th and 13th; he was concerned about the Second Panama Canal treaty, scheduled for a Senate vote in the next week.[57] The PRP study group assumed that time was not on their side—that it was too late for Carter to make changes in the McIntyre statement. The testimony was already written and copies made to take to the Senate the next morning.

At 7.30 a.m. the morning of the 14th, McIntyre and high-level PRP staff met with Carter. At that meeting, they were told to rewrite the testimony that they had prepared arguing for the narrow department and, instead, present an argument for the broad department of education. The testimony was scheduled to be presented at 10 a.m. Not surprisingly, the entire PRP and DPS group was flabbergasted. Speculation abounded about the reasons for the Carter decision—a decision that appears to have been his (or somewhat influenced by reorganization adviser Richard Pettigrew). At the least, the PRP study team felt itself to be vindicated and believed that it had, from the start, accurately assessed the President's perspective.

McIntyre arrived at the hearing of the Senate Committee on Government Operations a half hour late. As he was introduced, Republican Senator Charles Percy of Illinois noted that "it was impossible to get a copy of your testimony even at 10.30 when you were scheduled to be here. We await with great interest what you are going to have to say."[58] Percy's remarks were punctuated with laughter and Chairman Ribicoff further queried: "By the way, do you have more than one copy of your testimony?" Laughter again accompanied the question and Percy retorted, "Has it been typed yet, even?"

McIntyre replied, "The ink is still a little wet but it is typed, Senator, and we do have, Mr. Chairman, some copies on the way ... I apologize to the committee for not being able to get the statement to the committee ahead of time as is your rule and as is our custom."[59] McIntyre's testimony then included the argument for the broader of the two options for the department. The uncertainty that accompanied the testimony, however, cast a sense of indecisiveness over the administration's position. While PRP study team members believed that Carter was made to look indecisive when he had been consistent all along, there were a number of individuals in the room—members of Congress and their staffs, interest group representatives, and executive agency staff—who felt shocked and betrayed at what seemed to be a reversal of the administration's position.

Ribicoff, however, was pleased with the shift. As McIntyre finished his testimony, the Connecticut Democrat commented: "I want to take this opportunity to commend the President for the creation of a strong Department. I must confess that during the pulling and hauling I had considerable doubt about the followthrough, but it becomes apparent the President has opted for a strong Department of Education. ... As a matter of fact, I had a lot of questions I was going to ask you that I don't have to ask you now. ... I was all set for a big debate. Now I have just commendation."[60]

McIntyre's testimony kicked off a long train of statements before the Senate Committee from interest group representatives as well as from executive agencies. While some of the statements dealt with the general issues about the advisability of any type of department, most of the comments focused on specific proposals for transfer of individual programs—Head Start, Indian schools, and the child nutrition programs received the most attention.

The *National Journal* reported that "Of the five Cabinet departments that would lose ground to Carter's Education Department, four resisted. Among them is HEW, which stands to give up not only the Office of Education but also the Head Start program. ... James Parham, HEW's Deputy Assistant Secretary for Human Development Services, was pressed by the Senate Governmental Affairs Committee for his views on Head Start. After considerable hemming and hawing, Parham said, 'It is very seldom that anyone desires to give up a popular program.' Sen. H. John Heinz, III, (R-Pa.) found Parham's comment to be the 'most lukewarm, half-hearted statement in support of an Administration proposal I have ever heard from someone in that Administration.'"[61]

Agriculture Secretary Bob Bergland, while not commenting directly on the reorganization proposal, told the Senate Committee that food policy must remain focused in a single agency—his. Intense opposition to the proposal also came from the Bureau of Indian Affairs.

As the arena for the decision shifted entirely to Capitol Hill, the Carter reorganization group found itself tangled in intensive battles both within the administration and involving a broad array of interest groups. The spirit of cooperation between the Congress and the administration that appeared to be so strong as Ribicoff applauded the McIntyre testimony was shortlived. It was a sharp contrast to the deep skepticism and hostility awaiting the legislation as it moved to the House a few months later.

CONCLUSIONS

The activities that took place in the executive branch of government in the period before April 14th illustrate the opportunities that are created in the American political system as an issue moves from one stage of the process to another. This period can be characterized as a transition from the formulation stage of the process to the adoption stage—a movement that indicates a natural shift of predominant actors from the White House to Capitol Hill. It is hardly surprising that this transition provokes a set of tensions. In this case, the tension was illustrated by the relationship between Ribicoff and the

White House. The Connecticut Senator did want a department that was as broad as possible. However, his major imperative was to get a department enacted. The imposition of the April 14th deadline (a deadline that one can view as an acknowledgement that the movement to adoption would take place whether Carter liked it or not) forced a decision from the White House.

The movement to the adoption stage formalized a shift of venues; if Carter wanted to continue to exert a role of influence on the issue he had to be able to shift strategies. The ball was in his court as long as the formulation stage continued. When it moved down Pennsylvania Avenue, Carter had to think about a role of influence (rather than authority) as his leadership base.

In addition to the macro shifts between stages, the activities that took place within this period involving HEW Secretary Joseph Califano also illustrate the dynamic within the policy process. As the formulation stage unfolded, it created new opportunities for individual actors to reenter the process. While Califano's personal intensity was not a trivial factor in his activities, the movement within the stage naturally created new opportunities for him to enter the policy door.

The activities during this period indicated that the relationships between the various actors within the executive branch were complex and fraught with tension. The PRP staff was involved in a battle with the Domestic Policy Staff for the President's ear. Both groups believed that they accurately read the interests and concerns of the President and both invoked his authority as they argued their cases. The PRP also attempted to wrap itself in the institutional influence of OMB and what it believed to be a close relationship between OMB Director McIntyre and the President. HEW's interests were expressed in two very different ways. Secretary Califano argued for the maintenance of the Department, invoking his personal relationships (particularly with the Vice President and his staff) as well as developing an analytical case for his position. The program components within the executive branch (largely from HEW but also from Agriculture, Interior and NSF) resisted the proposed change and the shifts in bureaucratic politics that might stem from those changes.

In addition, the activities during this period also give some glimpse of the relationships between the President and his staff and the Vice President and his advisers. Mondale's role in this issue was always acknowledged to be important but it is difficult to pin down the specific areas in which that role played itself out.

As the proposals moved (however tenuously) into the adoption stage, the staff of the PRP confronted a number of conflicts between the culture of analysis and the culture of politics. It was clear that the issue was moving into a stage in which political feasibility assessments were essential. The PRP staff's strengths were not in this area and when events demanded that they make such assessments, they did not have enough experience to predict accurately the political consequences of their proposals.

As events unfolded, it was also clear that the PRP staff wanted to push for specific information and to assume that the interest groups and other actors involved would be explicit about their concerns. They believed that groups would specify their interests, conflicts between demands could be identified and, once identified, eliminated. They did not understand how the policy-making process and the political structure of separation of powers create and sustain conflict. It was difficult for the PRP to deal with symbolic actions and the tendency for political actors to redefine their positions as much as they could to create space for bargaining. They believed, for example, that the sponsors of the legislation could be depended upon for support and viewed their sponsorship as a literal endorsement of all specifics of the legislation.

The culture of analysis was also important in two other ways. First, analysts involved with reorganization were attracted to comprehensive grand schemes and, as they worked through the system, tended to overestimate the positive consequences of change. Second, the hierarchical structure of the decision-making process (both in OMB and in the White House) put the analytic perspective at a disadvantage. The chief spokespersons for the analysts were not specialists but, rather, were political generalists. These generalists were the voice for the technical analytic perspective and the analysts had to depend on them to interpret and give meaning to their proposals.

The interest groups' resistance to the analysts' desire for specificity indicated the difficulty that the PRP staff had in dealing with the interest groups during this period. The groups themselves played the political game, giving themselves as much space as they could to maneuver, devising coalitions with caution, and using their scarce resources very carefully. Although the PRP used the rhetoric of consultation and acknowledged the political importance of interest group support, they were also caught in the logic of their own position. One of the strongest arguments for the creation of a broad department was its ability to change interest group behavior and relationships—hardly something that the interest groups wanted.

The entrenched iron triangle relationships in the education field did not appear to be strong during this period. The relative silence of the career bureaucracy (one of the essential components of those relationships) suggests that the triangle may not operate as is often thought. Part of this may have been due to the difficulty of dealing with an issue as a reorganization question rather than a substantive policy question—a difference that was dramatically reflected in the shift of venues from the education committees to the government operations committees.

Finally, the activities during this period indicate the fundamental difficulty of dealing with education issues as reorganization questions. Reorganizing the structure was not a very precise way of making education policy and did not transmit very clear signals to the players in the issue field. Although PRP staffers argued, for example, that they wanted to include Head Start in the new department as a way of changing the education system (for education to become more like Head Start), the Head Start community saw the proposal as a way to dilute its approach and as a threat to its independence. Other problems of interpretation were also found with the Indian education and science education programs. Although the PRP pronounced that its rule of thumb was that "if it ain't broke don't fix it," the goal of changing American education was often in conflict with that operating rule.

NOTES

1. Keith M. Miles, "Memorandum to PRP Assistant Director Peter Szanton," (November 22, 1977).
2. Patricia Gwaltney, "Memorandum to OMB Chief McIntyre, "(November 28, 1977).
3. Brian McGovern, "Memorandum to Terry Straub," (December 2, 1977).
4. Patricia Gwaltney, "Memorandum to OMB Chief McIntyre," (November 28, 1977).
5. Nicole Jeffers, "Memorandum to Bill Hawley," (December 23, 1977).
6. James T. McIntyre, Memorandum to the President, "Subject: Next Steps on Education Reorganization," (January 7, 1978).
7. Stuart Eizenstat, Memorandum for Hamilton Jordan and Jim McIntyre, "Subject: Cabinet Level Department of Education," (January 9, 1978).
8. "The High Price of Cheapening the Cabinet," *New York Times* (January 16, 1978).
9. Bill Hawley, Memorandum to Patricia Gwaltney, "Subject: Speculation on the Program Content of a New Department of Education," (February 3, 1978).
10. President's Reorganization Project, "Outline for a Political Strategy for Establishing a Department of Education," (February 6, 1978).
11. Ibid., p. 1.
12. Ibid., p. 2.
13. Ibid., p. 3.
14. Ibid.
15. Ibid., p. 5.
16. Ibid.
17. Ibid.
18. Ibid., pp. 6-7.
19. Joseph A. Califano, "Testimony to the Senate Appropriations Committee," (February 2, 1978).
20. "Califano Suggests Under-Secretary as Alternative to Education Department," *Education Daily* Vol. II, No. 36 (February 22, 1978), p. 1.
21. James T. McIntyre, Director of OMB, Memorandum to the Vice President, Hamilton Jordan, Stuart Eizenstat and Frank Moore, "Subject: Secretary Califano's 'List of Agencies Considered for New Education Department,'" (February 24, 1978).
22. Dom Bonafede "Carter's Relationship with Congress ... Making a Mountain Out of a 'Moorehill'," *National Journal* (March 26, 1977), p. 456.
23. Patricia Gwaltney, Memorandum to Les Francis, "Subject: Committee Jurisdictions over Programs that Might be Included in the Education Department," (February 21, 1978).
24. Jimmy Carter, *Keeping Faith: Memoirs of a President* (New York: Bantam Books, 1982), p. 71.
25. President's Reorganization Project, Staff Paper, "Education and the National Science Foundation," (undated), p. 5.
26. Ibid., p. 8.
27. Arthur Sheekey, Memorandum to Willis Hawley, "Subject: Meeting with Frank Press on Science Interests," (February 10, 1978), pp. 1-2.

28. Ibid., p. 2.
29. Howard Carroll, National Education Association, Memorandum to Roz Baker, "Subject: Department of Education Media Campaign," (March 10, 1978).
30. Quoted in *NEA Reporter*, "NEA Gets Plum; AFT Munches Sour Grapes," (undated), p. 3.
31. Marian Wright Edelman, Letter to Vice President Walter F. Mondale, "Re: Reorganization of HEW—What are the Goals?" (December 4, 1977).
32. Ibid., p. 1.
33. Ibid.
34. Ibid.
35. Ibid., p. 2.
36. Ibid., p. 3.
37. Marian Wright Edelman, Memorandum to Vice President Walter F. Mondale, "Reasons Why Head Start Should Not Be Included in the Department of Education or Placed Under Educational Auspices in Such a Department," (undated).
38. Ibid., p. 1.
39. Marian Wright Edelman, "Letter to Harrison Wellford," (March 21, 1978), pp. 1-2.
40. Ray Marshall, Secretary of Labor, Memorandum for the President, "Subject: Employment and Training Programs and the New Department of Education," (April 10, 1978).
41. Patricia Wald, Assistant Attorney General, "Letter to James T. McIntyre, Jr.," (April 10, 1978).
42. Richard C. Atkinson, Director, The National Science Foundation, "Letter to the President," (April 10, 1978).
43. Joseph A. Califano, Memorandum for the President, "Subject: The Administration's Proposal for a Cabinet Level Department of Education," (circa April 10, 1978).
44. Irving Janis, *Groupthink*, Second Edition (Boston: Houghton-Mifflin, 1982).
45. James T. McIntyre, Jr., and Stuart Eizenstat, Memorandum for the President, "Subject: Establishment of a Cabinet Department of Education," (undated).
46. Ibid., p. 2.
47. Ibid., pp. 3-5.
48. Ibid., p. 5.
49. Ibid., p. 6.
50. Ibid., p. 8.
51. Ibid., pp. 8-9.
52. Ibid., pp. 9-10.
53. Ibid., p. 11.
54. Ibid.
55. Ibid., p. 12.
56. Ibid.
57. Joel Havemann, "Carter's Reorganization Plans—Scrambling for Turf," *National Journal* (April 20, 1978), p. 791.
58. Senate Committee on Government Operations, Hearings (April 14, 1978), p. 224.
59. Ibid., pp. 224-225.
60. Ibid., p. 232.
61. Havemann, p. 790.

Chapter 6 CONGRESS CONFRONTS THE DEPARTMENT

The morning that OMB Director James McIntyre testified before Senator Ribicoff's Governmental Affairs Committee marked the move to congressional action. Congress became the center stage to which all eyes were turned and energies directed in the struggle over whether a separate cabinet-level education agency would be created.

The change in venue from the executive branch signalled dramatic shifts in both the style and the substance of the decision process. As a reorganization issue, jurisdiction for the education department was in the hands of the Senate and House government operations committees rather than with the education authorizing committees—the Senate Human Resources and House Education and Labor Committees.

WHAT SHOULD BE IN A DEPARTMENT OF EDUCATION?

Most of the significant decisions about the programmatic scope of the department were played out during the first round of enactment activity in the Senate. Although support for the first Senate bill, S. 991, was extensive, it was characterized as being "a mile wide and an inch deep." As Senator Jennings Randolph (D-West Virginia), an early co-sponsor of the ED bill, quipped to one PRP staff member, "When we agree to support these things, we don't necessarily agree with everything that's in it."

The similar bills proposed by Senator Ribicoff and the administration for a broad department, including many education-related programs outside of the Office of Education and HEW, had abstract appeal for a number of constituencies, largely due to claims of better coordination, effectiveness and improved management. This was not the case, however, for other interest groups, some members of Congress, and the civil rights community, who vigorously opposed many of the principles on which the ED proposal was built.

OMB Director McIntyre's April testimony to the committee had evoked many highly negative reactions to the administration's position. Thus the department initiative was re-evaluated within the ranks of the administration. In a memo to the President, McIntyre recommended pressing for ED's enactment in 1978 but insisted that this "would involve investing your time and that of the Vice President and senior White House staff to enlist support for our proposal among interest groups and Members of Congress."[1] If the President were to put the weight of the administration behind the Ribicoff bill in 1978, however, lingering conflict among White House factions would have to be resolved. It was essential that the administration appear unified and committed to the ED proposal.

The most obvious crack in this presentation of a "united front interest" was Secretary Califano, whose opposition to ED was common knowledge at this point. When the Secretary was invited to accompany McIntyre on his second appearance before the Senate Governmental Affairs committee, even he deemed his own presence unwise, and yet his absence would have been of equal embarrassment. The consensus among the actors (Eizenstat, McIntyre, the congressional liaison team, and finally, the President) was a compromise: HEW Under Secretary Hale Champion would appear in person and as letter of testimony by the Secretary would be submitted for the record. Judging from the record of this day's hearings, the Senators were more preoccupied and concerned with the proposed transfer of Head Start than with who was sent by the White House.

Witness after witness in the eight Senate committee hearings devoted to transfer issues testified in opposition to the inclusion of their programs in the Education Department. The transfers which provoked the most controversy were child nutrition from the Department of Agriculture, vocational rehabilitation, and Head Start from outside the Education Division in HEW, Indian schools from Interior, and science education from NSF. Although each debate involved a different set of actors, most engaged representatives from the interest groups, Members of Congress, PRP staff, and other executive branch personnel. Strategies for or against inclusion of the individual programs varied in effectiveness and the intensity with which they were employed. Although these transfer debates had many elements in common, their outcomes were very different.

CHILD NUTRITION

PRP argued that the transfer of the food programs would give a new department a comprehensive flavor. Senator Ribicoff was a firm supporter of the transfer of the child nutrition programs from the Department of Agriculture to the new department for many of the same reasons as the PRP. Ribicoff became convinced that the programs could be better administered after seeing a report on the television program "Sixty Minutes" describing the corruption and fraud as well as the poor quality of the food and management of these programs. To his mind, this TV description told the real story of the child nutrition programs. To rectify the low priority of the programs in USDA, he proposed an assistant secretary for child nutrition in the new department.

As could be expected, the proposed transfer met with formidable opposition. The children's and commodities groups, fearful of the unknown, were reluctant to have to break into a new "iron triangle" relationship with education bureaucrats. The arguments being put forward by the PRP in favor of the transfer were not goals close to the hearts of the interest groups involved who had learned that a strong constituency could protect a program no matter where it was structurally located.

Opposition to the transfer was not to be overcome by a few phone calls (at the request of the administration) to the major interest groups from USDA officials like Secretary Bergland. On the contrary, in June 1978, the opponents mobilized into a coalition of 18 groups, which called itself "Save School Lunch." The coalition used practical arguments to allege the detrimental effects of such a transfer: higher prices for school lunches and other feeding programs—resulting from projected elimination of the commodity distribution program—and a low priority for child nutrition programs in the budget. The coalition even turned the linkages argument to its own advantage by underlining the importance of a coordinated food, nutrition, and agricultural policy.

"Save School Lunch" had some very powerful backers in the Senate and few real opponents among the administration. Members of the Senate Committee on Agriculture, Nutrition and Forestry, led by Senator Herman Talmadge (D-Ga.), wrote a strongly worded letter of protest to Senator Ribicoff in April of 1978, insisting that transfer of the child nutrition programs would be "detrimental to the programs, to the children of the Nation and to American agriculture." "It might well jeopardize the creation of the Department," they added menacingly in their letter to Chairman Ribicoff.[2] As he had promised, during the mark-up of S.991, Senator Charles Percy (R-Ill.) represented the interests of the Agriculture Committee members and the interest groups. He introduced an amendment to drop the child nutrition transfer, but it was defeated in a tie vote (8-8). The Washington newsletter of the National Farmers' Union reported that the Percy motion was defeated after Ribicoff made a concession to leave $560 million in funds used to purchase commodities for donation to the school lunch and breakfast programs in USDA while transferring the remaining $2.5 billion into the new education department.[3] Senator John Heinz (R-Penn.) had changed his vote to oppose the Percy motion afer the Ribicoff compromise was offered, casting the tying vote. However, the indication was that Percy and Talmadge would persevere in their protest in the full Senate. It came to pass that the Percy amendment was indeed introduced and passed by voice vote when S. 991 came to the floor in late September. Thus the child nutrition programs were not included in the Senate endorsed bill.

VOCATIONAL REHABILITATION

The PRP's recommendation for vocational rehabilitation had originally included VR programs in ED. But in the by now familiar sequence of decision making, the PRP was overridden by other OMB advisers. The administration appeared to be holding fast to its position to keep the programs out of the ED proposal. Once the debate came into the congressional arena, however, the administration abandoned the fight to retain VR in HEW. It did not try to make deals or to bargain. Senators Jennings Randolph and Muriel Humphrey represented the interests of the vocational rehabilitation community, and the Humphrey amendment transferring VR to the department and creating an Assistant Secretary for Special Education and Vocational Rehabilitation, passed by a voice vote in committee.

HEAD START

As noted in Chapter 5, the Head Start community had a very effective grass-roots network which was operating in full swing during this early period. One Ribicoff staff member reported a constant parade of Head Start mothers in and out of the committee offices. Even in the PRP, the question, "How many letters have we gotten about Head Start today?" masked with sarcasm the growing sense of doubt about the wisdom of the transfer.

When the administration's bill included Head Start, the interest group coalition was surprised, shaken and angered. Feeling betrayed by the administration, they turned to their supporters in Congress. The members of the Senate Subcommittee on Child and Human Development, with Senator Alan Cranston (D-Calif.) as their spokesman, and the Subcommittee on Employment Poverty and Migratory Labor, led by Gaylord Nelson (D-Wis.), had played a central role in ensuring Head Start's success and hoped that they would continue to do so. These legislators took the lead from the interest groups into the Senate, where, like the Agriculture Committee members on the child nutrition issue, their efforts to block the proposed transfer were successful. Senator John Glenn (D-Ohio) turned the PRP's rhetoric back on itself and maintained, "If it's not broke, don't fix it."

The administration was ultimately forced to concede to strong opposition from all fronts. Following the suggestion of a *New York Times* editorial, among others, Senator Ribicoff finally decided to "include Head Start out."[4] In one of the first actions on S. 991, the Committee voted without dissent to strike Head Start at the chairman's request.

INDIAN SCHOOLS

Despite the PRP's inability to develop support for its proposals, the Indian programs were incorporated into its design for a broadly-based department, along with other non-HEW education-related programs. Freed from the constraints of a recommendation based on a purely political analysis, the PRP tried to demonstrate that Indian education programs could be improved if transferred. It was not difficult to get most Indian representatives to admit that the BIA's handling of the programs fell far short of satisfactory. In addition, there was a good deal of overlap in functions between the two agencies responsible: the BIA and OE's Office of Indian Education. The PRP reversed its earlier position and recommended transfer of all Indian education programs to the new department. The Ribicoff bill limited its coverage to the BIA schools.

During this same period, Senator Ribicoff himself contacted over 300 Native American groups to request comment on the transfer. A letter from Ribicoff written in April drew approximately 300 responses, three quarters of which were opposed to the inclusion, although many mentioned the possibility of compromise if certain assurances were given.[5]

On May 16, 1978, the Indians had their day in Congress. Perhaps the best summary of the perspective of Indian groups toward BIA, the PRP attempts to involve them in negotiations, and the proposed transfer of the programs, was heard from Lionel Bordeaux, President of the National Indian Education Association:

> There is an old Sioux legend that my grandfather told me long ago, back early one morning. The story goes that a sparrow decided to fly south for the winter. Unfortunately, it got too cold and he waited too long. Finally, after much thought and deliberation, and very reluctantly, he started his southward journey. Ice began to form on his wings. He came crashing down in a barnyard nearly frozen. The sparrow thought it was the end. A cow came along and crapped on the sparrow. The sparrow definitely thought it was the end. Lo and behold, the manure warmed him, brought him back to life. Warm and happy, he began to chirp; he began to sing.
>
> A cat in the area heard the chirping sounds, investigated, cleared away the manure, found the chirping bird and promptly ate him.
>
> Three lessons are contained in this particular story. The first lesson: Not everyone who craps on you is necessarily your enemy. Not everyone who takes crap off you is necessarily your friend: and three, most importantly, if you are warm and happy in a pile of crap, you would do well to keep your damn mouth shut.
>
> Thank you. (Laughter)[6]

Both Democrats as well as Republicans in the Senate opposed the transfer and the programs were not included.

SCIENCE EDUCATION

On April 18, the Senate Committee heard from a panel of science and science education organizations testifying in opposition to the transfer of science education from NSF. These interests were represented by the American Association for the Advancement of Science; the Dean of the University of Illinois' College of Education (a leading science educator); the National Science Teachers' Association; and the National Academy of Sciences. This rather diverse group all opposed the transfer on similar grounds: the fear of being a small, neglected fish in the large education agency pond.

Unlike the Head Start or child nutrition situations, the administration saw a real opportunity to win this transfer debate. Despite the fact that the science community was unified in its position, it traditionally had very little lobbying experience, and never organized an effective opposition to the transfer. The spokesman for the science education community was Senator Edward Kennedy (D-Mass.), chairman of the Subcommittee on Health and Scientific Research, who wielded a significant amount of influence on the issue—in large part because he was in the unique position of supporting the ED bill.

Although the attempt to delete the science education transfers was defeated by a large margin, the final decision was a compromise, consistent with the administration's proposal to transfer only those programs aimed primarily at students and teachers in the elementary and secondary and undergraduate institutions and to transfer them specifically and intact to the Department's Office of Educational Research and Improvement.

THE SENATE DECIDES

As a result of interest group initiatives and congressional pressure, the bill which emerged from the Senate was a much trimmer version than the proposals of both Senator Ribicoff and the administration. The champions of the controversial program transfers had been only partially successful, but the debate had done little to dampen the enthusiasm of the senators for the bill itself. The ED bill was reported unanimously in mid-July to the full Senate, and with the adoption of the Percy and Stevens amendments (deleting child nutrition and Indian education), the Department of Education Organization Act passed the Senate by a vote of 72-11 on September 18, 1978. In light of this broad base of support, the onslaught of opposition from within the House caught ED's advocates almost completely by surprise.

Clearly, questions of program inclusion were the key issues dominating consideration of the bill in the Senate. How those programs would be organized within the department received relatively little attention in the upper House. By the time the legislation reached the House, however, these issues were important matters of concern.

There were structural issues that differentiated the administration and Ribicoff's proposals. The administration and the first Ribicoff bill differed on the organization in ED of intergovernmental relations, staff and cross-cutting support functions, the authority of the Secretary and the division into program components.

Attempting to respond to arguments that the department would take over all education in the U.S., the administration proposed the creation of the Intergovernmental Council on Education, which gave much more emphasis to strengthening intergovernmental relations than S. 991's National Advisory Commission on Education had done. While the mandate of the Ribicoff Commission would be to assist the Secretary in formulating policy, conducting evaluations, reviewing program administration and consulting with federal, state and local officials, it would not, according to OMB's McIntyre, "address sufficiently the need to improve intergovernmental relations." The administration stressed that this had to be the primary function of such an organizational body.[7]

Although the administration's design was to group together programs serving similar purposes, functions, or target groups, the study team had taken pains to ensure the authority of the ED Secretary by making the cabinet officer's administrative flexibility explicit in the language of the bill. For example, although a pool of 14 executive-level positions reporting directly to the Secretary was created, a real effort was made by the administration to keep these Assistant Secretary roles undefined.

As it was reported out, however, S. 991 designated an Assistant Secretary for each of the following offices: Special Education and Rehabilitative Services; Indian Education; Child Nutrition; Elementary and Secondary; Postsecondary; Occupational, Adult and Community Education; and Educational Research and Improvement. A Director for the Office for Civil Rights was designated, as well as an Inspector General and a General Counsel. As it stood, the Secretary would have exactly two Assistant Secretary slots available to align the remaining staff functions: policy development, evaluation, budgets, intergovernmental relations, congressional relations, and public and parental involvement. This was not exactly what the administration had in mind. When the Senate bill was amended in the full Senate and the Indian education and child nutrition programs were eliminated, this presumably would have afforded additional room in which the Secretary could maneuver.

ON TO THE HOUSE

One day after the Ribicoff bill passed the Senate, H.R. 13343, the companion to S. 991 introduced by Representatives Jack Brooks (D-Texas), Michael Blouin (D-Iowa) and Frank Thompson (D-N.J.) three months earlier, met with crippling opposition and came to a grinding halt as the Congress adjourned in October of 1978. As was evident from Brooks's views on the department, the House was going to be a much more difficult site in which to gain support. Many of the debates in the House had centered on the same program transfers that had occupied the attention of the senators, but the tone of the argument suggested that they had gone further than to object to the specifics of the bill.

As the legislation moved foward in the House, there was a strong presumption that the department of education could indeed come to pass, and this realization engendered the more abstract, ideological discussions in the House. As opponents began to bring their issues to the enactment debate, ED's advocates were forced to redefine goals and shift strategies.

One of the key actors on the House side was Congressman Jack Brooks, Chairman of the Government Operations Committee. Brooks had almost single-handedly thwarted Carter's reorganization agenda in the early days of the administration. Nor did Brooks have his Senate counterpart's personal involvement in or commitment to education issues. But his sponsorship of the bill was not negotiable as far as the administration was concerned. After months of meetings with the President, the Texas Democrat finally agreed to sponsor the ED bill on the condition that Head Start be removed. Several sources reported that Brooks's final decision to go along with Carter was made aboard Air Force I during Carter's visit to Beaumont, Texas, to dedicate the Jack Brooks Federal Building.

Committee Chairman Brooks saw his job as getting the ED bill passsed. He and his staff devoted litle attention to the programmatic scope of the department. The staff and members of the committee who were concerned most about the department focused almost exclusively on efficiency issues, having little or no familiarity with the specific education programs in question.

The perspective of the committee members in turn influenced the administration's testimony before the House Committee. The PRP found the efficiency arguments for the creation of ED appealing and attuned to its role as a part of OMB, but was hard-pressed to show convincing evidence for those arguments. At one point, for example, analysis showed cost savings of $100 million—less than 1% of the education budget.

OMB Chief McIntyre's first testimony before the House Committee, as contrasted with his first appearance before the Senate, confirmed the administration's new strategy. Although many of his general introductory comments in both statements were identical, one obvious difference was the language used to describe the projected outcomes of the creation of an education department. In the Senate, the outcomes referred to were more abstract. McIntyre spoke of greater visibility, high-level leadership, and improvement of educational quality. In the House, the outcomes outlined revealed that management concerns were assigned equal importance. The ED, McIntyre argued, would

Improve the management and coordination of education programs at the Federal level by bringing together programs now scattered throughout the government; increase the accountability of education and related programs to the Congress, President and the public, both as a result of increased visibility and status of education and related programs; and encourage broad and diverse approaches to education with increased involvement of communities and parents by bringing together a range of programs and constituencies in addition to those with a focus on elementary and secondary schooling.[8]

The "blame the bureaucracy" mood was an important element of the political climate and was fueled by President Carter's promises to reduce dramatically the size of the federal bureaucracy. In speaking of these concerns, McIntyre stated, "We are trying to be as frugal as we think is reasonable and practical in setting up this department. We don't want to set up a department that fails because it doesn't have sufficient management capacity."

As for the department's content, it was clear that opposition had forced the administration to incorporate certain concessions into its proposal. At Brooks's insistence, Head Start had been removed. The best guarantees the administration could provide to the other controversial transfers were high organizational status and visibility. To wit, the administration proposed that:

child nutrition programs would be located in an office reporting directly to the Secretary of Education;

OCR would be structured with provisions for a direct reporting line to the Secretary, with a level IV Secretary, appointed by the President;

science education programs from NSF would be kept intact, reporting directly to the Director of the Office of Educational Research and Improvement.[9]

As for Indian education programs, McIntyre was willing to provide for high organizational status, although he promised that these programs and the DOD overseas dependents' schools would report directly to the secretary.

As the House debate developed, a new wave of interests group activity was challenging the fundamental assumptions upon which the department was based. While the NEA and its team-mates worked to reinforce much of the pre-existing broad acceptance of an education department in the Senate, opposing groups—the AFT, conservative groups, the Catholic Conference and the civil rights community—conserved their limited resources faced with inevitable Senate passage. It became necessary, and more effective, to voice this opposition once debate reached the House—an arena where these constituencies had friends and advocates and where the ground work prepared by advocates was not so extensive. The opponents' silence during the Senate hearings had misled the administration, which was ill-prepared to counter these attacks.

Congressman John Erlenborn (R-Illinois) was the spokesman for the right-wing opposition in the House. Erlenborn was a formidable opponent of the administration because he represented a silk-stocking constituency on the outskirts of Chicago which did not rely on federal support. The conservatives' attack was based on three arguments. First, Erlenborn and his colleagues, Arlan Stangeland (R-Minnesota), Robert Walker (R-Penn.), and Dan Quayle (R-Indiana), accused H. R. 13343 of being a "political payoff in every sense of the word" to the education community, specifically the NEA. Second, the conservatives viewed the establishment of ED as a serious threat to local control: "The tentacles of the Federal Government are everywhere; they cannot be avoided. If we create this Department, more educational decision-making as to course content, textbook content, and curriculum will be made in Washington at the expense of local diversity." Finally, they warned that ED could be a "colossal bureaucratic blunder wasting tens of millions of dollars."[10]

Some liberal Congressmen like Ben Rosenthal (D-New York) were concerned about very different issues. They saw consequences of a federal education agency that would fragment the HEW coalition in Congress and thus diminish overall federal support for education. Many of the Black Representatives took the position that domination by professional educators and state and local officials would diminish the aggressiveness and scope of federal action, especially with respect to civil rights enforcement. Other liberals, like Ron Dellums (D-Calif.), however, were very strongly in favor of the ED bill.

The National Urban Coalition was the lone civil rights organization which stood in support of the department. This was apparently motivated by the belief that ED would help improve the situation of education and by the political advantage to be gained from supporting the administration's position.

In some instances loyalty to the AFT was more compelling than the idea of the department. This seemed to be true for most of the New York City delegation. The AFT had been on record since 1972 as opposing a federal department of education and was the most active interest group to work against the bill. It feared, among other things, that creating a separate federal education agency would produce a dramatic increase and expansion of the federal role in education. In this respect, the concerns of the AFT and the conservatives overlapped. In his letter to Senator Ribicoff in May 1977, AFT President Albert Shanker cautioned that

> Little evidence has been offered that indicates any improvement in federal education policy except for the status considerations that might accompany Cabinet-level status.
> A successful federal education policy cannot be devised and implemented in isolation from the development of health and welfare programs.
> If departments proliferate, it is more likely that the administration of programs will be fragmented and that their programs will overlap.
> The merits of consolidation have been recognized by Congress both in its committee structure which acknowledges the importance of relating programs and exercising broad authority.[11]

The AFT's more practical objections stemmed from a long-standing rivalry with the NEA, and its identification, as an AFL-CIO affiliate, with labor interests. The House Education and Labor Committee supported the AFT's education as well as labor interests in Congress. The fact that labor interests found a more sympathetic audience in the House was not a new phenomenon in constituency politics. It was feared that education reorganization would affect and realign committee jurisdictions.

The Education Coalition, an ad hoc group of private, nonprofit advocacy groups which had common experience working together on civil rights and education issues during the 1960s and 1970s, included representatives from the Children's Foundation, the Children's Defense Fund, the Alabama Council on Human Rights, the Federal Education Project of the Lawyer's Committee, the NAACP Legal Defense and Education Fund, and several other groups. The Coalition was dissatisfied with the treatment of civil rights issues in the education reorganization plans of the administration and in the Senate. Encouraged by the success of Head Start advocates, the Coalition targeted its efforts to House members and presented its demands for civil rights "safeguards," but did not actively oppose the department.

The Education Coalition was very effective at the committee level in large part because it had a long-time civil rights champion among its ranks. Representative Rosenthal. Rosenthal's amendments stipulated that the OCR component:

> be run by an Assistant Secretary reporting directly to the Secretary;
> submit an annual report to Congress summarizing OCR compliance;
> have authorization to collect and coordinate data;
> select and appoint staff attorneys;
> and have direct budget appeal to Congress.

Even though much of this language was adopted during mark-up of the first Senate bill, the Education Coalition was still cautious about endorsing the department. Its eventual support or opposition was wholly contingent on the administration's and legislators' initiatives to strengthen civil rights functions in the new department.

The position of the U.S Catholic Conference, as articulated by the Rev. Msgr. Wilfrid Paradis, their Secretary for Education, emphasized the threat of increased federal interference in education. The Catholic Conference argued that education was primarily a responsibility to be shared by parents and local school authorities. Furthermore, the creation of the department represented a "philosophy of education which runs counter to the nation's traditional acceptance of and respect for pluralism in education."[12] Despite the rhetoric of an ideological commitment to pluralism, the Conference believed that the new department would be dominated by public school interests.

Although the Conference, as a religious institution, did not "lobby" legislators with the same currency as other organizations, its legislative liaison team met personally with members of the House, working "hand in glove" with the AFT's government relations team. In addition, the Washington office of USCC contacted principals, teachers and parents of children in Catholic schools across the country to inform them of the Conference's long-standing opposition to the department.

It was clear from the array of actors that rallied to the education issue that the administration was up against much stiffer opposition than it had anticipated. Despite the fact that almost all of the interest groups had pragmatic motives for opposing the creation of the education department, the debate in the House was ideologically based. The specific elements of the proposal were largely lost in the heated ideological discussions in the House.

House committee members were more attuned to management questions than their Senate counterparts, and tended to view a Secretary's flexibility and discretion, coveted by the administration, as a positive management strategy. But the subject of ED's internal organization was as elusive in House discussions as it had been in the Senate. Priding themselves on their management expertise, the members bombarded McIntyre with queries on "vital statistics": costs, personnel and numbers. Roles and responsibilities never surfaced in these often heated debates. About the only significant decision on structure which emerged from the House was the mandate to reduce personnel by 500 by Fiscal Year 1980, although at this point in ED's adoption, the specifics had yet to be engaged.

NO GO IN THE HOUSE

As the House subcommittee began mark-up of the ED bill in early August 1978, liberal New York Democrat Ben Rosenthal and conservative Illinois Republican John Erlenborn joined forces in their effort to wipe the ED proposal off the administration's legislative agenda once and for all. They calculated that if enough amendments were added to the legislation, this would make ED unacceptable even to its firmest supporters.

During the first one-hour session of the mark-up, Rosenthal introduced his amendments to secure the integrity and independence of OCR. These were adopted by voice vote. In the second five-hour session five days later, Erlenborn took center stage. His tactics were less concerned with substance and more designed to delay the final vote. Twenty amendments were offered to the bill—nine of which Erlenborn introduced. Then Erlenborn demanded that the bill be read aloud in its entirety. At the end of the day, three amendments were adopted deleting the Indian, child nutrition, and science education transfers, and seven others pertaining to administrative and organizational functions were approved. Nonetheless, the final result was an easy victory for ED advocates. Republican Erlenborn, Democrat Rosenthal, and Black Democrat Conyers of Michigan were the only ones opposing. Brooks had shepherded the other seven subcommittee members into his fold.

H.R. 13778, reported favorably by the subcommittee, reached the full committee the next day. Mark-up went on for four days, during which time close to 50 amendments were introduced, debated, and voted upon. On the second day, opponents offered so many amendments and took up so much time that the committee couldn't take a vote. The longer the committee took to vote on the bill, the greater the chance that it would be too late for the leadership to schedule for floor action. On this same day, the committee voted 29-9 to move the vocational rehabilitation programs over to ED. The administration was still on record as opposing such a transfer. President Carter was the most adamant opponent, maintaining that just the reverse had been done in Georgia.[13]

On the third day, Vice President Mondale intervened, pressing the House committee for speedy action on the bill. Opponents ignored the administration's pleas. Chairman Brooks complained, "They're printing up amendments as fast as they can." The "filibuster by amendment" strategy looked very promising. The House Rules Committee's deadline for approving the bill for floor action had already passed, but Brooks told a *Washington Post* reporter that if the committee could manage a vote by the end of the week, it would still get to the floor.

On the fourth and final day, the committee approved the Department of Education bill by a vote of 27-15. Twenty-two Democrats and five Republicans had supported it; seven Democrats and eight Republicans had opposed. Out of 46 amendments, 20 had been approved. Most of them dealt with the authority of the Secretary (limiting it in most cases) and with personnel allotments and grading. Despite the wide margin of victory, however, the PRP legislative staff was cautious. In one of its memos to Harrison Wellford and Pat Gwaltney, the staff commented that many members of Congress, lobbyists and the *Washington Post* were "predicting the death of the bill."[14]

The NEA had been unable to counter the House opponents' strategies, but during the Labor Day recess, the organization shifted into high gear. The goal was to secure the chance for the ED bill to reach the House floor before Congress adjourned. The first indispensable step was to persuade the House Rules Committee to grant an open rule to hear debate. The NEA leaders met individually with each member of the committee in Washington, and then had their local affiliates lobby these members in their home districts. The opponents were just as busy working on this same set of pivotal actors through Shirley Chisholm of New York, a member of the committee. The final 9-6 vote to grant the rule camouflages the uncertainty which surrounded the outcome until only hours before the final tally.

When ED came to the floor, House opponents threatened to stall all House business unless it was removed from the schedule. Since the open rule provided that no amendments to the bill would be in order except those germane amendments printed in the *Congressional Record* at least one calendar day prior to the offering of such provisions, Representatives Quayle and Walker dumped 30 amendments into the *Record*. Some of these amendments were more colorful than substantive, such as one to rename ED the Department of Public Education and Youth, or DOPEY. The bill, scheduled for floor debate on September 29th, was pushed aside by Speaker Thomas O'Neill (D-Mass.) when opponents threatened to filibuster.

As one PRP memo described the situation, the Department of Education bill was "hanging by its thumbs." According to the recollection of one PRP staff member, Rosalynn Carter had even told reporters that she thought the bill had been dropped about a month before. The only thing which would prevent ED's early death was a hearty dose of lobbying by the administration. During the week of September 25th, the President and Vice President hosted a "pep rally" for congressional staff and interest groups in order to halt and, it was hoped, reverse the negative momentum building in the House. On Monday, the President met with key House members. The following Wednesday, the Vice President hosted a breakfast in the Roosevelt Room for civil rights leaders and an evening reception to which over 100 organizations and selected Senators and Representatives were invited. Briefing sessions were held throughout the week. In an effort to ensure a vote, Senate leaders, the NEA and members of the administration, including the President himself, lobbied House members and the Speaker. When the department bill appeared on the schedule along with 19 other bills, however, Representative Walker single-handedly led a crippling filibuster, to which the Speaker conceded for the second time. This was the fatal blow. Thus, when the House adjourned on October 15, 1978, the department of education bill had not come up for a vote.

REGROUPING AFTER THE 95th CONGRESS

Undaunted by the crippling opposition in the House, Senator Ribicoff and his staff used the few months between the 95th and 96th Congresses to capitalize on momentum from the ED bill's passage in the Senate. In December 1978, the Senate Governmental Affairs Committee produced a 25-page fact sheet on the Department of Education legislation, which included a history of the legislation, arguments for a department, positive press commentary and a list of organizations in support. This was distributed mainly by the interest groups to their constituents, but copies were sent to all members of the Senate as well. By the time the Congress reconvened in January, Senator Ribicoff again had over 40 co-sponsors for his new ED bill, S. 210.

But opposition in the House had been potent enough to prevent the bill from coming to a vote and continued to be problematic. The coalition of liberal Democrats and conservative Republicans illustrated the adage "politics makes strange bedfellows." Maintaining this bipartisan coalition was crucial to the House opponents' effectiveness, but it was also recognized that more sophisticated strategies needed to be developed to defeat the bill. Stalling techniques alone would not work for ED's opponents if the administration decided that passage of the bill was a domestic priority and a political necessity. Erlenborn, planning to take the lead again in opposing the ED legislation, met with incoming GOP congressmen before they even took office.

Confronted with what was likely to be a major battle in the second round of congressional activity and a potential political disaster, the PRP underwent a series of changes in strategy, personnel and articulation of goals for the new department. The original team of education analysts were superseded by political advocates. Passage of the department bill was of utmost importance. No further substantive analysis would take place. All resources would be devoted to negotiating and compromising. The immediate task at hand was to protect existing support and gain the support of those members who might be persuaded to change their views or who were still neutral.

By the end of 1978, there was only one large constituency from the "education community" undecided about its position. The higher education community, a diverse group of approximately 50 organizations with varying concerns, had yet to play a significant role in any of the formulation or enactment debates. This was not for lack of initiative on the PRP's part, which had met repeatedly with representatives across the higher education sector. A source of frustration for the PRP was the inability of these groups to agree on a set of federal education policy issues—a problem endemic to the diverse and fragmented nature of this constituency. This lack of a unified policy was one of the most frequent concerns articulated by higher education groups themselves during their meetings with PRP staff. The one point of consensus was the concern that the department would inevitably be dominated by the NEA and elementary and secondary school interests.[15]

Of the higher education groups which did take a position against the department, the most vocal was the Association of American Universities, an organization of 40 of the most prestigious universities. While representative of the elite institutions, the AAU was not known for exerting political strength or influence. Supporters included the junior and community colleges and the American Association of University Professors. The American Council on Education (ACE) steadfastly retained its neutrality on the issue of the department, though its Director of Governmental Relations, Charlie Saunders, was involved in an ongoing dialogue with the PRP and provided valuable information and suggestions on working with these groups.

The PRP carefully outlined its strategy for wooing the stubborn higher education groups over to the supporting side. It was viewed as crucial to indicate support for a strong Assistant Secretary for Postsecondary Education, chosen from the ranks of the higher education community. The newly created Office of Educational Research and Improvement, a stronger and elevated research arm, would also be used as a lure, as well as the continued support and improvement of the Fund for the Improvement of Postsecondary Education (FIPSE).

The outcome of the past House activity had left the cadre of interest group supporters disappointed and frustrated. Many of the core groups tried to figure out what had gone wrong. A Phoenix meeting of the Chief State School Officers in December turned into, as one representative put it, a "post mortem" on the failed education legislation. One of the conclusions reached was that the department was linked too closely to the NEA. If a new coalition were built, with an identity separate from the NEA, it would create the appearance of another front of support. Approval for this new coalition was sought and granted by the NEA, and Allan Cohen, a lobbyist for the State Department of Education in Illinois, was selected to head the Ad Hoc Committee for a Cabinet Secretary of Education.

The first meeting of the Ad Hoc Committee took place in December in Reston, Virginia—intentionally removed from downtown D.C. which was regarded as NEA turf—and was attended by 40 organizations and six White House staffers. Three committees were established to cover legislative, public relations, and outreach bases. The decision was made early on that the group would bypass any discussions of department content, and concentrate exclusively on achieving a legislative victory.

Another source of frustration shared by the interest groups was the lack of initiative on the part of the White House. The Committee tried to impress upon the administration the need to be more organized in its strategies and more forthcoming in its commitment to the department. The White House responded and the Vice President hosted the third meeting of the Ad Hoc Committee at the White House. More than 90 organizations with 130 individual representatives were present. In his opening remarks, Vice President Mondale sought to allay the criticisms of the interest groups:

> It's a sign of the importance I attach to this effort that I just came through a rain storm to be with you. I can't think of any meeting I would rather attend or any objective of our administration that the President and I place at a higher priority than the reason which brings us together today, namely harnessing the public support necessary to adopt and create at long last a Department-level for education.[16]

This meeting set a precedent for cooperation between the White House and ED supporters. After the third meeting, the Committee, which had expanded to over 100 organizations, began to meet weekly and was joined by several members of the White House staff.

The strength and determination of the supporting coalition contrasted sharply with the resources of the opposing groups as Congress prepared to reconvene in January 1979. It was not until after the 1978 elections and the defeat of the bill at the close of the congressional session that the AFT met with representatives from the U.S. Catholic Conference to coordinate lobbying strategies for 1979. During 1978, many more pressing pieces of education legislation had preempted the attention of the AFT legislative staff; reauthorizations for higher education, elementary and secondary education, and CETA, and the tuition tax credit debates were all considered more significant than the ED legislation. As the new session got under way, individuals and organizations that had expressed their opposition to ED were brought together in what amounted to a paper coalition. In much the same way that the NEA had created other committees to support ED, the Committee Against a Separate Department of Education was a symbolic, as opposed to activist, gathering of forces. The Committee never met formally or on a regular basis, and included the group of AFT, USCC and AFL-CIO lobbyists working to bring the ED bill to its knees. The conservative groups, however, were more adamant than these groups in opposing the legislation.

Even though the Senate and House had deleted most of the controversial program transfers, the possibility remained that with the new Congress, the administration would wipe the slate clean and re-submit its proposal for a broad department. In view of this uncertainty, the groups that had opposed the inclusion of "their" agencies within the department continued to put pressure on members of Congress and the administration. The most active at this point were the NSF and Indian lobbies.

The press became increasingly interested in ED's enactment when congressional debates revealed the extent of the controversy over the department's role and functions. A tidal wave of press activity both touted and condemned the department, and some of the most prominent journalists' voices in most of the major dailies were heard on both sides.

As time progressed, the media scales appeared to be tipping in opposition to ED. One of the most widely discussed pieces was David Breneman and Noel Epstein's *Washington Post* column, "Uncle Sam's Growing Clout in the Classroom," in which the authors contended that the "fundamentally political act" of creating the Department of Education was "not chiefly an issue of reorganization or consolidating federal education efforts" so much as it was "a backdoor way to establish a U.S. responsibility for education itself."[17] The authors' articulation of the federal control threat was picked up by many of ED's opponents and was even referred to by Congressman Erlenborn in his dissenting views in the H.R. 13778 report. The *Post* article was timed to coincide almost to the day that the House Government Operations Committee was marking up the ED bill.

In the first few months of the new session, three of the country's most prestigious newspapers published editorials sharply criticizing the education department initiative: the *Washington Post*, the *New York Times*, and the *Wall Street Journal*. On January 16, 1979, "An Illusion of Education Reform" appeared in the *New York Times*. It suggested that the disappearance of the ED bill from the House floor was a positive event for several reasons. First, education would carry even less clout than in its inadequate present form in HEW unless all the education programs across the government were included in a "Big E." Second, an intimate relationship would develop between the department and the NEA. Finally, creation of a cabinet agency for education interests would set a precedent for other special interest groups to follow. The editorial concluded with a gentle warning: the President "would be wise now to accept the House leaders' well-considered second thoughts and let the matter drop."[18] Both the *Washington Post* and the *Wall Street Journal* editorial pages expressed many of the same sentiments.

Several prominent members of the education, government, and public administration communities took issue with these editorials and columns against ED, in what evolved into an ongoing dialogue on the editorial and "op-ed" pages of hundreds of papers across the country. Reverend Jesse Jackson (Director of PUSH), Samuel Halperin (former Deputy Assistant Secretary for Legislation in HEW and then Director of the Institute for Educational Leadership), and James Farmer (former head of CORE and Executive Director of the Coalition of American Public Employees), were only a few of the many well-known individuals who tried to mollify unfavorable public opinion by praising ED in the press.

Carter's State of the Union address in January 1979 barely whispered a commitment to ED's enactment. The Carter domestic priorities also included a national health plan, hospital cost containment, deregulation of railroad, bus and trucking industries, and more jobs. On the international front, Carter aspired to a strengthened NATO alliance, congressional approval of the Multilateral Trade Negotiations, and Mid-East and SALT II agreements. The section of the address on ED was shrouded in Carter's government reorganization rhetoric:

> This year, we must extend major reorganization efforts to education, economic development and the management of our natural resources. ... There is no such thing as effective and noncontroversial reorganization, and reform can never be easy, but we know that honest and effective government is essential to restore public faith in our public action.[18a]

However, despite this apparent downplay of the ED initiative to the public at large, according to one high level PRP staffer, ED was one of two or three domestic priorities on the administration's unwritten agenda. ED's advocates, who were looking for a more vocal commitment in the State of the Union, had nonetheless been contented by the administration's oblique references to "major reorganization efforts."

THE SCOPE NARROWS

When Senator Ribicoff introduced S. 210 in January of 1979, it excluded the three most controversial transfers: Head Start, Indian schools, and child nutrition. With these programs out, the debate focused on the question of the department itself. Many of the issues raised in the second round of Senate activity bore a striking resemblance to debates that had been ongoing in the House. The benefits of greater public visibility, increased access to the President, and better coordination and management were claimed by supporters, and the threat of federal control and loss of civil rights protections were alleged by its opponents.

This came as no surprise to members of the administration; indeed, OMB Director McIntyre had predicted such a shift in focus in a January memo to the President.[19] While it seemed obvious that the administration's proposal to the Senate in February would reflect a leaner programmatic structure in keeping with the Senate bill, some of the program transfers continued to be considered among members of the Domestic Policy Staff and OMB. In his memo to President Carter, McIntyre summarized 1978 congressional action on the controversial transfers and submitted recommendations for final approval on science education, Indian schools, child nutrition, and vocational rehabilitation.

On Thursday, February 8, 1978, McIntyre appeared before the Senate Governmental Affairs Committee, flanked by several members of the administration: Harrison Wellford, Pat Gwaltney, Assistant Secretary of Education Mary Berry, Commissioner of Education Ernest Boyer, and Pat Graham, Director of NIE. McIntyre's testimony revealed only two points of difference on content between the administration's proposal and the Ribicoff bill. The administration had added the two migrant education programs but had not included the vocational rehabilitation transfer. McIntyre was quick to stress the administration's willingness to "pursue the issue" further with the committee. His discussion of ED's structure mirrored the previous year's—the administration tried to incorporate more organizational flexibility for the Secretary than S. 210.

After minimal debate on the few transfers which remained in the bill, the committee voted 13-1 to report to the full Senate. During mark-up, the committee also voted to strengthen language protecting against federal control, adopting amendments sponsored by Senators Bill Roth (R-Del.) and John Danforth (R-Missouri). In the minds of local control advocates, the Senate was fulfilling its traditional role as protector of the rights of states and localities in intergovernmental assurances. The only substantive amentment offered to the ED bill on the Senate floor, the deletion of the DOD transfer, was defeated by a large margin. In what had clearly become a partisan battle, the Senate passed the department bill on the last day of April by a vote of

72-21. The ten-vote gain by the opposition from 1978 included one vote by a Democrat.

President Carter's special education message to the House in mid-February 1979 outlined the narrowest version of the department yet supported by the administration. In effect, the administration deferred to the Ribicoff bill. There was not a separate administration proposal at this time. Moreover, Chairman Brooks had prevailed upon the administration to introduce its own House bill in the 96th Congress which he would then manage, reaffirming his reticence to be out in front for the ED initiative. The administration's veneration of organizational flexibility was sacrificed to political expediency; the administration designated four separate offices—Civil Rights, Elementary and Secondary, Postsecondary and Research and Improvement—to be headed by Assistant Secretaries.

Of all the education-related programs outside of OE, the administration's House proposal retained only two: the DOD overseas dependents' schools and the NSF transfers. The DOD transfer had stirred some controversy during the 1978 congressional debates, but garnered support from many fronts. The administration, prominent members of Congress, the European Congress of Parents, Teachers and Students, the National Parent Teachers' Association, and the NEA affiliate, the Overseas Education Association, all wrote, testified, or resolved to work on behalf of the transfer. Unlike other executive agency heads who were unenthusiastic or openly opposed to relinquishing their programs to the new department, DOD officials, including Secretary Harold Brown himself, endorsed the transfer. Members of the Senate Armed Services Committee were forthcoming in their support. And during the first day of hearings on H.R. 2444, Commander Michael Austin, Vice President and Legislative Chairman of the European Congress, stated his organization's reasons for supporting the transfer: "We want to come in from the cold. ... We see our closed, parochial military system drifting further away from the mainstream of the American educational process and the continued inability of our current organizational structure to make the requisite adjustments."[20]

Solutions to the NSF transfer issue remained elusive since hostility to inclusion of the Science Education programs was still running high among NSF staff, congressional advocates and interest groups. In his Senate testimony, Senator Ted Kennedy had finally come out against the transfer, introducing dozens of letters he had received into the *Record*. Kennedy went on to work with Office of Science amd Technology Policy staff to draft a mutually acceptable compromise, which was incorporated into the Senate report of the bill. Its language stipulated that "no mission-oriented research functions or programs of the National Science Foundation or of any other Federal agency shall be transferred by this Act." Finally, in response to a chorus of fears expressed about federal control, a section entitled "Prohibition against federal control of education" immediately followed the description of purpose in the administration's House proposal. This had been incorporated into the report of H.R. 13778 in 1978, and was seen as symbolic protection of the powers of state and local education agencies.

THE FINAL SHOWDOWN

Two years of work by the administration and over a dozen by Senator Ribicoff to create a cabinet-level education agency had come down to the moment of reckoning in the House of Representatives. At the end of February 1979, Congressman Brooks dutifully introduced H.R. 2444, President Carter's Department of Education proposal.

The administration's ultimate political calculation was that its most persuasive case for the department in the House would hinge on claims of improved efficiency, better management, and cost savings. In individual meetings with Representatives, the PRP and the White House found receptive ears. The administration's major prop, colored charts showing duplication of administrative functions in HEW, "worked like a charm," according to one PRP staff member. The management argument served a dual purpose: it was designed to rebuff charges that ED would mean more bureaucracy and greater costs, and supplied the representatives with a compelling, concrete argument to bring to their constituents. The administration came into the final round of hearings armed with numbers, costs, and figures. In a significant shift in rhetoric, in his last appearance before a congressional committee on ED's behalf, McIntyre called these administrative benefits and management improvements "the fundamental issue at stake."[21]

Much to the dismay of the strategists in the White House, however, the efficiency approach did little to inspire the supportive committee members. Moreover, about the only committee member to take issue with the administration's claims was New York Congressman Rosenthal. In his words, "The proposed new Department of Education meets virtually none of the standards required for the establishment of new departments and, in fact, violates every rule of good management, good organization, and even good politics."[22] One intepretation of this lack of interest in management issues was offered by a PRP staff member, who explained, "Congressional hearings are theater, and management doesn't make good theater." ED's advocates and opponents resorted to those abstract and symbolic arguments which were the most capable of stirring emotion. The issues of federal control and civil rights enforcement pre-empted all discussions, and left the administration at a strategic loss from which it barely had the time and resources to recover.

Underneath the ideological rhetoric in which the federal control issue was steeped, what was really at stake was the political advantage that the different constituencies stood to lose or gain by ED's adoption. Conservatives argued effectively, and in timely fashion, that ED would lead to increased federal intervention. Federal involvement in education implied categorical programs, and these were necessarily accompanied by heavy administrative burdens and restrictions on local managers. The conservatives were quick to point out the inconsistency of the Carter proposals. Another administration initiative—the regulatory reform proposal—was being advanced at the same time as legislation to create yet another federal bureaucracy.

For many conservatives the real issue was the federal role itself; they wanted to phase out federal programs entirely. Congressman Robert Walker (R-Penn.) demonstrated his point that ED would inevitably lead to soaring costs in the first of his series of "lessons" sent to his congressional colleagues. In Lesson #1, Walker's multiplication and addition tables computed that the proposed number of ED's supergrade positions times the cost of these positions would amount to a total salary figure of $4.5 million. He commented:

> At a time when cuts in federal spending and bureaucratic growth are being urged by the American public, I find the creation of 90 new bureaucratic positions with the accompanying price tag (of $4.5 million) completely unconscionable. How can we as public officials elected by a budget-conscious populace possibly justify the exorbitant expense involved with the creation of these new positions?[23]

Walker's Lesson #2 calculated that for the amount of tax money spent on one new supergrade bureaucrat in ED, 3.3 school teachers could be hired.[24] Lesson #3's intricate equation came up with a figure of $774 million for the cost of ED's paperwork.[25] For each of these math exercises, the administration drafted a rebuttal, but Walker's graphic techniques, which went on to include a mid-term and final exam, hit the mark for some members of Congress.

The liberal faction headed by the AFT was equally skeptical about ED's guarantees of state and local control. An official statement prepared by the AFT's Department of Legislation stated: "To assign the task of guaranteeing state and local control of anything to a new agency of the federal government is the equivalent of hiring a fox to assure the safety of a chicken-coop."[26] On the flip side of the federal control coin, some liberals were concerned that ED did not provide enough federal control. This was part of a larger issue. Left to their own devices, it was argued, state and local agencies would not be aggressive in ensuring civil rights protection.

While the National School Boards Association voted unanimously at its 1978 annual convention to support ED, by early 1979 a handful of the states broke with national leadership and testified that programs initiated and implemented at the local level were most succesful. The Pennsylvania, Kansas and Nevada school boards went on record in opposition to ED in

February of 1979. Other state boards wavered but did not eventually oppose the department—Michigan, Ohio and Texas.[27] The organization itself had expressed concern about federal control. The NSBA split gave a point of leverage to opponents.

Of all the objections lodged against ED, the administration had the most difficulty countering the federal control arguments. Not surprisingly, the sides were divided pretty much along philosophical lines—conservatives wanted less control and liberals, with the exception of the AFT, wanted to maintain existing controls. Strategists in the White House were not sure how to balance the factions. Intergovernmental relations provided the administration with a vehicle for trying to prove its commitment to state and local control. In addition to shoring up the language of Section 103, "Prohibition against federal control of education," the administration was asked by the interest groups most involved in these issues to consider several other proposals to strengthen relations. The National Conference of State Legislatures, in conjuction with NSBA, NASBE, CCSSO, the Education Commission of the States, and the National Governor's Association, submitted draft language to the administration for five amendments. The first three amendments would clarify the states' constitutional role in education, to be inserted in Sections 101, 102 and 103 of the bill. The fourth would give the Under Secretary of the new department the clear responsibility for the conduct of intergovernmental affairs. The final amendment would require the department to issue an "impact statement" for each legislative, regulatory or funding proposal that would have a significant effect on states, their local school systems or tribal governments.[28]

There was very little disagreement over incorporating most of these intergovernmental assurances into the ED bill. The interest groups were satisfied that state and local control would be enhanced by these provisions. This in turn motivated the administration to work hard to comply with this particular set of demands because it could be tied to a source of assured support.

Although related, many of the intergovernmental assurances written into the ED bill did not address the more concrete concerns of the civil rights groups. The day before Brooks introduced H.R. 2444, Children's Defense Fund head Marian Wright Edelman sent the chairman a letter on behalf of the Education Coalition expressing grave concerns about the effects of the department. The letter raised a series of questions for which she felt convincing answers had yet to be heard:

> Will the proposed department be any different than OE in administering and enforcing federal education legislation designed to improve educational opportunities for the most vulnerable students?
> How will the proposed reorganization improve the quality and quantity of services available to children in their schools, families and communities? Is it truly a constructive change in the federal role in education, or simply another shuffle of bureaucratic boxes in Washington?

Will coordination in fact be improved through a narrowly based department that is little more than the present Office of Education?

In a time of fiscal austerity and restraint in federal spending, who will pay the inevitable costs of the proposed department? Isn't it an invitation to more layers of bureaucracy?[29]

Copies of the Edelman letter were sent to all the members of the Brooks and Ribicoff committees, to the President and Vice President, more than ten members of the administration, and key interest groups. The Education Coalition was not formally opposed to the department, but it was clear that the administration was being held accountable by the civil rights groups and that it was expected to take an active role in constructing adequate civil rights assurances. In the following months, members of the administration drafted a point-by-point response to Edelman's letter. Although a formal response was never sent to Edelman herself, a copy of the draft was sent to Ann Rosewater of the Coalition by DPS Assistant Director Bert Carp, with the handwritten note, "Go easy on us."

Civil rights advocates Rosenthal, Conyers and Chisholm had distributed the Edelman letter to their colleagues in the House. They were dissatisfied with OCR provisions in the new House bill because they did not give the civil rights agency the power to appeal budgets directly as well as separate contracting authority, both provisions approved by the committee in 1978. Rosenthal and Chisholm had a two-part strategy: first, they worked to reinforce and strengthen the Rosenthal amendments; second, they urged their colleagues, particularly members of the Congressional Black Caucus, to make their support of ED contingent on civil rights assurances.

In a move to alienate civil rights advocates and preclude their support, Republican Congressman Walker and his colleague Republican John Ashbrook prepared to introduce a series of anti-civil rights amendments which the conservatives were endeavoring to attach to every appropriations and education-related bill during this time. Of all the opponents' strategies to defeat the ED legislation, it appeared that the introduction of these debilitating amendments on busing, school prayer, abortion, and affirmative action would be the most effective. The period from early April to late October 1979 was an uphill struggle for the administration and ED's advocates. At many stages of the adoption process defeat seemed imminent, and to prevent this, the administration was forced to make both small and large concessions at many critical points. Countless deals were struck, the majority of which will probably never be known. The ED initiative held the administration captive, usurping invaluable and irreplaceable White House resources while other issues of national and international importance were also in need of presidential attention.

The subcommittee mark-up was the first successful step for the ED bill on its long path to the floor of the House. On April 9th, the subcommittee

On April 9th, the subcommittee approved Congressman Horton's amendment to transfer vocational rehabilitation, some managerial and intergovernmental amendments, and agreed by a voice vote to report to the full committee.

The amended ED bill reached the full committee two days after the Senate's resounding approval of the department. According to a *Congressional Quarterly* poll taken just a few days prior to mark-up, the committee was evenly split 18-18, with three members undecided. On the same day that the committee was considering the legislation, two full-page ads appeared in the *Washington Post* from the opposing sides.

Around noon on the day of the mark-up, two senior Democratic Congressmen, L. H. Fountain of North Carolina and William Moorhead of Pennsylvania, revealed their intentions to switch their votes from the previous year and to vote against the measure. Moorhead was quoted as having come to fear "centralizing the control over ideas", echoing concerns expressed by Pennsylvania State Board of Education Executive Director Fred Heddinger. Fountain predicted that the new "monster in the federal government ... would grow and grow."[30] In the flurry of lobbying that ensued, Chairman Brooks managed to pick up the votes of three incoming Democrats and one Republican newcomer, handing President Carter a one-vote victory. Of the 19 votes against, seven were Democrats. After the vote, a spokesman from the White House asserted, "We have now passed the toughest hurdle in our efforts to establish a separate Department of Education."[31]

The months of May and June were spent preparing for the final showdown on the floor of the House. The more immediate target for both sides was the House Rules Committee, chaired by Democratic Missourian Richard Bolling. According to a PRP staffer, although Bolling himself was against the bill, he would agree to "take a walk" during the vote. Opponents had a few influential friends among the ranks of the committee—Democratic Representatives Shirley Chisholm and Leo Zeferetti from New York, and Bolling himself—but the final count was 9-5 in favor of granting the rule. According to a *Congressional Quarterly* article, however, the margin of victory once again masked the fact that only hours before the vote, sources were reporting that the committee was evenly divided.[32]

Floor debate began on June 11th, and the ED supporters watched as opponents pulled out all the stops. During a three-day filibuster by amendment, they succeeded in preventing the House from taking a vote. Although most of the dilatory amendments were killed, in what became a major stumbling block for the administration, all four of the anti-civil rights amendments passed by an average margin of 125 votes. Amendments to delete science education and DOD schools were not passed. Opponents had unsuccessfully offered amendments transferring additional programs to ED which would have renewed opposition from other camps. The hours of debate came to a head after midnight on the third day of debate when Representative David Obey (D-Wis.) offered a motion to strike the enacting clause of the bill. The motion was defeated (146-266) only after House Speaker O'Neill pleaded, "Do not let the bill go down this way."[33]

Failure to pass the bill promised to become a political disaster for the administration. The White House was forced to barter on programs and structure. Even a little lobbying by specialized interest groups paid off. More personnel cuts were promised and trades were made by the administration on other issues.

Indian schools went back to Interior in an effort to smooth over the widening rift between the Indians and the government over federal treaty issues;

An Assistant Secretary for Non-Public Schools was promised to gain support from conservatives and Catholics, who were being thwarted by the administration on the tuition tax credit issue;

Hispanics won a separate Office for Bilingual Education—a symbol of their growing political clout;

Museum interests were assured that their $13 million program would have a direct reporting line to the Secretary;

Certain science education programs were given back to NSF to win over adamant Members of Congress.

When the four days of debate were finally over in the House and opponents had managed to postpone a vote until after the July 4th recess, the outcome was impossible to predict. The reaction of the civil rights groups to the adoption of the anti-civil rights amendments could not have been better planned by the conservatives: they immediately announced their opposition to the ED bill. In a June 12, 1979 letter to Jack Brooks, the ACLU wrote that "in light of the drastic and damaging anti-civil rights and civil liberties amendments recently approved by the House, this legislation has become a mechanism to severely undermine this nation's commitment to civil rights and civil liberties. For this reason, the ACLU now opposes enactment of this legislation."[34]

The Congressional Black Caucus, however, was still maintaining its neutrality. Several members of the Caucus had received personal calls from the President persuading them that the clauses would be removed in conference. The administration argued that this was not the first time the House had supported such measures, and that there was considerable question as to their tangible effects. They were reluctant to emphasize the symbolic nature of the amendments lest the same criticisms be leveled at the language protecting against federal control.[35] Carl Holman, President of the Urban Coalition, remained loyal to the administration. He had convened a broad group of women, Hispanics and civil liberties representatives to work on civil rights issues while maintaining support for the administration's bill. At the Vice President's request, Holman was reported to have helped to prevent a very negative telegram from civil rights leaders to House members prior to the final House vote.

Head counts conducted by the administration the month before the recess bear out the effectiveness of the liberal/conservative coalition's strategies. By July 4th, although the NEA was predicting a five-vote victory, the administration's team had ED slated for a seven-vote defeat.

The NEA's measure of influence had diminished considerably since the early Senate debates and the organization's role in the final House proceedings was quite minimal. Although the organization enjoyed a good relationship with many members of the Senate, it had made very few inroads in the House. This partly had to do with the fact that the general arguments advanced by the NEA and the Ad Hoc Committee were clearly secondary to matters being discussed in the House. On the House side, every member's support was contingent on a specific provision of the legislation. In addition, AFL-CIO loyalists numbered significantly among ED's opponents in the House.

The NEA took advantage of what was clearly its strong point during the July 4th recess—grass-roots lobbying. The NEA Governmental Relations Office sent memos to all the local chapters urging its affiliates to phone and visit the Representatives in their home districts. The target list of the Ad Hoc Committee included over 70 members, most from the key states of Texas, Pennsylvania, Illinois, New Jersey, New York, and California. Leaders were designated to cover the House floor, including representatives from most of the Big Six and state education agencies.

The White House worked hand in hand with the NEA these last few weeks. The legislative liaison team put out "installments" of lists of members to phone, and delegated calls to swing members to the President, Vice President, Cabinet officers and White House senior staff. With the final administration count showing a loss by eight votes, the ED bill came to a vote on July 11, 1979. When the last vote was cast, the score was 210 for the administration, 206 opposing.

With the exception of the House bill's inclusion of the amendments limiting civil rights activities, the House and Senate versions of the department bill had just a handful of discrepancies. The House bill's language protecting against federal control was stronger than S. 210's, which more abstractly stipulated that establishment of the department "shall not increase federal authority over education or diminish the rights of states, local school systems, other branches of state government or tribal governments in the areas of education policy and administration ..."[36]

An analysis of the final vote reveals that the House opposing coalition was able to gain support from both the liberal and conservative camps, primarily because of the civil rights issues. The administration's legislative team analysis of the vote showed "a relatively unusual voting pattern," with "extraordinary support from conservatives, particularly in the South." The strongest regional support was in the South and Far West, and the greatest opposition from the mid-Atlantic states (New Jersey, New York, Pennsylvania, Maryland, and Ohio). Of 89 Democrats who voted against, 43 were from these five states.[36a]

In the final tally, more members of the Congressional Black Caucus voted for the department than against, despite the urging of Caucus leaders. Over 50 votes switched from 1978 to 1979. The New York contingent accounted for ten votes changed from favorable or leaning favorable in 1978 to opposed in 1979. Another five vote switches took place in Pennsylvania. In all, 36 Democrats and 20 Republicans decided to reverse their previously held positions and register their opposition to H.R. 2444.

According to the usual procedure for conference committees, following passage H.R. 2444 would be sent immediately to the Senate, which then would have the option to accept the House version, the Senate version, or to request a conference. If the Senate requested a conference, the House would then be required to vote first on the conference report, having the possibility of sending it back for revision. If the House requested a conference, however, the Senate would have to pass on the final version of the report before it could be returned to the full House. Then the House could only pass or defeat the legislation. It did not have the option of sending it back to conference.

Congressman Brooks knew that the conference must be requested by the House: given the opponents' desire to keep the anti-civil rights amendments in the legislation, the House would probably have sent the ED bill back to conference repeatedly. Furthermore, Brooks knew that Erlenborn would oppose any effort to get the unanimous House consent needed to request a conference. In an unusual parliamentary maneuver, Brooks went straight to the Government Operations Committee, getting approval to seek a conference. He then needed only a majority in the full House. The House voted to instruct the conferees to keep the controversial clauses in the bill and then passed the measure 236-156. In mid-July, the House and Senate appointed 14 conferees, nine Democrats and five Republicans: Senators Ribicoff, Percy, Javits, Glenn and Levin, and Representatives Brooks, Horton, Erlenborn, Fuqua, Moorhead, Fascell, St. Germain, Levitas and Stangeland.

The single most important issue to be decided in conference was whether to delete the controversial amendments. Given that Erlenborn and Stangeland were the only ones who voted for all the amendments, it would seem that all or most of them would be dropped. Pursuant to the request of the Government Operations General Counsel Bill Jones, the NEA conducted a survey of House members in August to determine the potential effect deletion of the amendments would have on final House approval of the Conference Report. According to their sources, while deletion would only pick up three votes, retention would cause a loss of 19 members who voted for ED in July. In addition, the NEA government relations team tried to assess how many votes would be lost if the amendments were taken out. Removal of the amendments was not seen to be a "risk-free enterprise," according to the administration's legislative staff, who had identified as many as 17 conservatives whose support was contingent on retention. In a two-and-a-half hour meeting, the conferees agreed to either delete the controversial amendments or to substitute language reaffirming principles of equal educational opportunity and local control. Liberal Republican Senator Jacob Javits of New York was instrumental in devising compromise wording on the racial quotas issue. Conferees voted 7-2 to drop the school prayer amendment, despite the fact that Representative Arlan Stangeland had urged his colleagues to retain it, arguing that "It is hard to quarrel with a permissive edict that allows a pupil to stop and reflect on the deity."[37]

The final program content agreed upon included the Education Division's 131 programs; six programs from the Rehabilitative Services Administration; two from NSF, the Department of Justice, and the Department of Labor; one from DOD, HUD, USDA (the Graduate School), and HEW's budgetary oversight for four special institutions. The legislation provided for the creation of Offices of Elementary and Secondary, Vocational and Adult Education, Postsecondary, Overseas Schools, Special Education and Rehabilitative Services, Bilingual Education, Educational Research and Improvement, and the Office for Civil Rights. The primary management concern under negotiation was the personnel cut, initiated by the House. The House had originally passed an 800-employee cut, which was revised in conference to 500.

On September 13, 1979, the House/Senate conference committee approved S. 210, which Erlenborn, Moorhead and Stangeland refused to sign. The following day, Erlenborn and Stangeland sent a 'Dear Colleague' letter to House members which began "WE TOLD YOU SO!" In their description of the conference committee meeting, they wrote: "Almost before the Chairman could shout, 'All aboard,' the train sped down the tracks. As the only two conferees who consistently defended the House position, we want to give you a report on how we were railroaded." The railroad image provided a catchy symbol with which to capture the attention of House members. In another of Walker's graphic antics, every day for a week he issued statements on the dissatisfactory results of the conference under the logo of a Department of Education car full of paper-ridden befuddled bureaucrats, being pulled along by the NEA Express. The caption of the first cartoon was, "Evidently the best way to get a Department of Education is to learn to run a railroad."

After the Senate passed the conference report, the last hurdle remaining for the ED bill was final House approval. However, the White House congressional team's count showed a dead-heat—214 to 214 with 7 undecided. But, despite the last ditch efforts of House opponents, the ED bill passed by an easier margin than expected (215-201) on September 27, 1979. A comparison of votes on initial House passage and approval of the conference report showed that removal of the controversial amendments made up in liberal support what it lost among conservatives. Fourteen Democrats and two Republicans switched from opposing passage to supporting the conference report. Three Southern Democrats and eight Republicans who voted for passage voted against the report, largely because the amendments had been taken out.[38]

As the voting came to an end, lobbyists from the White House and the NEA burst into cheers and applause on one side of the corridor leading to the House chamber, as glum and silent AFT lobbyists lined the other. It had been a good week for the President. Congress had passed the Panama Canal legislation and the House Commerce Committee had approved the hospital cost containment bill. Beaming from what was hailed as a major legislative triumph for the administration, Carter called ED's passage "a significant milestone in my effort to make the federal government more effective. We will now have a single cabinet department which can provide the coherence and sense of direction needed to manage U.S. dollars."[39]

In its most crucial vote, the House approved by a scant four votes the Department of Education Reorganization Act, a bill which was a pale shadow of earlier incarnations. President Carter had nonetheless delivered on a campaign promise, and was hailing the newly created department as the single most important achievement of the decade for American education. Of equal import was the fact that ED's adoption was seen as one of President Carter's rare legislative victories.[40]

CONCLUSIONS

As the department of education proposal moved to formal adoption in the Congress, a new set of problems, actors and issues emerged. The authority to determine the life or death of the department was in the hands of the members of the Congress, the body that had the formal authority to make this decision. As in other reorganization attempts, congressional unwillingness to delegate matters of organizational structure to the President meant that Congress—alone—could legitimate the proposal.

The path that the legislative decision-making followed was a highly stylized, quite open route. Deals could be struck in the proverbial "back rooms" but they had to be brought forward and legitimated in the open sessions of subcommittees and committees as well as on the floor of the House and the Senate. The legislative decision-making bodies are multiple and formalized; for a bill to finally emerge from the legislative labyrinth, it must muster agreement in a pluralistic setting from diverse actors who often hold conflicting views. Ability to build coalitions as a way of resolving conflicts is more than often the path to success. These coalitions are fashioned through two different sorts of skills—skills in building coalitions around vague goals (which are often abstract statements of principles) and skills in organizing coalitions that address diverse and even conflicting goals (with legislation emerging that has something for everyone).[41]

When the department of education proposal reached the Congress, it was thrust into an environment that did not pay deference to the work that had been done earlier. The work of analysts in the PRP (indeed, the work of analysts on congressional staffs) was relevant only when it supported the position of an actor already involved in the political fray. If there was a "correct" answer, it was one which allowed the legislative actors to come to some sort of agreement. After all, the congressional world was driven by the art of the possible, not by the elegance and logic of policy positions.

Thus the adoption stage of this policy process was strikingly different from the formulation stage that preceded it. The adoption stage pushed for agreement, not for opening of new issues and possibilities. It was formal and relatively open, not informal and played in closed bureaucratic corridors. It emphasized political interaction, not analytic competence.

The shift to this arena had consequences beyond the internal workings of the decision process. When the issue moved to Congress, it allowed the various interest groups to operate in a setting with which they were familiar and comfortable. In the case of the NEA, the public nature of the congressional decision process allowed it to maximize its resources and lobbying skills and, at the end, to "pull out the stops" to ensure the passage of the legislation. The fragmented nature of the congressional process also tended to push the issue away from a conceptual, comprehensive clarity to a situation in which sub-issues could be confronted one at a time.

Although the jurisdiction over the issue remained in the hands of the government operations committees, it had to be presented to the full House and Senate where other kinds of questions would be asked about the proposal. Even with the breadth of support for the measure in the Senate and Senator Ribicoff's deep commitment to it, there could not be a "pure" consideration of the general idea of a department. The Head Start, vocational rehabilitation, and science education program debates indicated the ability of specialized interest groups to raise their concerns, even within the confines of the Senate Government Operations Committee. Once these program debates were cleared away, however, the Senate was willing to look at the department proposal as a reorganization issue, emphasizing issues of improved efficiency and calculating the political advantage that might be gained from the symbolic elevation of the education field to a cabinet status.

When the issue came to the House, however, the ground rules changed. It was a proposal that could not be debated as an efficiency measure. To conservatives in the House, reorganization became a surrogate for increased federal control of education. To some civil rights advocates, reorganization was a way of diminishing the federal role in civil rights enforcement. Once the Pandora's box was opened, it was difficult to contain the question of the appropriate role of the federal government in a reorganization framework. The closeness of the vote in the House demonstrated this difficulty. The interest group activity in the House was much more complex, reflecting the interests of specific program advocates and their past relationships with one another (such as the case of the competition between the AFT and the NEA) as well as other more ideological questions.

By the time the issue was seriously considered in the House, relationships between Carter and the Congress were problematic. It was becoming increasingly difficult for a Democratic Congress to support the proposals of a Democratic President. Not only was the Congress skeptical about the issue of government reorganization, but it was finding it difficult to comprehend the strategy that Carter was employing in his relationships with the Hill.[42] Although the administration made serious attempts to consolidate its position and present a united front to the Congress on this issue, members remembered the differing views on the department that had been aired for almost two years within the executive branch. To the opponents of the measure, there was poetic justice in quoting a Carter appointee who had opposed the idea at an earlier time.

At the end, the Carter administration realized that the success or failure of the department of education proposal was a political question not incidently tied to a coming presidential election. The White House strategists came to the same conclusion as had Senator Ribicoff some months before: for political reasons, it was essential to have a victory on this issue. A department, no matter how narrow its scope, was better than no department at all. This was made possible, in the end, by the close relationships between the advocates in Congress, and the NEA during the last few weeks of the debate.

NOTES

1. James T. McIntyre, Memorandum to President Carter, "Subject: Department of Education Initiative," (May 10, 1978).
2. Senate Committee on Agriculture, Nutrition and Forestry, "Letter to Senator Abraham Ribicoff," (April 18, 1978).
3. National Farmers' Union, Washington Newsletter, Vol. 25, No. 29 (July 21, 1978), p. 1.
4. Editorial, New York Times (June 14, 1978).
5. Senator Abraham Ribicoff, "Letter to Native American Groups," (April 14, 1978).
6. Lionel Bordeaux, "Testimony to Senate Government Affairs Committee," Hearings on S. 991: Department of Education Act (May 17, 1978), p. 559.
7. James T. McIntyre, "Testimony before the Senate Committee on Government Affairs," Hearings on S. 991: Department of Education Act (May 17, 1978), p. 662.
8. James T. McIntyre, "Testimony before the Subcommittee of the House Committee on Governmental Operations on Establishing a Department of Education," (August 1, 1978), p. 400.

9. Ibid., p. 405.
10. *Dissenting Views Accompanying H.R. 13778* (August 25, 1978), pp. 45-47.
11. Albert Shanker, President, American Federation of Teachers, "Letter to Senator Abraham Ribicoff," (May 1977).
12. Rev. Msgr. Wilfrid H. Paradis, Secretary for Education, U.S. Catholic Conference, "Prepared Statement," *Hearings on H.R. 13343,* p. 551.
13. James T. McIntyre and Frank Moore, "Memorandum to the President," (August 17, 1978).
14. Patsy Fleming, Memorandum to Harrison Wellford and Pat Gwaltney, "Re: Congressional Action on Legislation to Create a Department of Education," (August 18, 1978).
15. Arthur Sheekey, "Memorandum to Patricia Gwaltney," (December 13, 1978).
16. Vice President Walter Mondale, "Remarks: Meeting of Ad Hoc Committee on the Department of Education," Old Executive Office Building (January 24, 1979).
17. David Breneman and Noel Epstein, "Uncle Sam's Growing Clout in the Classroom," *Washington Post* (August 6, 1978), D. 1.
18. "An Illusion of Education Reform," Editorial, *New York Times* (January 16, 1979).
18a. Jimmy Carter, State of the Union Address (January 23, 1979); Vital Speeches of the Day, Volume 45, No. 8 (February 1, 1979).
19. James T. McIntyre, "Memorandum to the President," (January 25, 1979).
20. Commander Michael Austin, Vice President and Legislative Chairman of the European Congress, "Testimony," *Hearings on H.R. 2444,* pp. 100-101.
21. James T. McIntyre, "Testimony," *Hearings on H.R. 2444,* p. 56.
22. Congressman Ben Rosenthal, "Statement," *Hearings on H.R. 2444* (March 27, 1979), p. 158.
23. Congressman Robert Walker, "Letter to Colleagues: Lesson #1," (May 16, 1979).
24. Walker, "Letter to Colleagues: Lesson #2," (May 17, 1979).
25. Walker, "Letter to Colleagues: Lesson #3," (May 21, 1979).
26. American Federation of Teachers, Department of Legislation, "Deficiencies in Federal Department of Education Legislation," (March 1979).
27. "School Boards Break Ranks on Education Department," *Education Daily*, Vol. 12, No. 31 (February 13, 1979).
28 Education Staff, National Council of State Legislators, "Memorandum to Patricia Gwaltney," (February 26, 1979).
29. Marian Wright Edelman, "Letter to Congressman Jack Brooks on Behalf of the Education Coalition," (February 26, 1979).
30. Spencer Rich, "Education Department is Approved," *Washington Post* (May 3, 1979), p. A1.
31. Ibid.
32. "Education Department Survives Crucial Test," *Congressional Quarterly* (June 16, 1979).
33. Ibid., p. 1149.
34. John Shattuck, Karen Christiansen and Laura Murphy, ACLU Washington Office, "Letter to Congressmann Jack Brooks," (June 12, 1979).
35. "Education Department Bill Delayed; Amendments Stir New Opposition," *Congressional Quarterly* (June 23, 1979), p. 1247.
36. Gary Fontana and Carroll Thornton, Memorandum to Jim McIntyre and Hubert Harris, "Re: Analysis of Department of Education Vote," (July 14, 1979).
36a. Ibid.
37. Reported in Beverly T. Watkins, "Separate Department of Education Nears Final Approval in Congress," *Chronicle of Higher Education* (September 24, 1979).
38. "Education Department Wins Final Approval," *Congressional Quarterly* (September 29, 1979), p. 2112.

39. Reported in Spencer Rich, "Congress Passes Bill to Establish Education Department," *Washington Post* (September 28, 1979), p. A1.

40. Ibid.

41. Nakamura and Smallwood, *The Politics of Policy Implementation* (New York: St. Martin's Press, 1980), p. 39.

42. Dom Bonafede, "Political Scientists Issue Their Report Card on the President," *National Journal* (September 16, 1978), pp. 1464-67.

Chapter 7   ORGANIZING THE NEW DEPARTMENT

President Jimmy Carter signed the act that established a cabinet-level Department of Education on October 17, 1979. The legislation that was placed before him at the signing ceremony in the East Room of the White House transferred 152 education programs from the Department of Health, Education and Welfare and five other federal agencies. The Department that was created as a result of this action took its place as the smallest of the 13 cabinet-level departments. ED, as it was to be called, had 17,000 employees, 11,000 of whom were a part of the Department of Defence Overseas School program. The 6,000 individuals who made up the Washington-based staff constituted a body that was smaller than the staff of the Office of the Secretary of HEW. It was also smaller than the professional bureaucracies of a number of school districts in the country. Despite its small size, ED was charged with the administration of a $14.2 billion budget—a budget that was the fifth largest of the 13 departmental budgets within the cabinet.

The legislation that emerged from nearly three years of activity within the Carter administration was far from the original proposals developed in the Executive Office of the President. However, the passage of the measure was viewed as a legislative victory for the President. As the Carter presidency had progressed, the Georgian was winning fewer and fewer victories in Congress. This action, thus, was seen as a significant step for Carter as well as a symbolic victory for the NEA and the other education groups that had fought so hard for the Department. Indeed, the day after the legislation was passed, the NEA endorsed Carter for reelection.

Carter's rhetoric at the occasion of the signing of the legislation emphasized the possibilities for the new Department. He proclaimed that the new Department "will profoundly transform ... the quality of education in our nation. ... I think there will be a bold escalation in the future of what the federal government can do in a constructive way to enhance education."[1] Carter noted that "Instead of being buried in a $200 billion a year bureaucracy, educational issues will now receive the top level priority they deserve. ... The time has passed when the federal government can afford to give second level, part-time attention to its responsibilities in American education." Carter proclaimed that the reorganization "will permit improved administration of the government's health and human services programs. ... It will allow the government to focus greater attention to the needs of those Americans who need it most—the poor, disabled, and elderly."[2]

The President commented: "Sometimes it didn't look as if we were going to make it. ... I don't know what history will show, but my guess is that the best move for the quality of life in America in the future might very well be the establishment of this new Department of Education."[3] Flanked by congressional advocates, 200 applauding education officials, and a class of 4th graders from Brent Elementary School in southeast Washington, Carter clearly enjoyed the taste of legislative victory.

Although one stage of the process was completed, the task of establishing the new Department had just begun. Indeed, the legislation creating the agency acknowledged the complexity of the next steps, providing more than seven months to prepare an ED to open its doors. That time period was to provide adequate transition for the movement of program components from one agency to another and for the appointment of the new officials to ED. Despite the detailed debate and analysis that had taken place in the nearly three years of activity within the Carter White House, planning for implementation would, inevitably, raise a series of new questions or demand new answers to familiar problems. The implementation of the bill forced policy-makers to move from general, abstract goals to the "nitty-gritty" business of structuring and organizing the Department. In addition, as new actors moved into center stage, charged with the implementation process, it was almost certain that issues thought to have been resolved at earlier stages of the policy process would be resurrected and would challenge the new cast of policy-makers.

As the ED legislation entered this new phase, it was difficult to characterize the activity that preceded the legislative victory. The bill's supporters had one goal during the adoption phase: devising a piece of legislation that would draw adequate support for passage. Grand expectations for change and improving educational effectiveness had to bow before the imperative of vote counting. Efficiency arguments were as strong as they were able to bring new votes or neutralize opponents. Political advantage goals and symbolic status goals were an integral part of the legislative strategy.

But as the President signed the legislation, it appeared that some of those earlier goals could take on a new life. The strong coalition of interest groups that led the measure to victory seemed excited at the prospect of addressing new issues and solving old problems through their legislative victory. And as Jimmy Carter's words at the signing ceremony implied, the White House appeared to be taken with the possibilities for change and improved educational effectiveness opened up by the new Department. Despite the modest scope of the ED, the tasks involved with planning for implementation provided an initial surge of excitement and potential. But the mood was not unanimously euphoric. Some felt that the process of achieving the legislative victory had deepened splits within the education community. *The National Journal* reported a comment by former Commissioner of Education Ernest Boyer: "The controversy over the department was so intense and the enthusiasm so limited ... there's going to be a fairly long period when the criticism outdistances the support."[4]

In addition to the conflicts among the interest groups that occurred during the period of heated lobbying and legislative debate, it was noted that the Office of Education had no legal head for two months. A battle had taken place over the appointment of an acting commissioner after Ernest Boyer resigned. Marshall L. Smith, Assistant Education Commissioner for Policy Studies, had been named by HEW Secretary Califano to be Acting Commissioner. But members of the Congressional Black Caucus had objected to Smith because he had participated in a controversial research project which concluded that programs aimed at equalizing education did little for the cause of Black education in the long run. Black Caucus members of the House threatened to oppose the department if Smith were named. As a result, Califano then named a Black woman, Mary F. Berry, Assistant HEW Secretary for Education, to serve as Acting Commissioner. Because she was already in a position within the Department, she was prohibited from serving longer than 30 days in that capacity. As a result, according to *The National Journal*, "policy-making and long-term initiatives have ground to a halt."[5]

The implementation tasks, thus, were viewed as a difficult challenge. The first agenda item, it was believed, was assembling a new team: finding a Secretary, Under Secretary and an array of both program and staff assistant secretaries. According to one observer, "After the initial flush of being Secretary, the agony of trying to put all the pieces together in a hostile atmosphere will make that job a joyless task."[6]

APPOINTING THE SECRETARY

Two days before the White House signing ceremony, *Education USA* (a specialized education newsletter) published an article entitled "Education Groups 'Construct' Secretary".[7] The publication noted that national education groups were submitting their list of qualifications for the new Secretary of Education to the White House. "While not stating outright that the nominee should be a practicing educator, several groups hint at it."

The newsletter reported that the Council of Chief State School Officers called for "knowledge of and experience in the field of public education." The National Association of State Boards of Education and the National School Boards Association noted that the Secretary should be knowledgeable about public elementary and secondary education "at the operational level."

While NEA was still drafting its proposals, the organization's representative commented that the NEA wanted a person who "relates to education ... not necessarily an educator, but someone who understands education." According to that individual, NEA wanted a Secretary "able to work in the political process. A person may be a good administrator but not understand the political realities of Washington."

Appointing the first U.S. Secretary of Education with less than a year before a presidential election was not an easy task. Speculation about that appointment had predated the actual passage of the bill. Indeed, in June 1979, while the measure was stalled on the floor of the House for the second time in a week, the *Chronicle of Higher Education* reported that the White House was beginning its search for a Secretary for the proposed agency.[8]

According to the report, the debate about the appointment included such questions as:

> Which would do more to help Mr. Carter's chances in the 1980 election—a woman or a man, a Black, a white or a Chicano?
>
> Should it be someone from within the Administration, or from among notable figures in education circles who could bring respectability and visibility to the new department?
>
> Should the new Secretary have a strong orientation to higher education or to elementary and secondary schools?
>
> Or should the post go to someone with a strong management background, even though he or she might have had little experience in education?

The report included "some of the names that have come up frequently:" Mary F. Berry, then Assistant Secretary for Education in HEW, a black female; Jerry Apodaca, former Governor of New Mexico, a Hispanic; Wilson C. Riles, then California Superintendent of Public Instruction, a black male; Harold Howe, II, a former U.S. Commissioner of Education and then a Ford Foundation vice president, a white male; Terry Stanford, President of Duke University and former governor of North Carolina, a white male.

Speculation about the appointment continued. It was reported that the administration had hoped to announce a name at the same time that the bill was signed.[8a] Ex-Governor Apodaca continued to be viewed as the leading contender for the post but, according to press reports, "talked himself out of the job in a meeting with President Carter."[8b] The *Washington Post* reported that no consensus candidate had emerged among the White House staff, but that a number of names were prominent on the list for consideration. That list, as reported, included Alan K. Campbell, Director of the Office of Personnel Management; Mary F. Berry; Wilson Riles; Rubben W. Fleming, former head of the University of Michigan; Clifton R. Wharton Jr., head of the State University of New York; Harold Howe II; and television journalist Bill Moyers.

The *Washington Post* quoted a White House aide as commenting, "The argument for a good manager, like Campbell, is that no one wants another

Department of Energy." At the same time, however, it was noted that politics would play a role in the choice of a Secretary.[9]

The Washington press did not appear to be the recipient of solid information about the probable appointee. But the speculation continued. Arguments were heard for a number of the reported contenders. Mary Berry was thought to be a logical choice since she was already part of the Carter education establishment and had solid support of Black organizations and tentative support from NEA. Wilson Riles was characterized as a strong political asset to Carter since he had received more votes in the last California election than had Jerry Brown. Harold Howe's previous position and his stature in the field was viewed as a strong asset. Alan Campbell's role as the strategist behind Carter's civil service reform campaign and his reputation as a strong manager were emphasized. But few had any real idea of the strongest contenders for the position.

THE CHOICE OF SHIRLEY HUFSTEDLER

On October 30, 1979 the speculation ended. The White House announced that President Jimmy Carter nominated Federal Appeals Judge Shirley Hufstedler of California to head the new Department of Education. The announcement was a surprise to all but a small group of White House staff and Carter administration officials. Judge Hufstedler was the highest ranking woman jurist in the U.S. at the time, appointed by President Lyndon Johnson to the Ninth Circuit Court of Appeals, sitting in California. As a judge, Hufstedler had demonstrated a strong commitment to civil rights and had authored a significant minority opinion (later sustained by the U.S. Supreme Court) advocating rights for limited English speaking children in the Lau v. Nichols case. She was a trustee of the California Institute of Technology (whose former president, Harold Brown, was Carter's Secretary of Defense), of Occidental College, and of the Aspen Institute for Humanistic Studies in Colorado.

Judge Hufstedler's support came from a number of sources—from Secretary Harold Brown, from Commerce Secretary Juanita Kreps, and from State Department official Warren Christopher. Her activity in the Aspen Institute had put her into close contact with a number of former Johnson administration officials.

The process of the selection was rapid. Once White House staff were assured that she was interested in considering the position, she was contacted by Vice President Mondale and invited to come to Washington to discuss the job. According to sources close to the Judge, she asked the Vice President whether acceptance of the cabinet post would rule her out of consideration for the U.S. Supreme Court if a vacancy occurred. When she was told no, the Judge agreed to a round of visits in Washington. Her first meeting was with an array of OMB officials and a few congressional aides. Subsequently she met with the Vice President, the President and top White House staff members. According to reports, the conversation between the President and the Judge was a friendly, low-keyed affair, focusing on Carter's personal commitment to education and on Hufstedler's concern about opportunities for young people.

Shirley Hufstedler's appointment provided the clearest clue about Jimmy Carter's view of the implementation of the new Department. In choosing a woman, Carter reaffirmed his commitment to affirmative action and the general area of equal opportunity. By deciding to make the first appointment to a non-educator, Carter sent up a signal that he did not expect the Department to become the "captive" of the education constituencies. *Time* magazine reported that President Carter "said he wanted a 'strong creative thinker.' He also wanted someone independent of the ubiquitous education lobbyists in Washington."[10] According to this account, Carter "reasoned that only a non-educator could pull together the department's elements, which represent primary, secondary and higher education constituencies that for years have competed fiercely with each other for federal funds."

The appointment was a frontal attack on the widespread belief that the Department was enacted solely as a political payoff to NEA. NEA was as surprised as the rest of the Washington community with Hufstedler's nomination. Indeed, her only affiliation with the education world had been through contacts with the higher education community. Her relationship to the worlds of elementary and secondary education came indirectly through her judicial responsibilities and through her service on a variety of committees and commissions for the California Board of Education. In addition, Judge Hufstedler had been working for many years developing curricula and inservice programs for teachers involving a Law and a Free Society project as well as a Constitutional Life foundation; these activities did bring her in contact with educators in elementary and secondary public schools as well as administrators in public school systems. Although she was clearly not a "professional educator," Judge Hufstedler had taught on both graduate and postgraduate levels throughout her legal and judicial career.

Hufstedler's appointment also signalled a decision by the President to bring in an administrator who had no role in the earlier stages of the process of formulating and enacting the new Department. This determination was not unique but strongly contrasted with the situation in the Department of Energy (when James Schlesinger played an important role in lobbying for the department), or in the creation of the Office of Economic Opportunity (when Congress knew that Sargent Shriver would be the first director of that office).

The President's choice of Judge Hufstedler indicated that he was putting a premium on her qualities as a brilliant and dispassionate jurist with knowledge about education but not about specific federal education programs.

Carter was attracted to Judge Hufstedler because of these characteristics and was not concerned about her lack of major administrative experience or of familiarity with the education establishment.

In his selection of Shirley Hufstedler as the first Secretary of Education, Carter once again emphasized the importance of bringing outsiders to Washington. He valued individuals who came to their positions without ties to the old political processes and alliances that were a part of the status quo. The President did not appear to recognize that it might be difficult for an outsider to Washington to be charged with the most insider job of all— implementing an administrative reorganization. For Carter the choice appeared to be cut and dried: reorganization was a vehicle for achieving change and change had to occur without the incumbrances of business-as-usual politics. It did not appear that Carter had paid regard to the difficulties of making a reorganization come to life—a task that would require support (or at least the avoidance of oppositon) from major political forces in the education field.

The initial reaction to Hufstedler's nomination was mixed. Senator Claiborne Pell, Democrat of Rhode Island and Chair of the Subcommittee on Education, Arts and Humanities, acknowledged that she was "intelligent, dedicated, diligent and extremely capable." However, commented Pell, "one of the major problems confronting the new department will be one of management and organization. I am not sure what skills Judge Hufstedler has in this area. ... I also note that Judge Hufstedler does not seem to have any significant experience with educational programs."[11]

The *Washington Post*, which had taken strong editorial positions against the creation of the new Department, hailed the nomination. The *Post* editorial of October 31, 1979 noted that "she is not a part or product of that particular hustling educational bureaucracy whose prospective influence was one of the better reasons for opposing the creation of the department in the first place."[12]

The strongest initial opposition to Judge Hufstedler's appointment came from the Hispanic community. Representative Edward Roybal of California and other Hispanics criticized the Carter administration for allegedly "being insensitive to the needs of the Hispanic community and for failing to appoint more Hispanics to important positions", pointing to the failure of Carter to choose former New Mexico governor Jerry Apodaca for the education post.[13] Similarly, the League of United Latin American Citizens also expressed their "disappointment" with Carter's action.[14] All critics, however, noted that their opposition was not to Judge Hufstedler personally but to the political decision made by the President.

Initial comments from the education "establishment" were less straight-forward. One report from an NEA staffer suggested that "it's all positive." Another NEA spokesperson was reported to describe a "wait and see attitude."

An official from the PTA organization reported that the appointment was only "a little bit of a surprise" since Judge Hufstedler "was viewed as a leading contender." According to one source, Phyllis Franck of the AFT called the appointment a "curious decision" but noted that the organization was keeping an open mind on the decision.

For nearly a month after the nomination was announced, Judge Hufstedler prepared for her Senate hearing. White House staff advised her on strategies for visits with various members of the House and Senate who were important to the confirmation process. Although the formal confirmation authority was in the Senate, it was acknowledged that key House members with authorizing and appropriations authority were also important to the Secretary-designate. In a memo to Shirley Hufstedler, Terry Straub, a member of the White House legislative staff, listed some of the House members that the Judge would be meeting. Straub advised the Secretary to be attentive to a number of House members and noted that

> in order to ease the Members' anxieties about the transition and implementation taking place without their personal input, we have asked (Congressman Bill) Ford's staff person, Tom Wolanin, to organize a small group of Congressional staffers who would be willing to advise you during this period. These individuals have exceptional institutional memories on the program and policy development of the education programs over the last several years. ... It would be advisable to form this group into a small ad hoc, informal committee that could meet with your office to offer counsel during the implementation process. The first meeting could serve the dual purpose of providing valuable expertise to you and your staff during the implementation period, and ease any anxieties the Members might have over the next few weeks as set-up of the new Department begins.[15]

Hufstedler's approach, following the advice of the White House staff, was to acquaint herself with the leading staff persons on both sides of the aisle, to meet them personally, talk with them candidly, and establish a relationship that would be helpful in future dealings with those individuals. Those meetings gave Judge Hufstedler an early information system; staff conversations allowed her to anticipate the questions that would be asked of her during the confirmation hearing.

The hearing before the Committee on Labor and Human Resources of the U.S. Senate on the nomination of Shirley M. Hufstedler of California to be the Secretary of Education took place on November 27, 1979. Committee Chairman Harrison A. Williams, Jr., Democrat of New Jersey, presided over the session and ranking Republican Senator Richard Schweiker of Pennsylvania joined Williams in opening the session. Judge Hufstedler was introduced by both members of the California delegation—Democrat Alan Cranston and Republican S. I. Hayakawa. Both Californians emphasized Judge Hufstedler's distinguished legal career; Cranston emphasized "the wisdom of the President's designation of a skilled and brilliant generalist, whose involvement in education has been extensive, but unsalaried."[16] Hayakawa, one of the minority of Senate members who voted against the establishment of the Department, noted that he had been concerned about the kind of person selected to run the new Department. "With President Carter's choice of Judge Hufstedler, I must say that my fears have been laid to rest. I was concerned that this Department of Education would be excessively dominated by products of schools of education."[17]

Secretary-designate Hufstedler's presentation to the Committee began with a recitation of her fundamental beliefs. She proclaimed:

> I believe in pluralism. The strength of our educational system is rooted in the primacy of State and local governments. Where Federal involvement is necessary, our goals should be maximum efficiency and cooperation, minimum disruption and domination.
>
> I believe in quality. The Department of Education can and should encourage excellence at every level—both by enhancing State and local efforts, and by supporting innovation and experimentation.
>
> We must create an environment where students can learn and teachers with ability and imagination can teach.
>
> I believe in equal opportunity. This is the cornerstone of our educational system and, indeed, of any just society. Federal responsibility has been clearly defined in areas ranging from eradicating race and sex discrimination to meeting the needs of the disabled.
>
> And I believe in the individual. Every policy of the Department of Education should be examined for its impact on the individual child in the classroom, and the individual student at all levels of education, which is, of course, a lifelong experience.
>
> It is far too easy for insensitive bureaucracies to see children in categories or as statistics, and even easier for children to become pawns in adult chess games.[18]

The questions submitted to Judge Hufstedler during the hearing (and in subsequent written requests) reflected the specific programmatic interests of a number of members. Questions were asked about the major education programs as well as a series of smaller programs (such as alcohol and drug abuse education programs) that were to be included in the scope of the new Department's responsibilities.

Several members, however, queried her about more general administrative matters. Chairman Williams noted that the education programs in HEW were "widely reported to suffer organizational deficits due to many vacancies and low morale and this situation is of some duration from the reports that we have had."[19] He asked Judge Hufstedler how she, as Secretary, would "deal with these morale problems" and in what ways she would "attempt to reinvigorate the personnel of the division."

Judge Hufstedler replied:

> The first order of business is to obtain enough names of people of outstanding quality representing the diversity and pluralism of the entire educational enterprise to be nominated for consideration by the President of the United States for the Presidential appointments to the Department.
>
> The second—which is proceeding right now—is to bring together persons who have been known for excellence in the existing Office of Education to assist, along with others from other agencies to define and outline the tasks and to suggest priorities for the attention of the Secretary of Education.

> The third is the commitment of the Secretary of Education at the first moment possible after confirmation to visit that Office of Education and to begin a personal contact with those who are leaders in the office and then to bring forward, as quickly as possible, commensurate with quality, teams to draw together the Office of Education as well as to fill the vacancies which now unfortunately exist.[20]

Senator Claiborne Pell, Democrat of Rhode Island, questioned the Secretary-designate about her management skills, noting that "when your nomination was announced, there was some concern about management, whether you had as much background in management as other Secretaries had had."[21]

Judge Hufstedler responded:

> Well, it is quite clear that I have never managed a bureaucracy of the size of the new Department of Education, nor a budget of the size involved in the Department of Education. I daresay unless one is a Cabinet-level officer of the United States or is a Governor of a very large industrial State, one would never have the opportunity to do it.
>
> I have had a significant amount of management experience, both in terms of contributing to the diagnosis of the ills and ails and of running major departments in very large metropolitan courts and in working on structures for judicial systems, developing management techniques for very seriously overburdened courts. ...
>
> I do not suggest that I am a master of such skills. I do suggest I am really quite a student, and my philosophy overall is not a particularly extraordinary one. It is that you find the very best people there are. You give them significant responsibility. You take responsibility for their mistakes as well as for their successes. You give them confidence where confidence is due. If they do not do their jobs, they are asked to leave.[22]

All of her years on the bench served Judge Hufstedler well in the confirmation hearings. She clearly enjoyed the colloquy with the members and was comfortable with the oral arguments that were presented. It was, however, a reversal of roles; she had been on the other side of the bench in previous encounters as the one who asked the question and pushed other participants in the judicial process to respond.

On November 29, 1979, the Senate Labor and Human Resources Committee unanimously confirmed Shirley Hufstedler's nomination. The Committee recommendation went immediately to the Senate floor and action was prompt. One day after Committee action, on November 30, 1979, the Senate voted to confirm her appointment by a 81-2 vote; only North Carolina Republican Jesse Helms and Texas Republican John Tower opposed the nomination.

As she assumed the position and began the preparations for the opening of the new Department, Education Secretary Shirley Hufstedler reinforced a theme that had been found in federal education activity for a number of years. Her emphasis on the importance of the federal role as a stimulator of educational excellence echoed similar pronouncements in earlier administrations (as well as administrations that followed). Indeed, in his action to establish a National Institute of Education, President Richard Nixon had called on the federal government to develop information that would provide models of effective practice to school systems throughout the country.

While her appointment began as a symbolically successful decision to disarm critics and establish an apolitical aura to the new Department, Hufstedler herself had strong views about what was needed to change American education. These views, once articulated and formulated, would not be able to escape the reality of American decision-making—a reality of strong political forces in both a partisan and interest group setting.

ORGANIZING A TRANSITION

The legislation that created the Department gave the administration until early June 1980 to set up the new agency. Thus as she assumed her new position, Secretary Hufstedler had seven months to shape the organization and to make decisions regarding its operation. These decisions were of three types: the development of the Department's organizational structure; the organization of staff functions and internal decision-making processes; and appointments to key positions.

Organizing for implementation is always a difficult phase in the policy process as an issue moves from the imperatives of agreement through the adoption phase to the imperatives of operation in the implementation phase. Actors who had a predominant role in formulation and in adoption are placed in a confusing position. Although they may believe that the seemingly mundane, day to day technical decisions made about organization and administration are important, they know that these decisions must be made by the agencies that are charged with the administration of the policies. At the same time, however, the predominant actors involved in the adoption of a policy— often the legislative branch—claim a role in the evaluation or oversight of those administrative determinations. The American system of government has made it legitimate for those with authority to create programs and policies to second guess those who are charged with the administration of those efforts.

If organizing for implementation is, by nature, a complex set of activities, organizing for the transition to the new Department of Education can only be described as a morass. Transition activities in this instance took place in four separate arenas. Activities in each of these arenas were orchestrated by a different set of actors; these efforts were sometimes overlapping in both time and function. For individuals and groups who attempted to follow these activities and influence their progress, it was not easy to determine who was, indeed, in charge of the Education Department transition.

The four clusters of activity that made up the transition phase of this policy were found in OMB (extending from the original President's Reorganization Project that played a predominant role in the formulation stage); in a small transition team that Shirley Hufstedler organized as soon as she was confirmed; in an official Program Organization and Implementation Group divided into a series of specialized task forces; and White House personnel.

While each of the cores of transition activity had its own set of dynamics and influences, each struggled with a similar problem. The clock had been ticking while the Department was being designed; Carter's reelection was a matter of increasing concern as time went on. Once again, two conflicting demands were being experienced: should decisions be made on the basis of complete and thorough analysis or should decisions be made on the basis of calculations about political survival?

THE OMB TRANSITION TEAM

As the Department of Education legislation was working its way through the Congress in April 1979, the President's Reorganization Project staff was beginning to focus on the requirements for activating an implementation plan for the proposed department. In a memorandum dated April 17, 1979, John McGruder of the Management Analysis Group in OMB (not part of PRP) devised a preliminary draft implementation plan for activating the proposed department. The memorandum, addressed to Don Boselovic of the PRP, suggested that following passage in the Senate, activity should include efforts to identify information needs, space needs and availabilities, OMB budget requirements, and to review the Act and its legislative history. As soon as Senate passage was achieved, he called for the "designation of persons to head the Task Force to put together the new agency. (Also helpful to establish early who will be the principal administrative officer and assign that person a key in the Task Force.)"[23]

According to McGruder, that Task Force should have two levels, "one comprised of the Cabinet Secretaries and heads of the involved agencies as the formal body with a working level of designees who will guide and review the overall effort."[24] Working groups, he advised, should include legal; policy, plans and programs; budget and fiscal; procurement and contracts; organization; field operations; personnel; facilities; information systems; security; inspector general; congressional, governmental and public relations; and records, correspondence and mail.

Also included in McGruder's analysis was a set of organization charts and specifications about qualifications for the major appointees to the inchoate department that were inferred from the pending legislation in the two bodies of the Congress. The Secretary, according to this memorandum, should be a generalist; of national stature; politically skilled; a team player; should not be seen as a "captive" of any education group; able to make decisions; should have experience as a chief executive of a major organization and a commitment to management; should show commitment and track record in civil rights; and should hold progressive views on improving the quality of education. Previous federal experience was deemed desirable but not necessary.

The Under-Secretary, according this formulation, would be a proven manager; experienced in managing a new or transitional organization; able to deal with a wide range of interest groups; able to make decisions; should have previous federal experience; commitment and experience with intergovernmental concerns; commitment and track record in civil rights; should show willingness to serve through to the end of the administration and to work out of the limelight; and should hold progressive views on improving the quality of education. This memorandum from another part of OMB (its permanent management side) appeared to trigger a concern within the Reorganization Project about implementation. Staff of the PRP were asked to review the literature on implementation to determine whether there were either academic or practical lessons to be learned from previous reorganization efforts. Conversations were held with individuals involved with the creation of the Department of Energy, the Federal Emergency Management Administration, and the Health Care Financing Administration reorganization. While finding the McGruder paper useful, the PRP staff seemed concerned about the political and bureaucratic strategies that would underpin the more technical administrative approach.

Attached to McGruder's memorandum was a document entitled *Notes On Implementation of New Agencies*, a paper prepared by W. S. Dinsmore of OMB's Organization and Special Studies Division, in September 1974. While written as a general identification and discussion of plans and actions to be considered whenever new federal agencies were legislatively created, the paper noted that "every case of agency implementation varies and has its own specifics which must be accommodated to (sic). Nevertheless, there is much commonality to the process in each occurrence and, therefore, some experience that can be passed on as general guidance."[25]

While emphasizing the importance of creating an implementation task force to coordinate the numerous planning and decision-making efforts that inevitably form part of a new agency reorganization, the paper noted: "There is a caution to be considered in terms of the direct participation of the prospective agency head. That is, he must be careful not to assume too prominent a role, particularly in controversial matters, before Senate confirmation has been voted."[26] As outlined in this paper, administrative management needs (rather than program or policy specifics) appeared to take preeminence in the implementation planning.

As the staff of the PRP began to focus on the implementation questions, it became obvious that there were very different perceptions about the appropriate role for the OMB group in the transition activities and subsequent implementation efforts. For some participants, PRP was created to serve an ongoing role; its functions would be institutionalized within OMB's management activities but it would maintain an identifiable separate status. The reorganization group would regularly scrutinize organizational arrangements in the new department as well as in other federal government agencies and departments. For others, the PRP was a temporary activity, tied to a specific president's personal agenda of a given period. As the campaign approached, the reorganization issues had less salience and thus were not expected to be institutionalized within the activities of the Executive Office of the President. Ongoing OMB management functions would pick up the issues.

PRP staff member Nancy LeaMond articulated the overall dilemma facing the ED transition in a memorandum to PRP Human Resources Chief, Patricia Gwaltney McGinnis: "Although all reorganizations are by definition pitched on management improvements, it is certainly clear that we are on record asserting that the main reason—the most compelling case—for the creation of a Department of Education is to improve the management of Federal education programs."[27] She noted that promises attached to the impact of this department on management questions may have contributed to a growing cynicism about the effort. Indeed, she commented: "The Administration's record with the Department of Energy and FEMA only increases the incredulousness about the potential benefits of reorganization. Fairly or unfairly, the Department of Energy is viewed as an administrative disaster. It is said that top management is poorly organized; that the Department does not have a completed organization chart; that civil service classifications have not been finished; and that internal communications are horrendous."

LeaMond continued: "In short, the climate seems more suited to failure and problems than to success. Unfortunately, the Department of Education implementation and transition will be taking place concurrent with the political primaries. To the extent that Carter runs at all on his reorganization record, adverse stories about the Department of Education could be painful."[28]

She advised moving on a number of fronts. Great strides would be made if they could:

— have agreement immediately on the person who will run implementation and give that person the authority to make decisions
— design an implementation task force that melds policy program, and management concerns.
— invest both political appointees in the affected agencies and career civil servants in the reorganization. (The lure of new supergrade positions may help with the normally lethargic or obstreperous types.)
— develop in the Congress, the press and the public some realistic expectations of implementation, and thereby perhaps mitigate some of the natural criticisms.
— accomplish a few symbolic things early. Eliminate egregious paperwork requirements, concentrate on the historically poorly managed programs first.
— concentrate early initiatives to areas where we have made promises for reform.
— try to adopt the bottom up open consultation reorganization process to implementation. (We must demonstrate a willingness to listen to interest groups' concerns about their statutorily protected offices without being captive of them.)
— involve all affected agencies in implementation so that there is not the perception that everything is being swallowed up by an exaggerated DE.
— appoint high level officials with a commitment to improving management and a willingness to serve until the end of the Administration.[29]

By early October 1979, when it appeared that the legislation was about to pass and the implementation concerns moved from the wings to center stage, activity intensified in the reorganization project. PRP Human Resources Division Director Patricia Gwaltney McGinnis was not directly involved in the effort because she was on maternity leave. Nancy LeaMond assumed the pivotal role.

A memorandum dated October 3, 1979 from Nancy LeaMond to PRP Director Harrison Wellford on the subject of "Implementation of the Department of Education," outlined her views on the tasks ahead. She noted that "several things are absolutely critical to a successful implementation of the Department of Education:"

> First, clearly understood relationships among the "players." ...
>
> Second, a strong signal from Jim (McIntyre), you and others that the Administration is committed to achieving the central purpose of this legislation: improved management of education programs. ...
>
> Third, a well orchestrated political strategy for implementation. This will require extensive consultations with the interest groups, Members of Congress and the affected agencies, particularly the Education Division at HEW. ... If we can make decisions on internal organization and general staffing for programs at approximately the same time that the major political appointments are being made, we may have the opportunity to make some important political trade-offs.
>
> Four, special initiatives to meet expectations and promises. ... If we fail to live up to any of these (promises)—the 500 personnel reduction, decreased paperwork burden on state and local officials, the elimination of duplication in staff function, the reduction in time for promulgating regulations—we will create negative reactions that will automatically outweigh any other successes. ...
>
> Fifth, a well managed and executed "nuts and bolts" effort to set up the Department.[30]

As the events moved toward a time when responsibility would be turned over to a new Secretary, OMB's role became both more complex and less clear. The PRP staff continued to play a role on the programmatic front, preparing the groundwork for the new Secretary to decide how the Department might be organized. The Education Study Group focused on substantive and liaison work, thinking about how the transition task forces might be organized to produce some options on organization and identify issues that would be of importance to the Secretary. At the same time, another office in OMB called Management, Improvement and Evaluation (headed by career staffer Howard Messner) was concerned about the operations and logistics side of the transition, identifying individuals who could begin to work on issues such as the budget, finance, space, personnel, and begin to develop options for systems for the Department.

Many of the individuals within the management side of OMB who worked on the Department of Education implementation had previously worked on the organizational issues involved with the Department of Energy. The Department of Energy was more complicated than the Department of Education because it brought together so many different programs from so many different places. Some of the stumbling blocks for Energy were avoided in Education—partly because of the experience that people had with it and because Education was a much simpler reorganization.

Because budget issues were never far from the minds of the administration, it was also viewed as important to involve the Budget side of the OMB structure, working with Division Director James Hinchman on education budget matters. Hinchman wanted to be able to brief the new Secretary on the budget that was expected to emerge from past discussions and, at the same time, to make the new official understand the importance of creating a separate Department of Education budget account (a requirement that was necessary because of the consolidated HEW account).

In the period just before the passage of the bill (and before the new Secretary was named) PRP chief Harrison Wellford became the spokesman for the administration on the plans for organizing the new Department. On October 10, 1979, Wellford conducted a briefing to the Ad Hoc Committee in which he reviewed the issues that were of current concern. He noted that there were major problems of disengagement in the Office for Civil Rights; that there were personnel distribution issues to be decided; that there were major space problems to be confronted as the Department plans proceeded. He commented that the Department had come out of the legislative process "more prescriptive than we want" but that it still was very broad in scope. Wellford noted that he had never seen a group as effective as the Coalition in his ten years in Washington and implied that once the legislation had been enacted, the group of supporters would be consulted with regards to a number of organizational and appointment decisions.

Several days later, Wellford met with HEW officials about the Department of Education implementation. At that meeting, it appeared that Wellford assumed that he would be the Director of Implementation and that Hinchman, Messner, LeaMond, Gwaltney, and others (not yet named) would be involved.[31] The activity within OMB continued through October 1979, up to the point when Judge Hufstedler's appointment was announced by the White House. At that juncture, OMB's role became much less clear.

THE HUFSTEDLER TRANSITION TEAM

During the first week of November, within four days of the time when Carter announced her nomination, Judge Hufstedler assembled four trusted personal advisers to work with her during the transition period. She believed that she needed individuals for whom she had strong personal respect who would be loyal to her and had no aspirations toward a permanent job in the new Department. Burt Gindler and Pierce O'Donnell were partners in Judge Hufstedler's husband's law firm and were well known to her; Richard Gilman, President of Occidental College (a college of which Hufstedler served as a member of the Board of Trustees) agreed to join the other two Californians in the task. In addition, Marian Otsea of the San Francisco Federal Reserve Bank and a good friend of Judge Hufstedler, came to Washington to assist the Secretary-designate during the pre-confirmation process. The California group did have some Washington experience: O'Donnell had gone to law school in D.C., worked for a Washington firm, and done a stint on the Hill; Otsea had spent a considerable amount of time in the nation's capital; and Gilman had been active in a number of education organizations involved with the creation of the Department. In no way, however, could one view the group as an "inside" Washington assemblage.

Hufstedler did realize that it was important to find someone with expertise in the Washington bureaucracy—a Washington insider—but had difficulty identifying such an individual early on. She asked former Social Security Commissioner Bruce Cardwell if he would take on the transition position but he was unable to make arrangements with his current employer for such a position.

As the confirmation preparation proceeded and she began to become more familiar with the lay of the land, Hufstedler believed that little had been done to prepare for the new Department (aside from the budget creation) and, at the same time, began to experience some resistance to her efforts to take charge of the transition. The Judge became suspicious of the counsel of some of the past OMB participants and quickly distanced herself from these individuals. While it has never been confirmed, it appeared that Hufstedler believed that Harrison Wellford claimed the Under Secretary position in the new Department and saw Hufstedler as a figurehead in the Secretary's spot. She was unwilling to become a figurehead Secretary and allow the PRP staff to move into the new Department.

The initial transition team that was assembled by the California advisers included very few individuals from the OMB staff; Nancy LeaMond joined Hufstedler's group just days after her appointment was announced and Patsy Fleming soon came to the staff to work on legislative matters. In addition, several individuals from the Office of Education (Marshall Smith, William Smith, Bill Dingledein among them) were asked to participate in the early Hufstedler transition group.

Hufstedler found it frustrating that she was unable to find out what her budget would be for the transition and that no one had thought about the space requirements for the transition group. She was amazed that, in a town where space is at a premium, there appeared to have been no thought about the location of the implementation planning staff.

One individual closely connected with the early activity characterized the situation as follows: Hufstedler "was coming into a completely unknown situation. She didn't know the people, she didn't know the issues, she didn't know the programs, she didn't know the budget process, she didn't know the bureaucracy. ... And she brought in a couple of her own people to head up the transition who were equally inexperienced in terms of these programs and the bureaucracy."

The relationship between the study team in OMB and the transition activities within the new Department was, necessarily, characterized by tension. OMB wanted to be more involved in calling the shots and designing the agency largely because it had become the lead agency developing the legislation. Normally in a piece of substantive legislation such as this, the Cabinet Secretary is the person who carries the ball. Because Califano was not interested in being the leading force in separating the two parts of his Department, consequently OMB became the lead agency. In addition, Jim McIntyre had made a number of personal and professional commitments on the management of the agency. The formal relationship between OMB and the Department was never worked out completely.

Different participants in the process did, necessarily, have varying perceptions on the worth of the early OMB implementation activity. Hufstedler was annoyed because there had been no final clear options on space and no budget for the transition. She felt that it was difficult for her to come in and deal with a host of bureaucratic issues without basic questions such as space and budget having been resolved. Actors within OMB, on the other hand, argued that many new Secretaries want to come in and begin without encumbrances—and they thought that their decisions on space and budget would be perceived as encumbrances.

As the early stages of the transition unfolded, Hufstedler attempted to develop a critical mass for the transition team and, at the same time, become more familiar with the broader issues in the education field. Two days before Hufstedler was confirmed, Nancy LeaMond outlined her thoughts about implementation in a memorandum to Hufstedler's confidante Burt Gindler.[32] LeaMond reiterated the concern that she had expressed earlier to PRP chief Wellford: "I believe that the Secretary will be judged primarily on her execution of the nuts and bolts of establishing the new Department. All other successes, albeit very significant ones—attracting high calibre people, initiating creative programs—will be minimized if the Department cannot live up to the central purpose of the legislation: the improvement of management of Federal education programs."[33] She made seven specific suggestions:

1. A clear statement by the Secretary of her goals for the Department.
2. A press strategy that conveys the realities and difficulties of creating a Department.
3. A manager of transition task forces.
4. A commitment to work with the bureaucracy (noting that there will be a "natural rivalry" between the transition team and the operating agencies).
5. A talent search within and outside government.
6. Use all of tools of Civil Service Reform (giving a Secretary improved management capability).

7. Development of a special management initiatives group within the transition team.[34]

LeaMond reminded Gindler about the Department of Energy "fiasco". "The major challenge will be to complete transition without egregious problems," avoiding the implementation problems faced by Energy: "a delay in securing space for the employees; a delay in the appointment of high level officials; inadequate coordination and communication among the principal elements of the new Department; and a lack of leadership by the Secretary."[35]

Hufstedler's past activities with the Aspen Institute brought forward some resources that would help her develop a broad substantive perspective on education issues. Aspen staffer and former Johnson White House education aide Douglas Cater along with former Ladybird Johnson press secretary Liz Carpenter arranged a two-day retreat at the Aspen's Wye Plantation. Former Secretaries of HEW and past Commissioners of Education provided the new Secretary with advice and sympathy. Additional conversations were held with individuals such as former HEW Secretary John Gardner who advised on bureaucratic, education as well as personnel matters. University of the District of Columbia President Lisle Carter joined the "inner circle" along with HUD Assistant Secretary Donna Shalala. Liz Carpenter was brought into the immediate staff to handle press matters. The original team of Californians was soon replaced; O'Donnell left in early December; Otsea departed after the confirmation hearings; Gindler left in January and Gilman stayed until February.

By early January, the major transition advice was provided by former HEW General Counsel Richard Beattie who returned to Washington to assist Hufstedler as Director of Implementation. Hufstedler found him to be the counselor she had sought being, indeed, a Washington "insider".

On December 11, 1979, the *Washington Post*, long a foe of the new Department, published an article called, "New Education Chief Knee-Deep in Territorial Wrangling."

The article began:

> When Shirley M. Hufstedler became the nation's first secretary of education last week she took over the federal bureaucracy's equivalent of a National Football League expansion team—mostly old faces, big hopes and glory first-year prospects. ... It is not likely that the former California jurist will spend much of her time in lofty arguments over education philosophy. Instead, Hufstedler must wrestle with such problems as how to pull together a department now scattered at 11 locations around the city—including six other existing Cabinet departments—and how to circulate a memo to her top staff members in less than the three days it now takes.[36]

The article went on to describe the difficulties of setting up a new Department—problems as mundane as space turf fights, bureaucratic resistance to moves from HEW officials, and availability of desks.

One of Hufstedler's first actions was to claim space in the old Office of

Education building, moving out of a dark office in the Old Executive Office Building to offices on Maryland Avenue (sharing the building with NASA). It was reported that several staff members in the Office of Education locked their doors and left so that the doors had to be knocked off the hinges in order to get the offices ready for the Secretary. That space claim also invoked the wrath of the Office of Education union which had an agreement with the agency that people had to be consulted prior to any major reallocation of space.

Through December and into January, less than a dozen individuals constituted the Hufstedler transition group. Donna Shalala served as the transition policy coordinator; Nancy LeaMond established processes that allowed information to be received and decisions made, setting the framework for the Executive Secretariat that would be put into place once the Department began operations. Although early appointments to the top posts were made largely through White House staffers, Hufstedler aides soon took over the appointment process, installing a new search process and screening efforts.

In an attempt to build her own relationships with the multiple interest groups and elements of the new Department's constituencies, Hufstedler began a process of meetings with groups all around Washington. For some observers the process was ludicrous; it put incredible demands on the Secretary's time and pushed her in front of groups when she had little detailed knowledge of their agendas or past history with the administration.

THE PROGRAM ORGANIZATION AND IMPLEMENTATION GROUP (POIG)

The establishment of a separate task force charged with planning the transition had been one of the major suggestions arising from the OMB implementation activity. Similarly, Nancy LeaMond had recommended that such a group be formed to assist the new Secretary focus on both structural and programmatic issues facing the new agency. When Hufstedler adviser Richard Gilman came on board, he was given the responsibility of conceptualizing and organizing the task force system as well as staffing the programmatic offices of the Department. Career OMB staffer, Paul Royston was brought over from the Reorganization Project to work as the day to day administrator for the effort. Royston had been in OMB for almost ten years and had done work on organizational studies involved with several other reorganizations.

The task force system that was devised—a set of 14 separate task forces established for each major programmatic area—was not exactly what OMB had envisioned. OMB staff thought that a small group of 10 to 15 individuals would come in to assist the Secretary plan for departmental operations. To some observers, the mushrooming size of the transition task forces represented an attempt by the Secretary to give Gilman an important job since he was the only person whom Hufstedler brought in who had a substantive background in education. However, as the task forces grew, space problems also increased. The only space available for the effort was an office building far from the center of the federal city—the Transpoint Building off in Buzzard's Point. Gilman would not move with the staff of the effort and lose his proximity to the new Secretary.

In December 1979 the move took place. Paul Royston moved with the staff. The physical distances between the other activities and the task force teams reinforced the tendency for the task force efforts to take on a life of their own. The location of the effort was open to ridicule. The staff feared that the *Washington Post* (which had called the idea of a department a "turkey") would carry an article with the headline, "Turkey Roosts in Buzzard's Point."

When Dick Beattie was appointed the chief of the transition, he took steps to attempt to curb the task force activities, believing that there would be minimal payoff from them. One observer characterized Beattie's view as "very negative", noting that Beattie felt that the task forces were "a circus with far too many people grappling for influence." Beattie was concerned that the activity in the transition task forces would have the effect of disrupting the day to day flow of work. According to one observer, he believed that it was imperative to move quickly to a basic organizational structure for the Department and allow the designated Assistant Secretaries to make the fine tuning decisions.

Despite Gilman's personal relationship with the new Secretary, he had to work through Beattie for access to Hufstedler on all transition matters. By the time that Gilman returned to Occidental College at the end of February 1980, the task forces had, indeed, taken on a life of their own despite Beattie's opposition to them because of their links to the career bureaucracy and various interest groups.

The task forces were staffed with a mixture of individuals from the past PRP efforts, from the operating agencies which would be moved to the new Department, and from some interest groups. The task forces began by looking at the enabling legislation creating the Department, funding levels for their program areas, and the staff allotments for the effort. The role of the task forces, as described by Royston, was fourfold:

1. To provide the Secretary with options regarding the placement of programs.
2. To advise the Secretary and the appropriate Assistant Secretary on internal organization efforts.
3. To look at critical relationships involved in the program area, and
4. To help set an agenda for the program area, including both long term and short efforts as well as management initiatives.

A memorandum that was sent to all Program Organization and Implementation Group (POIG) Task Force leaders by Paul Royston on December 28,

1979, illustrated the complexity of the assignment. By geographical necessity, the groups would have to operate independently since they were more than a half hour away from the other ED staff. But they were instructed that there were a number of coordination requirements involving the downtown staff. Staffing for the task forces, for example, required some advice and counsel from the Maryland Avenue group because the Secretary's office was concerned about a balance between "outside" experts and "internal" staff on the task forces. Contacts with congressional committees and the media had to be handled by congressional relations staffer Patsy Fleming and press aide Liz Carpenter, both of whom were operating out of Hufstedler's immediate office. All meetings with outside interest groups were also to be recorded and forwarded to the downtown offices.[37]

Royston envisioned a four stage process:

Phase I—Task Force Activation—involved organizing and staffing the program task forces and developing work plans and schedules. That phase was to be completed by January 4th.

Phase II—Analysis of Program/Placement/Organization/Relationships— would be undertaken between January 4th and February 8th. It would include analysis of policy, organization, management and coordination issues; consultation with program agencies, interest groups and congressional staff; development of papers on organizational options; and a final decision memo by February 1st. This phase was the substantive heart of the task force assignments.

Phases III and IV—Implementation Planning and Post Activation—were wind-up activities in which task forces would simply move to assist the designated Assistant Secretaries in their implementation concerns. Under Royston's plans, some aspect of the task force structure would continue until September 1980. As was true of the PRP plans, this follow-up never occurred.

Whether by design or default, the activity in the Transpoint Building at Buzzards's Point was never clear to the education constituencies that had labored so hard to ensure the creation of the new Department. For nearly three years, the interest groups had been courted by the White House and the PRP staff. Whether or not their advice was heeded, these groups did have access to top administration officials. PRP head Harrison Wellford regularly briefed the Ad Hoc Coalition on the OMB implementation plans up until Hufstedler's appointment when his role diminished rapidly. With the exception of Richard Gilman's contacts in the higher education community, the Hufstedler California team was unknown to the education establishment.

At the same time that changes were occurring with the entrance of the new ED team, relationships among the supporters of the Department were also shifting. During the adoption stage of the policy process, it was clear that the goal of all of the supporters of the Department was, simply, the creation of the Department. Although specific groups moved into and outside the coalition (responding to the shifting configuration of programs that moved in and out of the proposed legislation), the coalition core was both strong and consistent.

Once the legislation was enacted, it made sense for the coalition to reconstitute itself as the Transition Coalition, focusing on implementation issues that would emerge. The Big Six education groups (the National Education Association, Council of Chief State School Officers, National School Board Association, National Association of State Boards of Education, American Association of School Administrators and the National Congress of Parents and Teachers) were joined by the American Educational Research Association, the Council for Exceptional Children, El Congreso Nacional de Asuntos Colegiales, National Committee for Citizens in Education, United Negro College Fund, and the United States Student Association.

But the dynamics of transition planning made it difficult for the coalition to work as a body with one voice. Many of the issues that were confronted by the transition task force involved very specialized program questions. Some special interest groups became involved in issues of program placement, undergirding their original reason for supporting the creation of ED—an attempt to gain political advantage through the reorganization and maintain an increased or guaranteed status within the new organizational structure.

As one AASA member explained, "Things that could have been said with one voice, no longer could be." Without a single goal in mind—the creation of ED—the constant compromising required to keep the group together was extremely difficult to maintain.

The Transpoint POIG Task Force group was committed, at least in principle, to extensive consultation with the interest group community. Although there were many observers of the process who believed that the substantive output hardly justified the process, a staff member, Sandra Gray, was given the responsibility to head up the public consultation process and ensure that all affected groups would be involved in the transition planning. Like the PRP group before it, the POIG Task Force invested in both analytic activity and consultation efforts. It did, however, recognize that it was difficult for members of the public to react if focused and substantive information was not provided to them. Indeed, in a memorandum to Director of Transition Richard Beattie, Paul Royston noted that "the public process to date has provided very little guidance for comment." This February 21, 1980 report commented that "historically, with very few exceptions, it has not been within the nature or resources of these organizations to propose how the government should organize to implement its work. Once the government makes a proposal, however, they are well trained to offer a reaction on how the proposal will affect their particular area of interest."[38]

The observation grew out of the experience of the transition group with the public participation process. That consultation process was kicked off on January 9, 1980 with a three day meeting in the HEW North Auditorium to review the efforts of the Program Organization and Implementation Task Forces and to solicit input from interested parties. The auditorium was packed with representatives of interest groups, members of the task forces, and other interested individuals. Although Secretary Hufstedler opened the session, she did not stay at the meeting. She noted that the purpose of the session was twofold: to share information with interested individuals and groups and to invite questions and comments about the process thus far. She acknowledged that many of the issues confronting the task forces were difficult because they involved so many conflicting points of view. The Secretary promised to consider all views as she met with each of the task forces in the near future. Hufstedler concluded by reaffirming her commitment that the Education Department would "strive for the best," meeting high standards and, at the same time, ensuring sensitivity to the special needs of the handicapped and disadvantaged.

The opening session of the three day meeting was also addressed by Richard Gilman, Dick Beattie, Paul Royston and Sandra Gray. In his introductory remarks, Royston stressed the importance to the work of the task forces of "taking advantage of the expertise and long-standing interest of people like you (the people present at the meeting)." He noted that the implementation task was not a three to six month process but rather an effort that would unfold over the next two to three years. He emphasized the importance of working closely with the group assembled and viewed this meeting simply as a starting point in that relationship.

Public consultation staffer Sandra Gray likened the fledgling Department to "an infant who needs attention." The questions that were provoked by the opening session were largely an attempt by participants to get updated information on appointments, some sense of the timetable for decisions, and a reading about more general strategy questions. The specific questions that were raised at the 14 separate briefings by each task force group were much more detailed and reflected the specific concerns of the participants. Many of the sessions were packed and briefings such as those on civil rights had over 300 attendees.

By January 25, 1980, participants in the public consultation meetings received a rather detailed summary of the comments, recommendations and questions raised during the three day session. The summary indicated that many of the questions raised during the meetings went unanswered or received vague replies because they reflected issues that the task forces had not yet resolved or considered. For many individuals, this meeting was the first opportunity they had to see the new Secretary and raise questions that were of concern to them. Many participants wanted answers—not the joy of participation. Some skepticism was expressed informally by participants about the effectiveness of the transition efforts.

The response of the interest groups to these efforts varied enormously. The National School Board Association issued its own report on the Department of Education Implementation Task Force Meeting, releasing its summary of the meeting and each of the task force discussions four days before the "official" summary was released. In his cover letter to the report, NSBA Executive Director Thomas A. Shannon commented that "At this point, NSBA is concerned that the education community may not have the degree of involvement which should be required."[39]

NEA officials participated in all of the public hearings and events that were held concerning the new Department but did not have a real sense of participating in the decision-making process. While NEA acknowledged that it was not appropriate for them to have a place in the internal decision-making of the bureaucracy, they felt that all of their past work on the issue gave them a claim to more substantive involvement.

NEA itself had internal disagreement about the appropriate role it should play in lobbying on the transition activities. Its role during the enactment process had been to focus attention on general issues involving the Department—the symbolic importance of creating a department, the need for national leadership on education issues, and the political access that a department would give the organization. As the bill progressed in the House and became more specific, NEA became less involved in the political trade-offs. A similar dynamic occurred within the transition activities. When the goals and objectives for ED were being discussed, NEA felt it had a role to play. But the more specific the transition became, the less contribution NEA and the other major Coalition groups could make. As the transition progressed, aside from a few specific program decisions about which NEA had a concern (for example, the organizational placement of the Teacher Centers program and the Gifted and Talented program), NEA's role during implementation could be characterized as peripheral.

During the first months of its operation, the task forces operating out of the Transpoint building met with many concerned groups, extending the formal consultation process of January to a number of more informal meetings and conversations. As Paul Royston noted in his February 21st memo to Beattie, it was difficult to elicit responses from interest groups to non-decisions. The Transition Coalition was no longer a cohesive body but most of the groups believed that it was better to be involved in the transition activities than to ignore them. As one interest group representative noted, "It was probably better to be nominally involved in the transition than not at all." Another representative commented cynically that "the transition was an enormous smoke screen—but we continued to send people to meetings, nonetheless."

The location of the group in Buzzard's Point gave some groups the feeling that the "transition team closeted themselves away. Everyone had a sense that they were going to do what they darn well pleased. All the work done by the transition teams became file cabinet or waste basket stuff." Even when groups met "officially" with the transition teams, they were disappointed with the follow-up. The Chief State School Officers met with individual transition group teams in March 1980. According to one participant, the transition task forces "said they wanted input, but we never heard anything further. The task forces had long meetings which produced many questions that never got answered." Commented another individual: "in a way it's understandable; they were overwhelmed with questions and ideas. But the task force people tended to lack expertise, to be 'jack of all trades' sorts. The task forces seemed to be all PR and very little substance." While this perception was understandable, it failed to consider the task force commitment to information gathering. As with the PRP, the shadow boxing continued.

The interest group cynicism, although perhaps inevitable, did reflect the frustration that the transition groups themselves were feeling about the process. Because of their isolation, most of the groups viewed the task before them as a technical assignment—determining the optimal location for the placement of specific program components within the new Department. The process itself was quite cumbersome. Final recommendations for decisions were being made in February and March; a preliminary report on policy, program organization and management issues was forwarded to Beattie on January 30, 1980 and the final report was develped in mid-March. As preliminary recommendations were developed, task force leaders were bombarded by the press and the interest groups about where programs would be located.

The ground rules that had been established for POIG had mandated that task force recommendations be delivered to the Secretary as a package since many of the decisions on one issue affected consideration on others. Task forces could, because of the structure of their assignments, come up with conflicting recommendations about program placement. These disagreements, according to the ground rules, would be noted in the overview decision memorandum.

When they began their work, the task forces met with Secretary Hufstedler to discuss their agenda and to attempt to ascertain what her interests and concerns would be. Because so many of these issues were unfamiliar to her, the recommendations that were made played a role more as background briefing documents for her than as advice on decisions. As she proceeded, Hufstedler believed that she had very little leeway in these decisions, that the authorizing legislation virtually set the organization chart for the Department, even to designating grade levels for the higher level positions. Many of the decisions that were recommended by the task forces were obvious, reflecting the prescriptive nature of the legislation and the operating principle of minimizing disruption within the program components. The memorandum prepared for the Secretary concentrated on the issues that were controversial.

Before sending their final recommendations to the Secretary, task forces did hold briefings about the staff level recommendations with a number of outside interest groups. Hufstedler had instructed the task forces that she wanted them to touch base with the interest groups before she made final determinations on program location issues.

By the time that the decisions were made by the Secretary, some of the Assistant Secretaries were already designated. The designees were given the opportunity to appeal the recommendations of the task force before the structural decisions became final. One participant in the process estimated that the Secretary supported the task force recommendations in about 75% of the cases; there were strenuous objections to some of the recommendations by a number of the new Assistant Secretaries and decisions turned on the appeal of these individuals. Hufstedler seemed, to the transition group, to be uninterested. Aside from initial meetings at which she spent five to ten minutes with groups of key participants urging a focus on excellence and the fostering of innovation, she was largely invisible. The transition teams received no guidance about priorities which seemed to bear her imprint. Clearly, other matters (a handful of specific policy issues plus the budget) dominated her attention and interest.

The process, thus, was confusing even to someone closely involved with the issues. The Transpoint group operated from December through March with an extremely murky mandate. It behaved as if it were the major advice giver to the Secretary on program placement issues yet it operated in a technical, rather than political environment. Interest groups were not sure whom they should contact; indeed, during this period, some of the groups addressed their concerns to White House adviser Stuart Eizenstat, rather than to Hufstedler. The group that operated as Hufstedler's personal staff (or an extension of her personal staff) focused on personnel decisions, press, legislative relations and policy formulation processes.

Richard Beattie played a pivotal role as the linchpin between the exiled Buzzard's Point staff and the Secretary's team. Not only was he skeptical about the usefulness of these transition activities, but he was also viewed as an individual close to Joseph Califano, the former HEW Secretary, who had been a major opponent of the creation of the Department. For some interest group members, his track record was, thus, suspect. A few of the transition team leaders did assume positions of authority as the Department unfolded: Julie Lester, the leader of the Vocational/Adult Education Task Force, became the Assistant Secretary for Adult Education; Cindy Brown, team leader for the Civil Rights Task Force, became the Assistant Secretary for Civil Rights; Floretta McKenzie, the task force leader for Elementary and

Secondary Education, became a Deputy Assistant Secretary. Other task force leaders, however, were career officials who returned to their positions or individuals from the outside who were not given major appointments in the new Department.

In addition to the organizational morass that confronted the task forces, it was also obvious that these groups did not command a high priority on the new Secretary's agenda. She was much more interested in the personnel decisions that were required for the new Department than in determinations of organizational structure. She turned the briefings on organizational structure into sessions on programmatic concerns. Once she recognized that the enabling legislation for the new Department was quite prescriptive, she did not attempt to exploit the areas of discretion involving organization structure that were open to her. It was difficult to make her focus on decisions relating to staff functions or the processes of decision-making because she was largely unconvinced of their substantive outcomes.

One is hard pressed to identify a theory of organizational change that guided the transition effort. Neither Hufstedler nor the transition group saw organizational issues within a broader context. Although a few of the transition task forces did raise questions that linked structure to substance, the nature of their assignment emphasized an analytical rather than a political approach to the issues involved. Some of the transition staff members were individuals who had been involved in the PRP efforts of the past. But, for the most part, there was very little continuity between the earlier activities within OMB and the analysis that came out of the Buzzard's Point operation. At the same time, however, one can draw a clear parallel between the substantive work of the PRP during formulation and the substantive work of the transition task forces. In both cases, the analytical activity was emphasized and institutionalized. But in both cases, its advice was not always heeded.

REDISCOVERING ORGANIZATIONAL STRUCTURE

Unlike many reorganization efforts, most decisions concerning the ED reorganization structure were made in the adoption stage of the policy process by Congress. Form and substance were inextricably linked in the debate on the Hill and thus many technical questions regarding structure and program placement were answered in the congressional debate. Hufstedler's own appointment and her approach to staffing indicated that non-structural strategies would be employed to achieve her goal of making the federal education efforts more effective.

Organizational issues, however, were not completely foreclosed by the legislation. But these approaches did not stir much concern or capture the imagination of the leadership of the new Department. Internal organization strategies were not a high priority for the incoming Secretary. Few opportunities were taken to use organization as a mechanism for achieving change or assuring that federal education programs operated more effectively and efficiently than they had in the past.

The decisions that were made about organizational structure reflected a number of other considerations viewed as crucial by the Department's incoming leadership. The political environment of the time was punctuated by the impending presidential elections and the uncertainty of the administration's continuity in office. In addition, election year politics reinforced an administration commitment to hold the line on the budget. It was ED's job to do better with existing resources; program realignments could create new policy options and new costs for programs. This was clearly to be avoided.

While Hufstedler did not develop relationships with the interest groups that satisfied them, her decisions regarding program placement indicated a willingness to defer to their status quo arrangements. Unless there was a compelling reason not to do so, the Hufstedler decisions reflected a strategy of simply responding to constituent interests regarding program placement. In fact, questions of program placement generated very little interest among the groups because the decisions that were made did not disrupt the ties between agencies and their traditional constituencies. In reality, the creation of the Department did not reflect an expression of the need for change by these groups.

Another factor determining the organization structure decisions was the Secretary's concern for organizational continuity, avoiding any disruption in the flow of dollars to state and local governments and the enforcement of civil rights mandates. The new team recognized that there was a delicate balance to be struck between its mission of equal opportunity and its desire to improve intergovernmental relationships—it was risky to tamper dramatically with this tenuous balance.

Although there was little in the way of a conscious organization strategy or theory underpinning the structure decisions, it did appear that there were three principles used to guide many of the organizational determinations. First, the number of people reporting directly to the Secretary was to be minimized. Second, individuals at the assistant secretary level were to be given significant roles in the policy-making process. Several reasons were given for this decision: to utilize more fully the expertise existing at the program level (based on the assumption that assistant secretaries would involve their subordinates); to engage the collective talent of the principal officers in a cabinet-style decision-making process; and to attempt to discourage program level personnel from end-running to Congress and interest groups in pursuit of their objectives. Third, a decision was made to give greater emphasis to the use of evaluation resources in order to achieve program improvement.

One might expect that Shirley Hufstedler would have relied heavily on expertise and substantive analysis to assist her in decision-making regarding organizational structure. As has been described, she was very skeptical of several sources of such advice. The OMB analyses relevant to organizational decisions within the Department had very little impact on the structure of the Department. OMB efforts were never systematically considered by the transition group nor trusted by Hufstedler herself. Indeed, as is usually the case, the advice of the consultants was heeded when it seemed to fit the preconceptions of key decision-makers or when there was little opposition from politically influential interests. In addition, advice on organizational issues was often conflicting. Over time, there was not one but a series of groups that operated without substantial interaction or coordination and produced conflicting advice. When experts disagree, the legitimacy of their advice and the incentive to listen to them are undermined. During the transition, many decision-makers saw themselves as more knowledgeable or "expert" than the consultants that others had chosen. The experts' advice was also avoided because principal officers chose to develop their own plans for organizational structure and to rely for advice on people whom they identified as their—not someone else's—allies. The decisions that were made more frequently reflected the general disposition to get the Department in place with few hassles. The experts' "best possible" organizational structure could create difficult relationships with strong interest groups. New structures that opened up new issues were not in the cards.

The staff functions and decision processes that were established during the transition were, however, another matter. The legislation creating the Department was not at all prescriptive in these areas, giving the Secretary considerable latitude in molding internal processes. The Secretary had the authority to organize the structure of staff functions in areas such as budget, planning, evaluation, regulations development and management. The ability to address inefficiencies in this area—especially in the reduction of clearance steps in the regulations development process—was one of the major promises made by the Carter administration for ED.

The organization of the immediate Office of the Secretary reflected Hufstedler's past experience as a judge. The Secretary relied on having all views and positions made available to her in order to weigh the evidence and make judicial-like decisions. Although she established an Executive Secretariat—a body found in most federal departments that plays five basic functions: information gathering and dissemination; tracking and coordination; quality control; record keeping; and special assignments—she did not favor the centralized control by the Office of the Secretary that was found in a number of other agencies. She favored a more open and participatory structure involving all principal officers in the agency. In such an environment, the Executive Secretariat ran the process of information gathering and served as a conduit to the Secretary rather than as a depository where major policy decisions were made. Nancy LeaMond, a former PRP staffer, set up the ED Executive Secretariat and attempted to use it as a vehicle for channeling information from the transition task forces, operating components within the Office of Education, and other agencies.

In addition, a key role in the Office of the Secretary was played by former OE staffer, Marshall Smith, who assumed the role of Executive Assistant or chief of staff. This position was an important one as it dealt with sensitive and highly political issues. Smith's relationship with Hufstedler was excellent and he provided a strong force in the molding of substantive policy and decisions and in giving shape to the organizational arrangements that came to be.

SELECTION OF TOP LEVEL OFFICIALS

While organizational structure questions held no intrinsic fascination for Shirley Hufstedler, she was clearly concerned about assembling a team of individuals who she believed shared her goals for the new Department. Both the new Secretary and the President were convinced that appointments were the key to an effective administration and thus were particularly important to the operation of ED. Hufstedler's own selection had reflected Carter's commitment to bring in individuals who were not the "captive" of the traditional constituencies but were among the "best and the brightest."

PRP staffer Decker Anstrom, a key figure in the efforts to conceptualize the Department and work the legislation through the Congress, had moved to the White House Office of Personnel. Anstrom had been one of the individuals involved in identifying Hufstedler as a potential candidate for the Secretary job and assisting her through the interview and confirmation process. Indeed, before Hufstedler was in the position for very long, she received a "suggestion" from the White House that two individuals be "considered" for key staff Assistant Secretary positions. Hufstedler agreed to these two individuals without interviewing anyone else. When Hufstedler's second tier staff was assembled following her confirmation, several members of that team took over the personnel recruitment and selection process. For some period of time, relationships between the White House and the new Secretary's staff were hardly cordial, replicating the tension that was also occurring during that time between OMB staff and Hufstedler's group. The Hufstedler staff found that recruiting in the White House was being done without job descriptions, and choices were being made based heavily on personalities and personal preferences. As one participant put it, "the whole process had the characteristics of the Carter White House. It was amateurish and everyone was trying to get jobs for friends."

After the initial period of conflict with the White House, Hufstedler assumed control of the process. In a memorandum written soon after her confirmation, the Secretary detailed her views on the selection process:

> We must have a carefully defined process that withstands scrutiny, both as the process is occurring and after the fact. Key elements to be defined are: a definition of major responsibilities for each Assistant Secretary level position; appropriate and timely constituent group involvement; the nature and sequence of both preliminary and final reference calls; my interview process; Congressional involvement.[40]

The memorandum emphasized the importance of a "paper trail" on each major personnel action and noted that the Secretary wanted to be able to "recall with complete clarity the sequence of events and all pertinent facts and opinions with respect to each significant personnel decision." She noted that White House personnel staffers, Decker Anstrom and Dave O'Brien, would be senior personnel advisers reporting directly to her. In order to "benefit in an organized way from the wisdom available," Hufstedler established a panel consisting of Dick Gilman, Burt Gindler, and Pierce O'Donnell; in addition, Lisle Carter, Donna Shalala, Sam Halperin, and former PRP staffer Patsy Fleming would nominate candidates, evaluate them, and advise on the composition of "short lists" for her consideration. The Secretary also asked for congressional reaction to the three to five individuals who appeared on the short lists.

The criteria that appeared to be operating in the selection process emphasized the same two priorities that led to Shirley Hufstedler's nomination. Affirmative action goals and the infusion of new blood were seen as methods of striking a balance between insiders and outsiders, between "the good old boys" and women and minorities. Once again, the interest groups found the process a difficult one to break into.

Even before Hufstedler was named, the groups that made up the Transition Coalition forwarded a document to PRP chief Harrison Wellford outlining their criteria for personnel appointments to the Department.[41] The document did not focus on the Secretary's position but, rather, attempted to outline thoughts for all of the top positions. According to this request, the education groups believed that four criteria were essential for personnel named to fill top positions in the Department. First, these individuals must be advocates for education; "key staff members must have the ability to effectively justify and communicate educational and Departmental priorities among various agencies and offices in the Executive Branch and on Capitol Hill." Second, individuals must have a strong demonstrated commitment to equal educational opportunity regardless of race, creed, color, national origin, sex or handicap. Third, appointees must be accessible to constituent groups, particularly parents and students. And fourth, individuals should demonstrate strong program management skills so that policy and program can be effectively integrated.

As time progressed and the appointment process unfolded, it appeared that at least some of the groups were not sanguine about their ability to influence the new Secretary. Most of the positions were presidential appointments—and the White House was viewed as the point of access for lobbying efforts. The American Association of School Administrators issued an alert to its members to write to Stuart Eizenstat, Assistant to the President for Domestic Affairs and Policy, to express their concerns.[42] For, noted the alert, "as the largest constituency for the new Department of Education, it is crucial that we elementary/secondary folks ensure qualified individuals from *our ranks* are named to *many* key department posts at the assistant secretary and bureau administrator levels. ... We have been told that this important position may not be filled by someone from the K-12 field." As it turned out, the appointee as Assistant Secretary for Elementary and Secondary Education was someone very familiar to this group—the individual who had held the lower status but comparable position in the Office of Education, Thomas Minter. But in other cases, the fears of the interest groups were justified. There was a conscious effort to attract people without commitments to existing programs. Several appointees to key positions— particularly those who held non-programmatic Assistant Secretary jobs— were unknown to those active in the politics of federal education policy-making and program administration.

By February 2, 1980, the *Washington Post* reported that the "winnowing process has been going slowly, prompting some grumbling from members of Congress and others who are waiting to see if their choices are picked."[43] The *Post* noted that the only appointments to top staff jobs "have been administrative positions such as the choice of Liz Carpenter, a high-profile press officer during the administration of President Johnson, to head the new department's public information office." According to the article, "Education Department officials explain that the slow going has been due in part to the lack of familiarity by Hufstedler and her top staff with the huge and sometimes competitive education community."

In reality, there were only twelve appointments to be made at the Assistant Secretary level and one Under Secretary to be named. Indeed, job creation was particularly problematic since Carter had promised to cut 500 jobs off the federal education job rolls if the Department was enacted. In addition, accepting an appointment in the new Department could have been risky for individuals concerned about job security. The election was less than a year away when Hufstedler was confirmed; it was coming closer and closer as the selection process dragged out.

The individuals who were named to the top level positions within ED reflected a somewhat haphazard process of timing and accessibility. Shirley Hufstedler was determined to find an outstanding Black individual to become Under Secretary. She asked UDC President Lisle Carter to take the job; he refused but agreed to help Hufstedler with the transition activity. If one wanted an Under Secretary to function in a team fashion with the Secretary, it would have been useful to make that appointment early. As it turned out, Under Secretary Steven Minter—a person largely unknown to education interests—was not named to the position until early March—several months after the transition activity had begun and after several other individuals had already been appointed to their posts. Minter was an official of the Cleveland Foundation and a former Commissioner of Welfare in Massachusetts.

In addition to Liz Carpenter, Assistant Secretary for Public Affairs, the first appointees to positions were William Fischer, Assistant Secretary for Planning and Budget; and John Gabusi, Assistant Secretary for Management. Betsy Levin was named to be General Counsel in mid-February. Five individuals were named early in March: Steven Minter as Under Secretary; Albert Bowker as Assistant Secretary for Postsecondary Education; James Rutherford, Assistant Secretary for Educational Research and Improvement; and Thomas Minter, Assistant Secretary for Elementary and Secondary Education. Others were named through March, April and early May.

One position was particularly difficult for Hufstedler to fill. The job of Assistant Secretary for Civil Rights was offered to at least one individual who turned it down because she worried about the level of political support she would receive from the administration when the "going got tough" on the Hill and in other circles. Within a few days of an article appearing in the *Chronicle of Higher Education* entitled, "Secretary of Education Hufstedler Hit for Failure to Name Civil-Rights Aide," the appointment was announced of Cynthia Brown, former principal deputy of the HEW Office for Civil Rights and leader of the transition task force on civil rights.

The crew that was assembled by Hufstedler reflected a somewhat conflicting set of criteria. All of the major program Assistant Secretary positions were given to "insiders"—most frequently individuals such as Thomas Minter who had held comparable positions within the Office of Education. Appointment of those individuals clearly reflected a strategy to minimize disruption of the program components and play a program maintenance game. The individuals who were named to non-programmatic positions (such as Assistant Secretary for Planning and Budget and General Counsel) were outsiders to the education bureaucracy. Some, such as William Fischer, knew their way around Washington but did not have intimate knowledge of the education field. Others, such as Betsy Levin, were familiar with education policy issues but had minimal experience as federal government managers or policy-makers. It is worth noting that not one individual who had been involved in the PRP effort received a top level appointment in the new Department.

The appointments, thus, created the potential for a bifurcated staff within the Department. Most of the program Assistant Secretaries were likely to argue for more of the same while the staff Assistant Secretaries were likely to be strong advocates for change. Given her background and personal style, it appeared that the staff Assistant Secretaries were closer to Hufstedler's own preferences.

The naming of these individuals established a new set of actors who were likely to have different views about the operation of the Department from those of the individuals in the transition group or the PRP. Although program placement decisions of a skeletal nature were already made, this skeleton had yet to be fleshed out and new decision processes developed.

CONCLUSION

The activities required to organize the new Department illustrate the discontinuities found in the policy process. Issues which appeared to have been settled in the earlier stages of the decision process were reopened as President Carter named a Secretary and preparations were made for the implementation of the new agency. Carter's own view of himself as an outsider was mirrored by his selection of Hufstedler as the new Secretary and, subsequently, by the appointment of some of her sub-cabinet officials.

The period from October to May (when the Department was scheduled to open) provided the chronological space for the process of moving from a political, open policy conversation (the style of enactment) to a more technical, closed process (the style of implementation). During this period, the incoming Secretary had an opportunity to focus on implementation issues—particularly the organization structure and personnel questions that were required to make the reorganization come to life. However, this transition stage operated in somewhat of a limbo condition. Some of the formal authorities for action were still found in HEW and until the Department actually opened its doors, formal authority and informal influence were often in conflict.

One could, if one accentuated the continuities of the policy process, see the activities involved in organizing the new Department as the next step in a relay chain—a new set of actors was designed to carry the baton and move the policy from pronouncement to reality. As the story indicates, however, it is inaccurate to characterize these processes as continuous efforts that build on one another. Both the structure of decision-making and the individuals in positions of leadership mitigate against this; indeed, if there is momentum in the process, it appears to work against a stair-step process. One is hard pressed to see many continuities between the PRP and OMB activity and the decisions made by Secretary Hufstedler in the first few months of her service in the office. At the same time, Hufstedler began to acknowledge that she could not start anew on these issues, that there were sunk costs of both personnel and history that served as very real constraints on her decision authority. Despite this, one can see a shifting of goals during these processes, away from the goals of symbolic status and political advantage to effectiveness and change objectives.

The movement of the decision center from the White House to a new executive agency was not an easy one. First, there were tensions within OMB between the permanent management side of the agency and the young "upstart", PRP. Once Hufstedler was appointed, she was extremely suspicious of the advice and past actions of both parts of OMB. Then came the creation of multiple layers of transition actors providing different sources of advice to individuals both inside and outside of the government. The convoluted relationships that developed between Hufstedler's personal staff and the Transpoint Transition Team show how difficult it is for a new appointee to come into the executive branch and work out constructive relationships with career officials. Additionally, detailed negotiations were required with HEW officials, sorting out both personnel and policy responsibilities.

During this period, analysts returned to an earlier role through the transition group. Given the proximity of the coming presidential election, decisions had to be made that reflected political relationships and issues—but linkages between analysis and political calculations were hard to come by given Hufstedler's personal style. With her entrance into the scene, one saw that another culture was introduced—the culture of the courtroom. The legal adversarial process was familiar neither to the analysts nor the politicians.

As the process unfolded, the interest groups attempted to hold onto the effective coalition that worked toward enactment. Despite attempts to form a Transition Coalition, this coalition could not be sustained as the decisions moved into more technical and detailed forms. Groups moved in and out of the process. The most active groups during enactment could not determine what was appropriate behavior during this period. While they had become sophisticated in organizational matters through the congressional activity, the transition planning activities did not provide an understandable way for them to influence many organizational structure issues. At the same time, they were convinced that someone was influencing decisions—and they knew it wasn't them.

While all of this organizational activity was occurring in the transition phase, Secretary Hufstedler was attempting to focus on the substantive aspects of education policy and use her position to develop a more visible leadership role for the federal government in the education field.

NOTES

1. Skee Smith, "The United States Department of Education" reprint from *American Education* (undated).
2. Reported in Lynn Olson, "Education Agency Added to Cabinet by Carter Signing," *Baltimore Sun* (October 18, 1979).
3. Reported in Steven R. Weisman, "Carter Signs Measure Creating a Department of Education," *New York Times* (October 18, 1979).
4. Rochelle Stanfield, "Getting the E Out of HEW—The Trauma Has Only Just Begun," *National Journal* (October 6, 1979), p. 1649.

5. Ibid., p. 1650.
6. Ibid., p. 1651.
7. "Education Groups 'Construct' Secretary," *Education USA* (October 15, 1979), p. 54.
8. Lorenzo Middleton, "Who Will Be the First U.S. Secretary of Education?" *Chronicle of Higher Education* (June 25, 1979), p. 14.
8a. Michael J. Sniffen, "Search for Education Secretary Widens; Ex-Gov. Apodaca Said Out of Running," *Washington Post* (October 20, 1979).
8b. Ibid.
9. Ibid.
10. "Carter's Choice: A Judge for Education," *Time* (November 12, 1979).
11. Betty Anne Williams, "Reaction to Shirley M. Hufstedler," *AP Story* (November 1, 1979).
12. "The Hufstedler Nomination," Editorial, *Washington Post* (October 31, 1979), p. A.20.
13. Robert Pear, "Hispanic Leaders Rap Carter for Choice for Ed Secretary," *Washington Star* (October 31, 1979).
14. "LULAC Unhappy at Choice for Ed Secretary," *Albequerque Journal* (October 31, 1979).
15. Terry Straub, Memorandum to Shirley Hufstedler, "Re: Hill Visitations," (November 7, 1979).
16. Senate Committee on Labor and Human Resources, *Hearings on Nomination of Shirley Hufstedler to be Secretary of Education* (November 27, 1979), p. 19.
17. Ibid., p. 20.
18. Ibid., p. 21.
19. Ibid., p. 32.
20. Ibid.
21. Ibid., p. 37.
22. Ibid., pp. 37-38.
23. John McGruder, OMB, Memorandum to Don Boselovic, PRP, "Preliminary Draft Plan for Activation of the Department of Education," (April 17, 1979).
24. Ibid., p. 2.
25. W. S. Dinsmore, OMB, "Notes on Implementation of New Agencies," (September 1974), p. 1.
26. Ibid., p. 2.
27. Nancy LeaMond, "Memorandum to Patricia Gwaltney McGinnis," (undated), pp. 2-3.
28. Ibid., p. 3.
29. Ibid., pp. 3-5.
30. Nancy LeaMond, Memorandum to Harrison Wellford, "Subject: Implementation of the Department of Education," (October 3, 1979), pp. 1-2.
31. Nancy LeaMond, Memorandum to Harrison Wellford, "Subject: Meeting with HEW Regarding Department of Education Implementation," (October 15, 1979).
32. Nancy LeaMond, Memorandum to Burt Gindler, "Subject: Thoughts on Implementation," (November 28, 1979).
33. Ibid., p. 1.
34. Ibid., pp. 2-3.
35. Ibid., p. 1.
36. Bill Richards, "New Education Chief Knee-Deep in Territorial Wrangling," *Washington Post* (December 11, 1979), p. A2.
37. Paul Royston, Memorandum to POIG Task Force Leaders, "Subject: Task Force Work Plans and Schedule," (December 28, 1979), pp. 1-2.
38. Paul Royston, Memorandum to Richard Beattie, "The Report and Recommendations of the Public Consultation Team Regarding Tab B and the Beattie Memoranda Issues," (February 21, 1980), p. 1.
39. Thomas A. Shannon, Executive Director, National School Board Association, "Cover Letter to Report on Department of Education Implementation Task Force Meeting," (January 21, 1980).

40. Shirley M. Hufstedler, Memorandum to Staff Members, "Subject: Selection Process for
     Presidential Appointees," (undated), p. 1.
41. Rosalyn H. Baker, "Letter to Harrison Wellford on Behalf of 12 Education Groups,"
     (October 25, 1979).
42. American Association of School Administrators, Legislative Alert, "Crucial Nominations
     to Come Soon: Time to Act is Now," (undated).
43. Bill Richards, "Thousands Seek Non Existent Jobs at Education Department,"
     Washington Post (February 2, 1980), p. A5.
44. C. M. Fields and L. Middleton, "Secretary of Education Hufstedler Hit for Failure to
     Name Civil Rights Aide," *Chronicle of Higher Education* (April 21, 1980), p. 13.

Chapter 8 IMPLEMENTATION

On May 4, 1980 the new Department became a reality. ED opened its doors one month ahead of the deadline set by Congress for the establishment of the new Department. The event was marked by a week of activities orchestrated to make the American public aware of the potential of the new agency. These activities were diverse, including the issue of a special postage stamp, visits to area schools, seminars, and a cultural event honoring teachers that involved numerous popular entertainers. The key event of the week was a ceremony on the lawn of the White House attended by members of the Cabinet, Congress, and the White House staff, representatives from major education associations, senior Education Department staff, media and "friends" of education from all over the nation.

The events of the week were reminiscent of the mood of a presidential inauguration, celebrating the possibilities attached to a new cast of characters. However, unlike a new president, the Department of Education was faced with a rapidly ticking clock. The agency did not have the guarantee of four years before it. Given the President's poor showing in popularity polls, the Iranian hostage situation, and the decline of support for Carter within the Democratic party, the new Department could not assume any more than six months of operation before November when the American public would decide who would be the next President of the United States.

This chapter deals with the implementation of the reorganization effort during the six months before the November election. It describes the structural decisions that promised a new set of relationships within the federal education community; and it focuses on the internal decision processes that were developed for the agency. All of these activities took place in an atmosphere of budgetary, political and programmatic pressures.

HUFSTEDLER OFFICIALLY BEGINS HER JOB

Although Secretary Shirley Hufstedler had been hard at work as Secretary of Education before the Department officially opened, the formal transfer of authority now gave her a set of programs and a staff for which she was responsible. The Department was expected to move into high gear immediately; the transition period was viewed as adequate time to set up the work of the new agency.

However, as Jimmy Carter also found, it is not easy to anticipate the sorts of demands that confront a new official when invested with the mantle of authority. Secretary Hufstedler's first days in the Department were characterized by enormous demands. There was legislation pending in the Congress— the new Youth Employment and Education bill and the Higher Education Reauthorization Act. The budget impasse in the Congress meant that a budget for Fiscal Year 1981 had to be prepared at the same time that Fiscal Year 1980 appropriations problems were still unresolved. The Carter administration was in the middle of a battle with Congress over the practice of congressional veto of regulations, arguing that Congress was overstepping its authority when it gave itself the power to veto executive branch regulations. Four education programs were affected by that battle.

But the problems were not found only on Capitol Hill. When the new Department opened its doors, it was headquartered in inadequate space. Negotiations were underway with OMB, the General Services Administration, and the Congress about a permanent home for the Department. As the *New York Times* reported, "The country's top education officials work in a Federal building whose heating system was designed to take advantage of the movement of the sun. Unfortunately, the builders turned the axis 90 degrees, so there are only brief periods every year when the system fulfills its designers' expectations."[1] The doors of the Department were opened without desks, telephones and other basic office equipment for some of the top officials in the agency.

Although Secretary Hufstedler emphasized the crucial role of individuals as she conceptualized her approach to the Education Department leadership position, she found that she had very limited ability to name individuals beyond the top positions. And not all of the personnel in those top positions were on board on May 7th. Some of the Assistant Secretary designees were awaiting Senate confirmation and others had just been appointed. In a May 7, 1980 editorial, the *Washington Post* wrote that the new Department brought together 7,000 or so people from five different agencies "who may or may not wish to come, removing many of them from their accustomed offices, superiors, subordinates and perquisites, and trying to mold them into a newly efficient and enthusiastic unit."[2] The Secretary had only 22 positions available to her in Senior Executive Service roles. And she was stuck with personnel ceilings established for ED and a mandate of a reduction of 500 employees by the end of Fiscal Year 1981.

EDUCATION DEPARTMENT

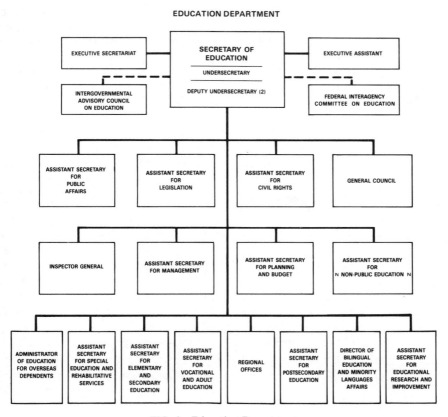

FIG. 3   Education Department
May 1980

PLACEMENT OF PROGRAMS

The organizational structure which was in place at the opening of the department represented the outcome of the debate that had been going on for several years (see Figure 3). The legislation creating the Department had made only marginal additions to the cluster of programs that had been housed in the Office of Education and the Office of the Assistant Secretary for Education within HEW. The imperatives that had influenced the recommendations and decisions of the transition group tended to minimize any disruption and thus kept individual program units and staff relationships in place. Nonetheless, there were a few exceptions to the "don't touch" rule of program placement and there was an attempt to establish new decision processes within the Department that would represent Hufstedler's views about the agency's creation.

Structural changes did take place in three major program areas: creation of the Office of Educational Research and Improvement; creation of an office to house the vocational rehabilitation programs; and an upgrading of the status of the bilingual education programs.

THE OFFICE OF EDUCATIONAL RESEARCH AND IMPROVEMENT

A concern about the status and direction of the educational research and improvement effort within the federal government had been present in the work of the PRP's education effort. Although the issue was a constant theme in the analytic work of the PRP, there is little indication that it ever became a major concern of the political actors, largely because the interest groups in this area had minimal ability to influence congressional votes.

The PRP staff wanted to organize the many fragmented federal education research and development programs in a new way for two reasons. First, they believed that a centralized office would improve coordination and make the research and development effort more relevant to policy and practice than it had been in the past. The reorganization also sought to make more efficient use of limited research dollars and direct some portion of a larger concentration of funds to more basic research.

Second, they argued that because research is intrinsically vulnerable (particularly in a budget cutting environment) and does not have an effective outside constituency, it needed to be protected by the development and dissemination programs.

As it examined the range of programs that might be clustered in such an office, the PRP recommended that about 50 programs in research, program development, demonstration, dissemination and professional development be included in a new Office of Educational Research and Improvement (known as OERI). This configuration would include most of the discretionary programs within the Office of Education.

Although there was very little controversy surrounding the creation of an OERI (with an Assistant Secretary at its helm) during the formulation and enactment stages of the policy process, the structure and content of the Office was hotly debated within the OERI transition team. This team included several individuals involved in the issue earlier, providing a thread of continuity between the PRP and the transition.

The Research and Improvement Transition Task Force worked closely with the relevant interest groups (particularly the American Educational Research Association) and then with the Assistant Secretary designate, James Rutherford, who moved from NSF to the new Department. The major task before the transition group was to figure out a way to bring together the more than 50 independent, autonomous programs and construct an administrative superstructure that would give the array some cohesion.

The National Institute of Education, established by Congress in 1972 with a separate advisory council (the National Council on Educational Research) proved to be one of the most difficult programs to integrate into a new OERI. Designed to operate as an autonomous research unit, over the years the NIE had become quite removed from the other elements of the federal education bureaucracy. Indeed, unlike most of the other operating programs within HEW, NIE had reported to the Assistant Secretary for Education rather than to the Commissioner of Education.

The separate status of NIE did not guarantee it a reputation as an effective body. Almost from its inception, doubts had been raised about NIE's usefulness and contributions to knowledge. Its budget had been dramatically reduced over the years reflecting an absence of support from groups outside the education research community. The transition group had to decide whether to include NIE within the broad OERI or keep the research unit as a separate umbrella unit within the Department. The decision was made to place NIE within OERI, providing NIE with more visible support. Indeed, immediately following her confirmation hearings, Secretary Hufstedler testified at the NIE reauthorization hearings. Her presence as an advocate for the agency appeared to offset some of the congressional budget cuts that had been anticipated.

There were similar issues in the debate about where to place the National Center for Educational Statistics. Established in 1965 as an agency responsible for education data collection and information gathering, the NCES also had a separate Advisory Council on Education Statistics that acted to oversee its operations. The Center and its advisory group did not support a proposal to place it within OERI and, instead, backed an option to locate it within the Office of the Secretary as a staff unit. Such a unit, they believed, would facilitate coordination of all federal data collection related to education and would view data as more than a research driven enterprise.

The decision arrived at during the transition phase was to put all of the NCES operation into OERI—a position that the PRP had also favored. It was believed that this structure would strengthen the technical expertise of the research, dissemination and technical assistance functions of OERI through its exchange with NCES and, at the same time, bolster NCES's role in fostering change and adding to knowledge about education.

There were a number of difficult decisions to be made about other program units, related both to the status of the units and the functional and programmatic effect of placing them within OERI. The decision to include the Fund for the Improvement of Postsecondary Education (FIPSE) in OERI appeared to some to downgrade the visibility of the Fund. There was also dispute about the placement of the Office of Libraries and Learning Technologies (which included programs serving schools, universities, and public libraries) in OERI or in a separate location.

The largest cluster of programs within OERI was found in the Office of School Improvement, a unit that was largely a transfer of efforts from the Bureau of School Improvement in the Office of Education. That Bureau had housed over 20 small discretionary programs, including the Women's Educational Equity Act Program, the Ethnic Heritage program, Arts in Education, Metric Education, the Teacher Corps, Teacher Centers, Basic Skills, Environmental Education, Alcohol and Drug Abuse Education, and Consumer Education.

There were several reasons why changes in organizational structure occurred in the research and improvement area and not in other parts of the Department. The programs had relatively small constituencies and, thus, opposition to change was difficult to mobilize. Indeed, some of the bureaucrats attached to these programs believed that movement out of operating program units (which were primarily involved in the distribution of federal funds) would give them more attention. OERI provided a symbol of increasing commitment to fostering "quality" without being intrusive. The movement could be justified in claims that there were no important political costs incurred by the program movment; that programs could be freed from their previous constraints, and could be placed in an agency whose ethos was one of knowledge development and change. In addition, the proposals for the OERI received continued analytical support because members of the PRP study team were directly involved in the implementation task force for OERI.

THE OFFICE FOR SPECIAL EDUCATION AND REHABILITATIVE SERVICES

The congressional decision to move the vocational rehabilitation programs from HEW to the new Department also included a determination that these programs would warrant an office at the assistant secretary level. Thus the selection of programs for placement in the Office for Special Education and Rehabilitative Services (OSERS) was a relatively straight-forward exercise, based on the attributes of programs, specific service approaches and a desire to meet the congressional concern that the vocational rehabilitation programs be kept distinctly separate from other programs.

The transition group did consider the possibility of locating the Gifted and Talent program in OSERS, since it had been located in the Bureau of Education for the Handicapped in the Office of Education. That program, which provided special services for children with a high potential for intellectual achievement and creative academic pursuits, was being administered in about half of the states through state agencies for special education. However, the transition team recommended against placement in OSERS because it believed that the new unit would be concerned primarily with the delivery of services to handicapped children and the program might lose visibility and support in that setting. Although there was a strong argument to place the program in OERI (because it was a small experimental effort), the decision was made to place it in the Office of Elementary and Secondary Education instead.

THE OFFICE OF BILINGUAL EDUCATION AND MINORITY LANGUAGE AFFAIRS (OBEMLA)

The Department of Education Organization Act authorized an Office of Bilingual Education and Minority Language Affairs headed by a director appointed by the Secretary. Although there had been an attempt by New York Congressman Robert Garcia (and others) to upgrade the position to an Assistant Secretary level (appointed by the President), the enacted legislation did not include such a provision and the Secretary resisted such demands.

The major bilingual education program had been administered in the Office of Bilingual Education in OE, a unit that was in the Office of the Executive Deputy Commissioner for Education Programs. More than 20 programs had bilingual education activities that were scattered throughout the Office of Education.

The transition group considered three different conceptual options for the type of office that would be created: staff, advocacy or program administration. The structure that was chosen contained elements of all three options. OBEMLA was given increased status and direct access to the Secretary; in the past within OE, the director was required to go through four offices before reaching the Secretary's level. Although the director did not have an Assistant Secretary appointment, on the official organization chart of the Department, the Office was depicted as equal to that of the other programmatic assistant secretaries. The advocacy option was addressed through the assignment of a coordinating function to the office. And the unit was given the responsibility of administering specific program grants.

Although the decision process involving the organizational structure of these three offices revolved around arguments about program effectiveness and change, most of the program units within the new Department looked very similar to the configurations in the old Office of Education. Individuals examining the Department from the outside could see very little that was different; OERI was, of course, an exception to this pattern. However, to the career bureaucracy within the department, even slight alterations produced a measure of anxiety about potential disruption and change. Some bureaucrats interpreted even the smallest change in location as a shift in status and visibility for their programs.

DEVELOPING NEW DECISION PROCESSES

While Secretary Hufstedler chose to minimize disruption as she made program location decisions, she did not shy away from instituting rather dramatic changes in the internal decision processes within the Department. These changes involved the legislation development process, the budget development process, and the regulations development process. The systems that were put in place by Secretary Hufstedler were part of an attempt by the new Secretary to develop a comprehensive view of policy formulation and implementation. Hufstedler had asked Donna Shalala, then Assistant Secretary for Policy Development and Research in the Department of Housing and Urban Development, to assist her in conceptualizing the policy formulation process for ED. Working closely with Michael O'Keefe, Deputy Assistant Secretary for Planning and Evaluation/Education in HEW, Shalala gave program task force leaders an opportunity to participate in this process.[3]

Arguing that the Department needed a comprehensive view of policy, the paper conceptualized a complex system of policy-making that depicted three activities: policy formulation, implementation and assessment. This attempt to integrate the various pieces of the policy process led the Secretary to group responsibilities of two of her staff Assistant Secretaries in a somewhat unusual way. The HEW pattern had been to combine policy analysis, planning, research and evaluation within a single unit (the Office of the Assistant Secretary for Planning and Evaluation). Similarly, the budget and management functions were grouped together (in the Office of the Assistant Secretary for Management and Budget).

By contrast, the ED assignment of responsibilities combined planning, programming and budget in the Office of the Assistant Secretary for Planning and Budget (a coupling that was beginning at the Office of Planning and Budget within OE); personnel, program evaluation, financial management, and contracts and grants were given to the Office of the Assistant Secretary for Management. Assistant Secretary for Management Gabusi fought hard to administer program evaluation within the Department. For the most part, other staff offices maintained the assignment of responsibilities that was familiar in HEW, without the problem of balancing concerns about education with those of health and welfare.

THE DEVELOPMENT OF LEGISLATION

As the architects of the new Department sought to devise a system for the development of legislation they were, understandably, reacting to the system that had been in place in the Office of Education and HEW. The legislative activity within OE included a diverse array of functions: to plan and prepare specifications for new legislation; to serve as a liaison with Congress (sometimes through or coordinated with the HEW Assistant Secretaries for Education and Legislation); to provide the Commissioner of Education with information on the status and progress of legislative proposals involving education; to coordinate suggestions for new legislation; and to serve as a liaison with governors, mayors, state legislators and others concerned with intergovernmental affairs.

The process by which education legislation was developed within HEW depended on the scope of the legislative proposal. If the program was large (for example the reauthorization of the Elementary and Secondary Education Act), proposals were developed by special task forces appointed by the Secretary of HEW. If the program was smaller in scope, legislation would be developed by the responsible program unit within OE, but the process of soliciting comments about the proposals would be managed by the Office of the Assistant Secretary for Planning and Evaluation. Depending on the issue, a multiplicity of offices would be involved from OE as well as the HEW Office of the Secretary. For example, comments might come from program offices, the OE policy office, the program development office of the Assistant Secretary for Education, NIE, the Assistant Secretary for Legislation/Education, and the Assistant Secretary for Management and Budget.

A decision memo would be sent to the Secretary and the final decision would be made in the Office of the Secretary. The actual drafting of a proposed bill would be done by the Office of the General Counsel; once drafted, the bill would be sent to OMB for clearance and then to Congress. The process tended to concentrate power at the HEW level. Program office staff often complained that the process by-passed their involvement, despite attempts during the Carter administration to get program people and interest group representatives more involved (for example, by instituting Regional Office hearings on proposed legislation). There were frequent criticisms that the Office of the Assistant Secretary for Planning and Evaluation had too much influence on the process.

During the transition period, there was not a separate task force that looked at the operation of the legislative development process. A recommendation had been floated to pair the legislative process with the policy development activities, but this was rejected. It was assumed that the management of the legislative development process would be centralized under an assistant secretary.

When former Congresswoman Martha Keys was appointed Assistant Secretary for Legislation, she brought together a core staff drawn from the HEW legislative office, from OE and from the Office of the Commissioner as well as from program and research units within OE. The staff reflected the attempt by the new office to draw together the legislative functions and expertise that were scattered around OE and HEW. The goal of the centralization of functions was to present issues of educational policy with one voice to Congress and to be able to respond to congressional requests in an efficient way.

While the new unit viewed itself as providing a service to the program areas (as well as to Congress), it was not always easy to convince those components of this centralizing approach and to build up the needed measure of congressional trust in the office and the Department in general. The Youth Education and Employment bill, one of the major initiatives of the Carter administration, was having a rough time in Congress even before the new legislative office was in place. And the Higher Education Reauthorization was in progress before the new relationships were developed.

Some program units did perceive some—albeit marginal—change from the new system. The vocational rehabilitation programs did not see much of a change as a result of these efforts; the process was opened up slightly and outside consultants were brought in to help with the drafting of legislative proposals. As in a number of areas, there was not enough time to know whether the centralization of the process made a substantive difference in the way that the Congress responded in the education area.

DEVELOPMENT OF THE BUDGET

The budget process that was developed in ED was a reaction to the complex and convoluted process that had been in place in HEW. That process went through a myriad of steps, moving back and forth between the Office of the Commissioner of Education, the program agencies, and units within the Office of the Secretary of HEW.

The HEW process began when the Commissioner, through the OE Office of Planning and Budget, called for issue identification papers, highlighting salient issues expected to be raised in the year's budget process. Program offices responded to this request, identifying issues of interest in general terms without specific budget figures attached. Using that input, the Commissioner, along with program and staff deputies, met to discuss general policy directions and determine their priorities. Those priorities became the subjects of detailed issue papers, written by program and staff offices (separately or in combination). Program staff offices were also asked to submit their Zero Base Budgets, submissions that specified at least three possible funding levels for their activities.

At this point, the Commissioner's Planning and Budget staff assisted program staff with their budget development with deputy commissioners and other middle level officials often involved. Usually decisions about priorities within the program components were made at this level by program staff and budget officers who were familiar with the programs. The balance of influence depended on the program area; in some cases the program staff exerted the most power while in other cases the budget staff prevailed. At this point, it was also common for interest groups and other constituent representatives to be aware of the process and to lobby for their interests. As a rule, unless the budget issue was particularly controversial or tied to the interests of a high official, the Commissioner's office and the HEW Office of the Secretary were not involved.

About this time in the calendar the "bottom-up" budget development met the "top-down" budget marks established by OMB and the Office of the Secretary of HEW. These budget marks provided OE with a target which served as an indicator of expectations about expenditure levels for education programs and provided general policy guidance to the budget architects.

The Office of Education Planning and Budget staff then reviewed the submissions, analyzed the requests and required the program people to justify their demands. On the basis of earlier discussions with the Commissioner and program deputies, Planning and Budget then developed a tentative ranking of the programs. The next step in the process involved the Spring Planning Retreat, a meeting attended by the Commissioner, the program and staff deputies, and some Planning and Budget staff members. During this session (where program directors were not in attendance), the proposed ranking was debated and reordered. Program directors did have the opportunity to appeal these rankings directly to the Commissioner. Based on the decisions made at the Retreat and subsequent meetings, Planning and Budget established a recommended budget and submitted it to the Commissioner (who sometimes modified it).

This budget was then submitted to the Assistant Secretary of Education; although that individual did not have formal power over the budget, the role gave that person the opportunity to attach comments to the OE submission before it moved into the HEW decision environment and to solicit comments from NIE staff and others who might not have been involved in the earlier process.

Once submitted to the HEW Office of the Secretary, comments were solicited from various staff offices. Although there were education budget specialists within the HEW Office of Management and Budget, the primary influence on the process traditionally came from the Office of the Assistant Secretary for Planning and Evaluation. At this point, the Under Secretary of HEW issued a tentative budget, using the OMB guidance to set a general ceiling on HEW spending. Following this issuance, the HEW Secretary accepted appeals of these recommendations, held meetings to discuss them, and finally came to a decision on a total HEW budget. The HEW submission moved to OMB which, in turn, made recommendations to the President. At this point, the Secretary of HEW did have the opportunity to appeal the recommendations of OMB directly to the President.

The complexity of the HEW budget process appeared to many education program people to work against their interests. Individuals who knew something about the program design and operation were involved early in the process but their concerns appeared to be washed away by the time the decisions were made in HEW. Even under the best of all possible conditions the process was convoluted; the impasse between the President and the Congress over the budget made the problem even more complex.

Although few education program staff could document their claims with specific illustrations of budget cuts, many of them believed that education programs received short shrift in the Office of the Secretary when tradeoffs had to be made to satisfy the overall HEW budget mark established by OMB. The decision process at the Office of the Secretary level was mysterious to a significant number of education program staff members.

A budget process for ED had been discussed during the transition activities. The linking of planning and budgeting had begun in OE and transition team members found it to be a preferred path. Although there was some attraction to a system in which program plans and budget estimates would be decentralized to the program Assistant Secretaries, in fact this did not occur. But there continued to be concern about the way that program staff would be involved in budget development.

The appointment of William Fischer (a former OMB budget examiner) as the Assistant Secretary for Planning and Budget signalled a commitment to link policy analysis activities and budget formulation. Fischer actually began work on the Fiscal Year 1981 budget before the Department opened its doors. He was faced with the task of revising the 1981 budget by the end of March, dealing with major program issues (such as increases in Title I monies and in student assistance).

When the Department actually began operations, Fischer was attempting to deal with a hostile Congress and to educate a new Secretary to the federal budget process at the same time that he was pulling together a staff drawn from five very disparate offices in OE and HEW. Fischer's strategy was to minimize the conflict between staff and program personnel by establishing a framework of participative decision-making. He sought to coordinate the development and presentation of the budget, working closely with the program Assistant Secretaries. At the same time, he saw the role of the Office as one which provided the Secretary with independent analysis and advice on education needs and problems and alternative federal programs to respond to those needs. Such an office, he believed, should not have a programmatic mission axe to grind.

The centralization of the budget process within ED did appear to increase the status that education programs had in this decision process. OMB was now dealing directly with the Secretary of Education on budget issues and the program Assistant Secretaries, in turn, had greater access to the Secretary.

The budget process, like the legislative development process, did not operate long enough to indicate whether or not it could have made any difference. The relationships with program officials had just begun to develop and required time to mature. The coupling of the budget and policy planning functions was designed to bring about an analytic and decision process that would encourage change and innovation in the federal role in American education. Its proponents hoped that this process would be able to offset the entrenched set of relationships that stemmed from the various education "iron triangles" (where interest groups, congressional members and staff, and career bureaucrats worked to thwart the changing of priorities and the reallocation of resources within programs). Before this theory could be tested, the Carter administration was out of office.

THE REGULATIONS PROCESS

More than any other decision process in the new Department, the regulations development process underwent the largest transformation and stirred the most controversy in the first months of ED. It was not surprising that a Secretary who was a former federal judge would be interested in the formal process of rule-making and would give attention to this procedure. Expectations were also great that a new Department would be able to change the overlap, duplication and delay that characterized the process of federal education regulations development.

The changes that were instituted in the regulations process within ED were constructed on a series of activities that were already underway within the Carter administration. Early in the presidential term, the White House issued a directive to all departments to streamline the federal regulatory process and make it more responsive to the public. No cabinet secretary took this directive as seriously as did HEW Secretary Califano; in September 1977 he instituted "Operation Common Sense." Within seven months Califano announced that he had eliminated many of HEW's 6,000 pages of regulations and streamlined the process of regulations development.

By the time that the ED legislation was being considered in Congress, advocates of the new Department argued that a proposed education regulation had as many as 14 levels to clear before it could be approved; on an average, the process took 519 days before the regulation was actually published. This was despite a provision in legislation that regulations should be published within a 240-day period.

Not surprisingly, there were few within OE or HEW who defended this process. However, given the complexity of the decision system, most players did not believe that the 240-day limit established by Congress was possible to meet. The causes of the delays, however, appeared to be in the eye of the beholder. Program staff tended to blame staff in the Commissioner's office or in the Office of the HEW Secretary. Staff offices complained about the inadequate time they were given to comment and noted that late comments were usually ignored. All complained about a lack of personnel who were able to draft, edit and type the regulations in an expeditious manner.

The process usually began with program staff, but, as the process developed, this staff often perceived that they had no control over their own regulations which were redrafted by OE and HEW staff offices without final consultation with program specialists. As one transition document noted, "The current perception is that it is easier and quicker to enact legislation than it is to implement it by regulations. This must change."[4] A new process was envisioned that would assist in program policy formulation and the grant award process, allow legal review of each regulation, and produce simple and clearly written policies developed with opportunity for "genuine" public participation.[5]

The transition group outlined four options that could be considered by the Secretary as she decided on the organizational placement of the regulation function. Option 1 would place it in the Office of Management and Budget; Option 2 would put it in the office of whatever assistant secretary was given the overall responsibility for development of departmental programmatic policies; Option 3 would place it in the Executive Secretariat and establish a regulations division within the office of each program Assistant Secretary; Option 4 would place the function in the Office of the Under Secretary.[6] The option preferred by the drafters of the memorandum was for the location of the regulations function in the unit responsible for the development of policy.

Secretary Hufstedler was not convinced by this transition group recommendation. In early February, she sent a memorandum on the regulations process to the Commissioner of Education, the deputy commissioners, the Transition Task Force leaders, and the staff of her immediate office. She echoed the goals articulated by the transition group:

> ... one of my highest priorities as we organize the new Department is to develop a model regulations process. The Education Department should prepare its regulations promptly and efficiently. Regulations should be prepared with as much public participation as possible, and they should be designed to minimize the burden placed on the education community and the public. And, most importantly, they must be written in clear, understandable English. ...
> At the same time, we must be sure that basic policy issues raised by ED regulations are thoroughly considered by all relevant offices and that policy decisions are made at an appropriate level of responsibility.[7]

Hufstedler ignored the options presented to her and, instead, decided to place the regulations process in the Office of the General Counsel, where it had been found in HEW. Hufstedler was attracted to that location as a lawyer and former judge and had confidence in the individual she had chosen for that position, Betsy Levin. Some program staff disagreed with the decision, believing that lawyers already exerted a disproportionate influence on the process.

REGULATIONS: MORE THAN AN ADMINISTRATIVE PROBLEM

Although most of the discussion about the regulations development process during the transition period emphasized internal efficiency questions, that approach to the regulations process tended to minimize the political problems associated with regulations development. The Hufstedler team confronted those problems quite early in its tenure; the legislative veto issue (the provision that was placed on some programs by the Congress in which the legislative body gave itself the authority to veto executive branch decisions about regulations) and the development of the *Lau* regulations (requirements related to bilingual education) illustrate the problems that the new team experienced.

The Legislative Veto

While both the general and education press tended to describe the issues related to the legislative veto as an isolated event, it was—in fact—just one episode in the continuously problematic relationship between Congress and the education agencies. Until 1968, most education programs did not have formal regulations; they were governed by draft regulations, guidelines and an assortment of other informal types of instructions. Most clients of the programs had little complaint about the process and passively supported the informal practices.

Around 1968, however, things changed. The Bureau of Elementary and Secondary Education began to enforce guidelines as regulations in its dealings with states over the Title I Compensatory Education program. Complaints from the states made Congress aware that the Office of Education had not been required to follow the stipulations of the Administrative Procedures Act and to formalize a rule developing process.

Congress stipulated that all requirements which were given the authority of regulations must be published in the Federal Register and that a 30-day comment period was needed before published requirements would go into effect. Despite congressional action to mandate these requirements, OE largely ignored them. In 1972, Congress responded to what it perceived to be inaction on OE's part by adding further stipulations. Under this action, OE was directed to study all regulations, guidelines, orders, directives and interpretations of rules since June 30, 1965 and revise and republish them. Public hearings were required on each program's regulations and the results of those hearings were to be reported to Congress. If necessary, the regulations were to be rewritten, republished, and then take effect 30 days after the second publication.

In 1974, Congress claimed even more control over the process; it required that whenever regulations had to be rewritten because of new legislation, OE had 60 days to give Congress a schedule which detailed when, in the following 180 days, new regulations would be published. The Commissioner of Education could request additional time if "unforeseen circumstances" were confronted.

Also in 1974, Congress added a step in the process that was known as the legislative veto. Congress gave itself 45 days following the publication of the final regulations to review the proposed regulation. If Congress did not act within that 45-day period (by joint resolution as well as through normal legislative procedures), then the regulation could go into effect. Although he signed the legislation containing this stipulation, President Gerald Ford stated that he did so despite his view that the legislative veto provision violated the doctrine of separation of powers between the legislation and executive branches. In a June 1978 message to Congress, President Jimmy Carter also expressed his view that the legislative veto provision was unconstitutional.

The legislative veto resulted from Congress's lack of trust in the Nixon administration to write acceptable legislation. Congress, thus, believed it had to write legislation on its own. Once required to become involved in the details of programs, Congress became less likely to simply react to administrative proposals and, instead, initiated its own suggestions, including more and more detailed restrictions and proscriptions in the law to prevent the executive branch from "subverting" its legislative intentions. The congressional urge to exert increased control over regulations can be seen as one more manifestation of a general tendency by the legislative branch to seek control over the administration of programs.

Carter's administration, thus, inherited a set of tensions between Congress and the federal education establishment which grew out of the distrust that had developed during the Nixon years. The Nixon strategy was to change the close relationships that existed between political appointees, career civil servants and Congress. The Nixon plan was to separate the career program staff from the political appointees and to limit the ability of program staff to deal directly with Capitol Hill. In some cases, these attempts at change highlighted the role of interest groups who became the conduit through which Congress and program staff could work together.

In February 1979, in the midst of the transition planning efforts, Hufstedler's staff became aware of rumors that the staff of the House Committee on Education and Labor was thinking about exercising its legislative veto authority over several rather minor education requirements. The first threat of veto was avoided; transition staff, representatives of the Commission's Office and the Office of the Secretary of HEW met with congressional staff members and were able to address the congressional objections.

Soon after, however, another threat appeared. It seemed to some transition planners that the congressional staff was acting to get the attention of the "new kids on the block", as one observer put it, "to flex their muscles and make ED roll over."

In mid-May, just days after ED opened its doors, the House passed resolutions to veto four regulations of education programs, none of which had active interest groups or articulate constituencies and all of which had been developed earlier in HEW before Hufstedler came on the scene. Congress charged that all four regulations exceeded the statutory authority which it had given to the executive branch. The Secretary and her advisers feared that the Congress (particularly through Jack Jennings, staff director of the House Education and Labor Committee), would continue to arrange such vetoes.

Although the Department of Justice had already issued an opinion on this issue, Secretary Hufstedler wrote to Attorney General Benjamin Civiletti, asking for a more complete opinion on the matter. (She was aware that both the White House and the Justice Department believed that the issue had to be viewed as a matter of legal principle and not dealt with in political bargaining terms.) Once she received the strongly worded opinion from the Justice Department finding that the veto should be ignored, Hufstedler had to declare the regulations effective. Hufstedler instructed her top aides to treat the disapproved regulations as final and effective rules, beginning immediately. This elevated the issue from a situation in which congressional staff were flexing their muscles before the new Department to a public struggle between members of Congress and the Department. Irate members of the Senate and House education committees wrote to the Secretary accusing her of arrogance and contemplated retaliatory measures, such as suing the executive branch or cutting off funds for programs in question.

By the end of June, although her public position was still one supporting the legal principle, Hufstedler appeared to be backing away from a full scale battle with Congress. It was clear to all that she could not win such a battle since Congress controlled the Department's purse strings and could also use its authorization and oversight authorities to make the Department's life quite uncomfortable. While the regulations were still valid and final, the Secretary ordered a quiet review of the four sets of regulations, with the possibility of making changes in them. Ultimately, Hufstedler ordered one regulation revised, began a detailed review of two others and left the fourth unchanged.

These activities took a significant amount of time and expenditure of political capital in the Department. Congressional demands in the regulations development process were not simply efficiency expectations; they were clear indications that Capitol Hill wanted more legislative control. Devising new ways of speeding up the internal regulations development process could not satisfy this demand.

The Lau Regulations Controversy

Controversy in the regulations process also surrounded the development of regulations requiring bilingual education for non-English speaking students. Although much of the press tended to view the Development of the *Lau* regulations as something that the "new upstart" Department was doing, these issues were a matter of discussion long before ED was created. In 1974, the U.S. Supreme Court had ruled in a San Francisco case, *Lau vs. Nichols*, that the 1964 Civil Rights Act required special instruction for children with limited English speaking ability. Because the issue was so controversial, HEW had failed to issue regulations that would implement the Supreme Court decree; despite several rounds of drafting and redrafting of the regulations, the issue was stalled within the HEW machinery.

An adversarial relationship between the Office of General Counsel and the Office for Civil Rights in HEW contributed to the impasse; the General Counsel's Office was viewed as the conservative force in the decision process while OCR was characterized as the advocacy unit. In addition, the civil rights enforcement machinery was bureaucratically separated from the education program establishment; OCR had responsibilities that were HEW wide (although it did have a specialist education staff) while OE looked only at education programs and policies.

When ED opened its doors, there was pressure within the Department as well as from the education and civil rights communities to deal with the issue. Moreover, Secretary Hufstedler herself had been directly involved with the San Francisco case; she had written the minority opinion on *Lau* that was eventually supported by the U.S. Supreme Court. When it was determined that the Department of Education Organization Act had, indeed, given ED the authority to issue civil rights regulations, a task force was established to develop options and a recommendation for the Secretary.

The draft regulations that were published in the Federal Register on August 5, 1980 have been both praised and damned by actors within ED, Congress, and the interest groups. Most of the actors involved in their development believe that the essential substance of the regulation would not have been different if they had been issued by HEW. However, the regulations were issued sooner (because of the streamlined process possible in ED) than would have been possible in HEW. Speed in this case was not necessarily a positive force; Hufstedler was under some pressure from the White House to issue the regulations before the November election to show Hispanic voters that the Carter administration was sensitive to their needs. As it turned out, because of the controversy of the subject matter, it might have been better for the administration if the regulations had been issued after the election.

There was some internal debate within ED about the substance of the regulations. The impetus for the effort came from the staff in the Office for Civil Rights who had been involved in the earlier HEW drafting attempts. Thus the issue was viewed as a civil rights problem rather than an education issue. Some questions about the wisdom of promulgating regulations that were bound to be opposed by the state and local education establishment and other education interest groups were raised within the Department. One participant noted that while many individuals within the Department were concerned, no one made it their business to stop the regulations in the same way that OCR advocates pushed to get them through. Indeed, one group of officials wrote a cautionary memorandum warning the Secretary to move slowly on the issue because of its sensitivity; according to one observer, they were called racists.

One would have expected the Director of OBEMLA to play an active role in these discussions since the program area concerned was bilingual education. He, however, left the advocacy of the issue largely to OCR. Most of the specific decisions on the regulations were made personally by Secretary Hufstedler who did have prior interest and background on the issue. One participant noted that the process would have been different if it had taken place in HEW because that system would have forced compromise further down the chain, particularly at the staff level.

The regulations themselves were intended to tackle the condition that was addressed by the Supreme Court case. Estimating that 3.5 million children were in need of bilingual education, the regulations specified how students in need of bilingual education would be identified, assessed and served and how long they would remain in those programs. The regulations did not specify the methods to be used, only the results expected to be attained. School districts that received any federal education funds would be covered by the regulation, no matter how many or how few limited English speaking children were enrolled. Schools were not required to provide qualified bilingual teachers at the high school level, only at the elementary school level. The regulations did provide for a waiver if schools could demonstrate that they had existing alternative programs that served these children.

The *Lau* regulations were thrown into a political context that was not receptive to the changes required. The past decade had seen growing concern in many parts of the country over the immigration of Asians and Hispanics and some communities were fearful that the new pattern undermined the "melting pot" concept of the U.S. culture. The regulations did try to make it clear that, eventually, all students were expected to learn English. But the election year atmosphere clouded the issue. Carter had been under attack by the Hispanic community for failing to appoint a Hispanic to the ED Secretary position and wanted to show his commitment to that community.

The controversy over the regulations was as much a political battle over the federal role in education as it was a dispute about the substance of the requirements. The opponents of the Department who had argued that creation of ED would mean increased federal intervention pointed to the *Lau* requirements as clear evidence of that movement.

Six hearings were held around the country during the 30 day comment period after the regulations were proposed. Few of those who testified opposed the practice of giving special consideration to children with limited English speaking ability, but many opposed the direction required by ED. Representatives of the Big Six education groups—the major education interest groups that had been the strongest advocates of the creation of the Department—expressed concern about the tendency of the regulations to limit the ability of local districts to assess the needs of their children and choose the specific programs they deemed to be effective. In addition, some Hispanic groups criticized the regulations for failing to support education efforts in a student's first language.

It was not surprising that the proposed regulations were immediately thwarted in Congress. A bill was introduced in the Senate to direct the Secretary to withdraw the regulations. A floor amendment was attached to the Labor-HHS-Education appropriations bill to prohibit the Secretary from issuing any regulations addressing needs of limited English speaking children other than by intensive instruction in English (it passed by a 231 to 194 vote after minimal debate). Before it recessed for the campaign, Congress gave the Department clear marching orders to back away from the proposed *Lau* regulations.

AN ASSESSMENT OF THE ED REGULATION PROCESS

Depending on the perspective of the evaluator, the assessment of the ED regulation process varied from "great success" to "disaster". The new process did not really address the problems that were confronted in the legislative veto question or the *Lau* issue. But many participants argued that these experiences were not typical. A significant number of interest group representatives and ED staff (including both program as well as staff people) acknowledged an improvement in the process. The streamlining of the system and the reduction of the number of clearance levels resulted in a speedier process. One participant estimated that it took four months in 1978 to produce two education regulations; in 1980, 56 were completed in the same period of time. Others, however, did not experience this improved time frame. The vocational rehabilitation staff acknowledged that although the regulation development process in HEW was slow, it was a relatively simple process because the regulations were generally viewed as "harmless" and noncontroversial. The changed process that was developed in ED was viewed as "tortuous"; the vocational rehabilitation programs did not fit the education model and, as a result, the staff viewed the ED bureaucracy as "heavy handed." One observer commented that the vocational rehabilitation regulations developed in ED took four or five months longer than they had before the Department was established.

For most of the education program staff, however, the new process gave them a "day in court" before a judge who was their advocate, with a personal stake in the educational content of the regulations. The system did assist in defining a more uniform interpretation of the development process, less duplication of data collection efforts, and fewer conflicting signals to regional managers. The Title I regulations, for example, travelled a very smooth and expeditious path, with compromises worked out between program staff and the legal officers before the recommendation was transmitted to the Secretary.

CHANGE IN THE DECISION PROCESS: WHAT DIFFERENCE DID IT MAKE?

The policy processes that were devised for the new Department centered around the Office of the Secretary and the various functions (e.g. budget, legislative development, legal counsel, management) that were attached to that office. Although most of the program units had their own, well institutionalized relationships with Congress and their relevant interest groups, the formal lines of authority within a federal agency required that the program views be funneled through the Office of the Secretary. New legislation, budget requests and regulations travelled a formalized path and whether they liked it or not, the program staff had to follow that procedure.

From the Secretary's point of view, these procedures were among the major tools available to develop a Department-wide perspective, to mesh the separate agendas of the various program components, and to conceptualize those views from the perspective of a cabinet member who was part of the Carter administration. One could expect, thus, that the processes instituted represented an attempt at control and the program units within the Department (both the political appointees as well as the career bureaucrats) would be expected to resist them.

Secretary Hufstedler's policy development processes relied on the personal relationships between the various actors within the Department. In this area, as in others, her belief that people make a difference became an essential part of the new system. When the system did work, as a number of players believed, it seemed to be because of specific individuals in particular roles.

But the processes themselves—like the organizational restructuring that occurred—were not institutionalized. The time available before the election was not adequate for the career bureaucracy in programs as well as the staff offices to work out the standard operating procedures that appeared to be predictable, established and well organized. It is interesting to note that one element of the Hufstedler strategy had been the linking of program evaluaion to the day to day management activities. Routine collection of information and regular monitoring of programs were unrealized hopes in the first six months of the Department's life. Neither Assistant Secretary for Management, John Gabusi nor Secretary Hufstedler emphasized that aspect of the decision process.

WHAT ABOUT STRUCTURE?

There were only three areas within the new Department in which organizational structure played an important role. The creation of OBEMLA—the Office of Bilingual Education and Minority Language Affairs—signalled a change in the status and mission of bilingual education programs. This status was believed to reflect the recognition of the importance of bilingual populations and the office appeared to be responsible for several new programs in that area. Although the programs were relatively small in scope, they were viewed as important innovations within a budget-cutting environment.

The Office of the Assistant Secretary for Special Education and Rehabilitation Services, despite complaints about the new decision processes, also experienced a change in the status that its new structure provided. As one key player in that office commented, the creation of an Assistant Secretary position with sole concern for the disabled brought the field a heightened sense of status and visibility. This was particularly important to a program area which often experienced exclusion and discrimination. The visibility of the office also gave the program staff the ability to participate in open program coordination, working with White House staff as well as others concerned about programs for the disabled.

Both OBEMLA and OSERS had strong and active interest groups who were able to use the visibility of the new structures to their advantage, highlighting their legislative and administrative concerns. Although both offices contained programs drawn from diverse past bureaucratic settings, it did not appear that either Assistant Secretary attempted to push them into a unified program mold. Thus the day to day administrative disruption within the offices appeared to be minimal.

Efforts within the Office of Educational Research and Improvement were quite different. Assistant Secretary James Rutherford linked the increase in status and visibility created by the new organizational unit to the improvement of the quality of education within the U.S. Rutherford's agenda for coordination and centralization confronted a diverse array of programs that had been free standing and administratively autonomous.

Rutherford did have the most consolidation to do. He decided to start from scratch—as a good scientist who trusted his own analyses. Thus he set up a study team and consulted with a number of "experts" before the new structure was formalized. His problems were complicated by a constant battle with the Assistant Secretary for Management over the allocation of space. Rutherford wanted to stay in the same building with the Secretary and resisted attempts to move OERI out of that location.

Not surprisingly, Rutherford's centralizing strategy for OERI met with resistance from a number of programs. As one participant commented, "OERI was not managerially strong and the centralization of all functions is not necessarily good management." But unlike either OBEMLA or OSERS, the programs within OERI did not have strong or visible interest groups that might have exerted some pressure against Rutherford's centralization strategy.

CONCLUSIONS

Of all of the stages of the policy process, the implementation stage contains activities and functions that are most dependent on time. Implementation in the federal government is thrust on large and complex bureaucracies that require the investment of time and sustained attention if changes in standard operating processes are to be accomplished. This stage requires attention to detail and knowledge of the plodding nature of large organizations.

The implementation stage of the policy process can be viewed as a microcosm of all of the stages: when a policy or decision is to be implemented, those in charge of the implementation travel through agenda setting, formulation, adoption and then—finally to the activities that allow a policy to be put into operation.

Within this framework, Secretary Hufstedler did have opportunities to refocus ED. She was required to develop her strategy within boundaries set by the formal legislation, but—like the actors who preceded her—she had opportunities to put her own imprint on the policy. The strategy that she emphasized was twofold: the appointment of key staff people whom she felt shared her view of change and the development of decision processes that provided opportunities for both coordination and control. She gave minimal attention to the organization and development of new structural units.

But time was Shirley Hufstedler's enemy. The strategy that she had chosen could not be accomplished in a few months. She relied on individuals who (like herself) might be forced to leave in January 1981. She instituted decision processes that were both new and complex; she did not emphasize the issues and processes that would give the Department an institutional memory beyond election day.

The mode of implementation that she chose was difficult to undertake in a volatile political environment. In most areas involving specific program units, she believed that she was minimizing the chance of political back-lash by agreeing to continue business as usual—appointing individuals to head program units who were known to the interest groups and to congressional actors and keeping the organizational structures administering those programs similar to those found in HEW.

But politics could not be removed from this stage of the policy process; power battles between the Congress and the agency were played out in the conflict over the legislative veto, the *Lau* controversy, and—to some extent—in the few changes that were made in organizational structure. Another form of political conflict was found in the clash between the career bureaucracy and the new political appointees, as new actors attempted to impose their agendas on career staff members. Secretary Hufstedler, like all of the Carter cabinet members, could never forget the forthcoming presidential election and the political climate which that created.

The analysts who were important in this stage included a group with a methodology and approach that was new to the ED issue. Because of Hufstedler's legal background and the nature of the issues that were on the agenda during this stage, legal analysts took on a new importance, particularly in the confrontation with Congress over the legislative veto. But some of the familiar analyses also appeared, emphasizing the efficiency imperatives that drove the development of the regulations process. Analysts justified the creation of the Office of Education Research and Improvement as a way of increasing the effectiveness of existing programs. But the ED analysts (and their client, Secretary Hufstedler), failed to acknowledge the linkage between the processes and structures they were creating and the politics with which they were entwined.

One is not surprised that the essentially political nature of these decisions was recognized by the political actors. During this stage, interest groups focused on their own specialized concerns; most of them were satisfied with Hufstedler's decision to minimize disruption. Those affected by the organizational structure decisions agreed to them when these actions appeared to support their agenda (such as the efforts to create a separate structure for the vocational rehabilitation programs and the increased status for bilingual education). If proposals for organizational change (particularly centralized control) disrupted their power relationships, some interest groups had enough influence to minimize the impact of—or even to stop—those proposals.

As the Department began operations in the last months of 1980, even the most modest efforts to change procedures involving federal education policy-making indicated that reorganization was a formidable task. It required a redistribution of influence which, in turn, expressed new relationships in status and visibility for program officials, actors within the legislative branch, and clients of programs.

EPILOGUE

After January 20, 1981, nothing was quite the same. Jimmy Carter attempted to use the creation of the Department of Education as evidence of his effectiveness as President. But despite the strong support of the NEA, he was soundly defeated by Ronald Reagan in the November elections.

Reagan ran on a Republican platform that called for the elimination of the Department of Education (as well as a number of other education planks that minimized the federal role in education). The death of ED became a real possibility with shifts in the Senate, giving the Republicans control of that body for the first time in 25 years, as well as the change in the White House.

For the first years of the Reagan administration, the advocates of ED were required to invest their resources and energy in survival tactics—saving the Department. The existence of ED had become an important symbol of the status of education within the American society. Even the education groups that had been lukewarm about the creation of ED were not about to support Reagan's position. Despite attempts by the Reagan administration (and the Heritage Foundation, a conservative think-tank) to eliminate the cabinet status of ED, members of Congress were able to thwart the administration's move.

But while the structure of ED could be defended, it was more difficult for supporters of existing policies to withstand other moves for change. The ED that remained at the end of the Carter administration was not a strong organization. Its internal decision processes had not been institutionalized. Many of the top staff were outsiders who did not find strong support for their positions and views within the career bureaucracy. And although interest groups continued to maintain their relationships with the specific program units within the Department, they had been effectively closed out of the deliberations of the Office of the Secretary.

When the administration changed, it left behind a weak organization which was unable to defend itself against new demands. The program pieces were subject to the budget pressures and program shifts of the Reagan administration. The coordinating mechanisms that had been an essential part of Hufstedler's strategy were not in place. There was no ability to create a setting which valued career staff and where the legitimate and conflicting perspectives of career and political appointees could be aired.

The Reagan strategy for change in the education field was waged on a number of fronts. While the attempt to kill ED failed, the administration was able to make dramatic changes through its appointment route. The Reagan appointees were even further removed from the Washington education establishment than the Carter officials. Block grant legislation (a consolidation of many of the smaller federal programs into a single grant) was introduced to shift the federal role so it would defer even further to state and local agencies. Through this program change, a number of specialized ED program staffs were eliminated; many of them were in the Office of Educational Research and Improvement and lacked strong constituency support.

The strategy that proved successful within the Reagan administration can be described as the reverse of that employed by Carter. Reorganization— changes in organizational structure—was viewed by Carter as the way to achieve other sorts of changes in the federal system; that is, to achieve goals of improved efficiency, increased effectiveness, and changing the federal role in education. Reagan, by contrast, used substantive changes in policies (formal as well as budget allocations) to achieve changes in the structure and organization of the Department.

NOTES

1. E. Fiske, *New York Times* (May 11, 1980).
2. Editorial, *Washington Post* (May 7, 1980).
3. Michael O'Keefe, "Draft Paper: Policy Formulation and Implementation," (December 7, 1979).
4. Office of General Counsel, Education Division, Memorandum, "Suggestions for Department of Education Regulations Management System," (December 31, 1979), pp. 4-5.
5. Ted Sky, Office of General Counsel, Note to Stewart Baker, "Re: Suggestions for Regulations Management System," (December 31, 1979), p. 2.
6. James Pickman, Deputy Commissioner for Resources and Operations, Memorandum to Stewart Baker, Special Assistant to the Secretary, "Position Paper on Reorganization of the Regulations Development Process," (January 4, 1980), pp. 6-8.
7. Shirley M. Hufstedler, Memorandum, "Subject: Regulations Process for the New Department," (February 7, 1980).

Chapter 9   CONCLUSION

We conclude this volume with three sets of observations. First, we return to the goals that various advocates sought to achieve by establishing a Department of Education and review the ways that they moved through the decision-making process. Second, we return to the five themes which were introduced at the beginning of this volume—the stages of the policy process; the politics of the executive branch; the culture of analysis vs. the culture of politics; interest groups and issue networks; and education policy and the federal role. We believe that the case study which has been presented provides insights about these issues beyond the specific example. Our third set of observations is cast as a set of lessons for two kinds of readers of this volume: those who see themselves as policy analysts and those who might, one day, be in the role of reorganizers.

THE GOALS OF REORGANIZATION

When Carter prepared to assume the presidency, one could identify five general concerns or goals that were associated with the proposal for a new department. These goals reflected the range of actors and issues that were involved in the advocacy of the department and, as they were played out, shaped the organizational alternatives that were considered. The expectations about the possible impact of ED varied tremendously, depending on which goal was predominant. As we have noted, each of these goals—symbolic status, political advantage, efficiency, effectiveness, and change—contained arguments that had been made in favor of a new department for many years. The nature of the goals (or combination of goals) shaped the character of the political activity through which they were pursued.

Symbolic Status

Those who argued for the creation of a separate cabinet-level structure for education because of the symbolic status of a department were attempting to address what they believed to be a simple problem: the U.S. was the only nation in the world that did not have an education ministry or department. For some, thus, creation of ED was a political end in itself. For others, the status of a department would have instrumental value. The creation of a cabinet-level department would provide the education sector with a status comparable to other sectors in the society which did have their own place in the president's cabinet. Some advocates of this position believed that higher status, visibility, and a place at the cabinet table would translate into future federal funding for education and, in general, greater public attention to the needs of students and educators.

As the story of ED has unfolded, this argument for change was omnipresent. While few of the proponents of the department rested their case on this argument alone, it was present in every stage of the process. The power of this position explains NEA's expenditure of resources, Carter's eventual willingness to accept a narrow department, congressional compromise and bargaining, and—finally—the ability to withstand the proposal to kill ED during the Reagan administration.

Edelman and others have emphasized the importance of the symbolic uses of politics. At the most basic level, government plays an important role in the construction of the social reality around public problems. Edelman has noted that "government affects behavior chiefly by shaping the cognitions of large numbers of people in ambiguous situations. It helps to create their beliefs about what is proper; their perceptions of what is fact; and their expectations of what is to come."[1] These means are most often described in their attachment to the *processes* of governing. This case indicates that symbolism is alive and well in the *substance* of specific policy proposals. The value of the symbolic status argument as a political goal is that it can encompass many actors at once in a way that allows them to imagine different consequences of their support. As long as the issue remains at a symbolic level, the consequences of these differences are muted.

Sometimes the symbolic status goal was the sole motivation for activity and some of the department's proponents were willing to invest simply in the attainment of ED, believing that status and visibility were important enough to warrant such an effort. Others combined the symbolic status goal with other goals; indeed, they believed that the symbolic status goal did not warrant the expenditure of political capital and (particularly for analysts) achieving this goal alone was worse than doing nothing at all.

Political Advantage

The advocates of reorganization of the federal education programs often linked the symbolic status arguments to their calculation of political advantage for personal, partisan and interest group agendas. It is clear that Carter's interest in the department was motivated by his interest in attaining the support of the NEA during the 1976 campaign. The political know-how and resources of the NEA were (and continue to be) considerable and provided Carter with a unique political machine that had functioning parts throughout the country. After the campaign, this goal appeared to be less important to the Carter administration—until the time came to plan a reelection strategy. And, once again, during the 1980 Democratic convention, Carter's support from the NEA was essential to his political fortunes.

The White House also attempted to calculate political advantage as it worked with the Congress on this issue. Carter's team had difficulty maintaining the support of a Democratic Congress on a broad range of issues. As the proposal for ED developed, the White House analysis could not be limited to simple vote counts on various proposals related to the structure and functions of the department. The calculus also had to include the impact of votes and positions related to ED on other issues on the President's agenda that the White House considered to be more important. The determination of political advantage, thus, had to include the entire range of Carter's domestic and foreign proposals. The White House tried to maintain a public position that would convince advocates and the Congress that the President gave high priority to the establishment of ED without sacrificing other goals that were, in fact, considered to be more critical to the nation's welfare.

Political advantage was also an essential goal for members of Congress as they determined their positions on ED. As long as the issue could be posed in general terms (simply a department), the organization and power of the NEA and its supporters played an important role in securing the votes of many members of Congress. However, as soon as the question before the members focused on specific programs and structures to be included or excluded from ED, then a range of other issues came to the fore. Members were, understandably, more concerned about the disruption of their long term support from various groups than they were about the short term advantage they might gain in supporting the President's position.

The goal of political advantage was an element that—like symbolic status—was not always openly articulated by the actors involved with ED. It was particularly difficult for Carter, given his unique approach to politics, to acknowledge that he was operating in an environment in which his survival was more dependent on accurate calculations of political advantage than on "good" or "correct" ideas. Carter's style of political leadership was not one which lent itself to the calculation of political advantage. He appeared to his critics to be a middle-of-the-road politician whose administration seemed indecisive and lacking focus. As Knott and Wildavsky had predicted[2], his personal style created a perception of a political leader who did not understand the process of governance. In addition, his concern about detail combined with an inability to take into account opposing viewpoints; the result was the perception of a president who was not able to control the advice that he received within the White House.

Efficiency

It is not surprising that supporters of ED argued that a cabinet-level department would make the federal education bureaucracy more efficient. Arguments based on increases in efficiency (assertions of reduced costs and more expeditious action) are the most common public positions taken to justify administrative reorganization. This position asserts that reorganization is needed because of overlap and duplication of functions; these result in complex and slow decision processes that produce costly and inadequate services.

This set of arguments focuses only on the *process* of the agencies, not on their substantive output. This approach was the path that justified the existence of a free standing PRP, theoretically connected to the substantive decision-making process but, in reality, separate from the substantive aspects of the Domestic Policy Staff or even from the budget staffs of OMB. It was also the reason for the existence of the congressional government operations committees—bodies that focused on the *how* not the *what* of federal government operations. As long as these arenas were the location of decision-making, the efficiency arguments would have some salience. In addition, in a budget-cutting environment, arguments that promise to achieve "more bang for the buck" take on some prominence. Moreover, they go down well in public because of the widespread belief that government is inefficient and wasteful.

The venue of decision-making, therefore, explains much of the attractiveness of the efficiency argument for ED's proponents. Indeed, this argument was one of the major reasons for support from the two congressional government operations committees. Efficiency arguments allowed the committees to differentiate their approach from that of the substantive committees and to justify their "meddling" in education matters. However, as has been shown, it is difficult to make a case for the creation of a department such as ED resting only on arguments of efficiency. Tortuous decision processes are not unusual in the American political system; indeed, they are a result of the complex structure of separation of powers that defines the U.S. system. Thus when the ED proposals travelled to the floor of the House, the efficiency arguments lost their power.

Although the PRP always attempted to include efficiency arguments in its analysis, the particular group of individuals assembled to work on ED did not find these arguments to be particularly convincing. The reorganization group was a part of the management "side" of OMB but many of the PRP staffers did not believe that management questions—unlike budgets—were important. The structure of PRP more closely resembled the substantive organization of the budget "side" of OMB than that of the management "side" (which saw the government in terms of broad management issues).

The PRP did recognize the arguments for improved efficiency were good public relations ploys and it was difficult for anyone to argue against them. The PRP position was not unlike that of the transition group and the strategists within ED. While they used the efficiency argument, it did not represent their major case for change. The emphasis on efficiency in the House deliberations left the administration with a weak case. The efficiency arguments used to support ED were innocuous and somewhat vapid; they did not point to scandals, examples of gross misspending or other forms of "horror" stories about management of federal education programs.

Effectiveness

Advocates of ED who argued from this goal rested their case on the belief that the creation of a separate department would improve the quality of educational services within the existing structure and level of resources already found in the federal government. Focusing on the growing skepticism within the U.S. about the ability of existing programs to address education problems, those who argued this position alleged that a new department would be able to take the programs that were already in place and make them work "better."

The effectiveness arguments were difficult to sustain in the ED decision process. First, advocates of this position were implicitly criticizing the status quo, even if they looked only to marginal and incremental changes. Proponents of the status quo were often the very groups who supported the concept of ED on other grounds. The education interest groups—especially the NEA—were found in this position. This argument also appeared to be an attack on the ability of the Washington career bureaucrats—important allies of the interest groups—to do their job.

Second, the argument often seemed trivial. If the problems in American education were significant, the effectiveness argument seemed to be placing a small band-aid on a large wound. If there were problems, it was argued, why not address them in more comprehensive ways? Those who were attracted to this argument (particularly the PRP staff and Hufstedler's staff) did find it difficult to rest with the scope of this approach. While they did want to appear to be improving American education, they were also aware of the political constraints and did not want to cause a large scale disruption of the system. This was not an easy position to hold.

Third, because the jurisdiction for the reorganization proposals was in the government operations committees in the Congress, substantive arguments (no matter how modest) were difficult to raise without violating the boundaries of the authority of those committees. Indeed, to raise some of these questions was perceived to be opening a Pandora's box. Once open, that box let loose criticisms of federal education programs, civil rights policies and other requirements that seemed to constrain state and local policy-makers.

For these reasons, the effectiveness arguments had only limited power to influence the development of ED. Despite Carter's own personal attraction to this type of argument (it acknowledged problems but did not suggest large scale action by the federal government), the decision process contained neither the arenas nor the actors to make this argument a major rallying point.

Change American Education

The proponents of this argument had much in common with those who diagnosed the problems of education in terms of effectiveness. But this argument made some of those diagnostic elements more explicit. Its proponents believed that a separate department would assist the federal government to develop a new role in the way that it addressed American education issues. The problems that currently existed, they argued, were largely caused by the school administrators and teachers who had a professional monopoly in the field. These critics believed that the providers of "schooling" were more concerned about their own professional status and conditions and the defense of failed policies than they were about the educational performance of the students in their classrooms.

Because many of the arguments made by these supporters of the department were explicit statements of issues that were implicit in the effectiveness goal, the boundary lines between the two are difficult to draw. The analysts within PRP gravitated to the change view because it seemed to be logical outcome of their analytical work. Those who used the change argument were attracted to the idea of a broader department. Carter's personal skepticism about Washington insiders gave this position some salience. At the same time, Carter was politically indebted to one of the most inside groups in Washington—the NEA—the very organization that seemed to reflect the interests and needs of the professional monopoly. Carter's selection of Shirley Hufstedler and her subsequent selection of top aides indicated his attempt to avoid the insiders.

Although the supporters of ED played down the importance of the change argument, its opponents picked up the implications of this approach. Some of ED's detractors argued against the creation of the department because they believed that it would be a captive of the professional monopoly that they believed already dominated American education. For example, this argument can be deduced from those who held out against the inclusion of Head Start in ED and, as well, from some of the civil rights advocates who feared that ED would not enforce requirements affecting state and local education bodies.

The argument was also used by conservatives who opposed ED because they believed that a cabinet-level department would, indeed, change American education and would make the federal role stronger in the intergovernmental system. When ED came up on the floor of the House, its opponents argued strongly that the creation of a separate department would mean a dramatic change in the structure and content of education.

In summary, if one believed that a cabinet-level department would accomplish an increase in symbolic status for education, that goal was met simply by the creation of ED. If one thought that creation of ED could provide political advantage, it appears that this goal was partially met, depending on the actor involved. However, Carter's loss to Reagan in 1980 does indicate that (from his perspective) the goal was not successful.

As has been discussed, it is difficult to judge whether the efficiency arguments might have been accomplished because of the short time frame available to the Department before the change in administration. The information that is available appears to show that the regulations development process within the new Department was, indeed, more efficient. The accomplishment of the effectiveness and change goals are also difficult to assess. It did appear that it was easier for the Reagan administration to make changes in the program and budget of the federal education machinery simply because a cabinet-level department provided a base for this attention. Ironically, ED became a "pulpit" for arguments for change even while its very existence was under attack. The educational reform movement that was undertaken by Reagan's two Secretaries of Education—Terrell Bell and William Bennett— would have had a difficult time emerging from other than the position of a cabinet secretary concerned only with education issues.

STAGES OF THE POLICY PROCESS

We have described a policy process that is full of paradoxes. It is, at once, both predictable and chaotic. It is linear yet circular. Informal sources of power define most relationships, yet formal authority is essential. The system churns out regular "choice opportunities" (as Cohen, March, and Olsen call them[3]) yet the vagaries of uncertainty influences the environment in which decisions must be made.

We have attempted to paint a picture of a fragmented, pluralistic system of policy making that, almost despite itself, is pulled along by relatively predictable behavior of multiple actors who must deal with the imperatives of political demands, time and deadlines. This process does not work like a Weberian machine but neither is it totally capricious. The garbage can metaphor, for example, does not capture the elements of predictability that lie within the decision-making process.[4]

This analysis of the creation and implementation of ED has depicted a policy process which contains distinct and sequential stages that have their own imperatives. While the stages can overlap (in this case, that occurred when ED moved from formulation in OMB to adoption in the Congress), they are predictable in a number of ways. This study suggests that it is natural for participants in the policy process to have a sense of *deja vu* as they move from stage to stage.

What, then, has this study told us about the stages of the policy process? We review the findings.

Agenda Setting

This case study has described an agenda setting process that was closely linked to the development of support for a political candidate. While the arguments for the establishment of a cabinet-level department had been around for years and had strong congressional support, the issue made its way to the active political agenda for two reasons: the desire by NEA to move into presidential politics and Jimmy Carter's need to gain the support of a strong grass roots organization with a well educated and active membership. This stage began with Carter's campaign rhetoric: he announced unequivocally that there would be a department of education if he was elected. And he asserted that such a department was in the "public interest"—an allegation that spoke to the symbolic status and political advantage goals associated with the creation of the department. The timing of the campaign promise—early enough to give adequate time to use NEA's resources but not so early as to dissipate those resources—was an essential component of this stage.

Formulation

Once in the White House, the primary considerations for this policy moved from political questions to an analytical phase. The development of the proposal for ED within the PRP was a long term activity that focused on two questions: should there be a department of education and, if so, what should be included within it? As we have shown, the actors within the Executive Office did not blindly accept the campaign promise. Rather, the imperatives of this stage (which attempts to define a problem carefully and assess alternative ways of dealing with it) pushed them back to the original question. We believe that this process is natural; but it provided ammunition for the perception that Jimmy Carter was indecisive and was ignoring his own strong campaign rhetoric. New actors joined the process and analysts attempted to predict the effects of alternative decisions that might be made.

In the fragmented decision system which characterizes federal policy making, analysts may try to respond to the expectations of multiple actors.

The PRP viewed Jimmy Carter as its client—but knew that Carter did not have the formal authority to make a decision come to life. As the boundaries between the formation and adoption stages became blurred, the policy analysts, concerned about the reception their ideas would receive, felt increasingly torn on the issue of whether the client for any analysis should be Congress or the President.

The predominant actors in this stage—the PRP staff members—exhibited the analyst's natural urge: a desire to amass as much information and data as they possibly could. In many ways, the collection of information was an end in itself and the analysts had some difficulty recognizing that others saw their data search in a more political light. Only when some external force reminded them that they were operating in a calendar-sensitive environment (e.g. when Ribicoff threatened to take the initiative or when campaign realities hit home) did the PRP recognize that timing was all important. In this case, deadlines had a positive impact on the work of analysts, forcing them to come to decisions. The tendency for analysts is to operate slowly and deliberately, taking their work very seriously. The PRP group wanted to believe that the decision-making process rested on rational analysis, even though the data that they were using hardly warranted such precision. Given this mind set, the analysts were drawn to the substantive aspects of the reorganization goals (effectiveness and change) rather than the symbolic or political goals.

Adoption

Although the adoption stage overlapped with the formulation stage in time, the two stages had distinctly different functions within the decision-making process. Actors sometimes found that they had different perspectives on issues depending on whether they focused on adoption or formulation questions. For example, when congressional staffers were involved (as secondary players) in the formulation stage, they did not view the world much differently than did the PRP staff. But when the proposal moved away from analysis and to the Congress for formal adoption, congressional staff followed most members of Congress in concentrating on one thing: getting agreement on establishing a department.

The proponents of the department searched for the coalitions and legislative language that would achieve passage. It was irrelevant whether or not an issue had been considered in the earlier stages. If it helped ED's advocates to gain support, the issue would be reconsidered. The congressional actors were, of course, constrained by the decisions and rules of the legislative arena, their formal authority, and the political realities of their relationships with interest groups.

Unlike the actors involved in the formulation stage, the legislative strategists were interested in information and data only when it was pertinent to specific positions of powerful actors and when that information predicted the behavior of those actors. The decision processes in this stage were characterized by bargaining and other forms of interaction between the multiple participants.

Again unlike the formulation stage, time was a constraint in the adoption stage. Members of the House perceived time in a two year reelection format and the regularity of elections made them extremely sensitive to time dimensions. The White House did not immediately recognize the importance of time during this stage; in the early phases of this stage there did not appear to be a recognition of the political clock. At least part of the tension between the Congress and the White House revolved around the differences in perception of time. Congress sought a decision in the fastest way possible. By the end of this stage, however, reelection panic set in and the White House was willing to accept any kind of a department.

As others have pointed out, the legislative process appears to push proposals to incremental rather than broad or comprehensive proportions. The legislative actors, recognizing the multiplicity of interests involved, sought to minimize the level of disruption or change perceived by those involved and to finesse the conflicts that existed among the players. The advocates of ED within the Congress sought to downplay the change and effectiveness goals and, instead, to emphasize the other goals as they sought support for the measure.

Implementation

Once passed, the ED legislation began the implementation process. This process began with a distinct set of activities that were involved in the transition from the adoption of the legislation to the operation of the Department. This transition, as it unfolded, provided an illustration of a characteristic of the implementation stage. That is, when the stage begins, it opens up a series of stages within itself. The transition activities began with agenda setting activities (the legislation); formulation activities (within Hufstedler's own staff and in the transition task force process); adoption (when Hufstedler put together a staff and made both structural and process determinations); and finally, the actual operation of the Department.

Throughout the debate on the creation of ED, both its proponents and opponents had made a number of assumptions about the way in which the new department would be implemented. But when the legislation actually passed and reached the implementation stage, the nature of the decision process moved from securing agreement on relatively general pronouncements to determining concrete, technical and detailed management issues. The implementation process provides the opportunity for the implementors to raise many of the same issues that seemingly had been resolved earlier. At this point, however, the issues were usually raised in the guise of technical determinations about specific administrative and policy problems. The search within this stage is for what "works". It is a process that requires attention to detail and knowledge of the plodding nature of complex organizations. As we have commented earlier, implementation takes time. And neither Hufstedler nor Carter had conceptualized an implementation strategy that recognized the implications of the clock for their activities.

We have emphasized that each stage of the policy process seems to cycle back to issues that had, seemingly, been resolved in an earlier stage. Sometimes this recycling occurs because the new stage demands that decision-makers look at the issue in new ways; sometimes it occurs because new actors are involved in the process. While the predominant dynamic in the system moves in a fragmented fashion, it does appear that there are forces which link the elements together. This case study has shown that interest groups—which never have formal authority to make public policy decisions—can provide the communication linkages between the stages. In other policy cases, the President has been able to establish the informal linkages between the elements of the stages and to serve as a "fixer".[5] Neither Carter (nor others in the Executive branch), played that role with ED.

THE POLITICS OF THE EXECUTIVE BRANCH

This volume has dealt with three aspects of the politics of the executive branch: the activities within the White House; bureaucratic responses to change; and the strategy of reorganization. As we have shown, over and over again, the multiple actors and institutions within the White House play an important role in policy-making. The conflict between the PRP and the Domestic Policy Staff, and the internal disputes within OMB between the PRP "upstarts" and the more institutionalized budget and management operations have been described in some detail. Moreover, this case provides an illustration of the competition within the White House staff for the President's attention, his time, and his voice. As the decision process proceeded, it was never clear to anyone on the outside who, indeed, spoke for the President. This, in turn, resulted in a perception by the press and the Congress that the President was indecisive. At the outset of his administration Carter did retreat from his commitment to establish a department. After November 1977, many observers of the process believed that he was personally clear and consistent about his views. But Carter was not able to communicate his desires to the White House advisers who were concerned about the political effects of creating ED. An issue that was perceived to be of greater importance—like disarmament—probably would not provoke such challenges to presidential positions. But no one in the White House saw the establishment of ED as an issue that would affect the course of human events or even the nation's welfare. Because the issue was perceived in almost wholly political terms by the White House staff, its impact on other political issues dominated substantive considerations. Ironically, perhaps, the major impetus for effectiveness and change goals within the White House came from the President himself.

The case also provides an example of the fragility of the coordinating mechanisms within the White House. The various actors within the executive branch (in this case best illustrated by the actions of Joseph Califano) have both incentives and opportunities to work their own agendas, irrespective of the coordinating attempts within the White House. As we have discussed, the openings provided by the stages of the policy process create opportunities for "disloyal" behavior.

The ED example indicates that attempts within the White House to set out comprehensive plans or agendas are inevitably short lived. Despite Carter's personal predilections for order and rationality, even the transition activities he organized before the inauguration came to naught. The government-wide approach set forth in the plan to establish an advisory committee for the PRP did not materialize. The idea that the PRP would operate as a "regular" unit in OMB had fizzled out even before the end of the Carter administration. Carter's grand plans confronted what every president has experienced—a turbulent political environment in which seemingly unrelated issues were often tactically joined.

The second aspect of this theme focuses on bureaucratic responses to change. Kaufman has noted that barriers to change inside bureaucracies fall in three categories: acknowledged benefits of stability, calculated opposition to change, and inability to change.[6] This case study appears to emphasize the first of these barriers: benefits of stability. It does not indicate a blind defense of the status quo and a resistance to change *qua* change. The bureaucracy, particularly the career public service, will support change if it believes that the proposed shifts will give it advantage and, indeed, may stabilize its operations and support mechanisms. Bureaucrats, through their interest groups and supporters in Congress, welcomed the move of the vocational rehabilitation progams out of HHS and into ED, believing that this move would help them achieve stability. While this type of behavior is often interpreted as self-interested protection of turf, it is more often motivated by the conviction that others, rather than they themselves, will lose out or benefit because of the disruption that occurs with reorganization.

The popular press finds it comforting to highlight bureaucratic inability or unwillingness to change. But we tend to ignore the accountability mechanisms that make it rational for bureaucrats to be skeptical of change. Indeed, the mechanisms that have been developed to assure the accountability of the bureaucracy push against change through formal means (congressional oversight) as well as informal techniques (interest group activity).

The third aspect of the theme dealing with the politics of the executive branch focuses on the strategy of reorganization itself. This case study has emphasized the importance of recognizing the consequences of the shared authority between the executive branch and the Congress in issues involving reorganization. However, despite its limitations and its mixed track record, one can expect new executives within public agencies to use reorganization as a strategy for influencing policy. Peter Szanton has noted that reorganizers frequently want to "shake up an organization to demonstrate the decisiveness or managerial reach of a new executive or simply to place his (or her) mark upon it."[7] Reorganization is used to symbolize change and new forms of control within an agency. Whether or not the symbol is taken literally, the reorganization effort does communicate a new set of relationships and priorities while demonstrating, presumably, that the chief executive is determined to "get things done."

But the experience with ED was different from previous reorganizations attempted in the executive branch. It was part of a strategy to develop a continuing reorganization activity, to establish reorganization as an end in itself, separate from the substantive programs and policies affected rather than to attach it to specific substantive policy proposals. The case of ED suggests that such a strategy is pointless. Reorganizations involve political choices and, if they are to have significant influence, cannot be divorced from the environment of politics.

In this case, as in many others, one is impressed with the capacity of the political environment to resist grand schemes for reorganization based on abstract principles of "good management". Indeed, Congress's unwillingness to delegate unlimited reorganization authority to the Chief Executive reminds one how futile it is to pursue such comprehensive schemes. Once again, the fragmented political system has the power to drive away or to reformulate comprehensive approaches to organizational structure. When reorganization has been effective, it has used the needs, sanctions and rewards that are a part of the standard operating procedures of a specific organization to reinforce the goals of the structural change.

But does organizational change make any difference? We have noted that this case study reflects two general theories about bureaucratic change that might result in different outcomes in the way that programs are implemented: one that focused on altering organizational structures and one that emphasized the individuals who provide leadership to an organization. This case study suggests that the two strategies might be linked, although Carter and his aides did not appear to consciously conceptualize such a relationship. Changes in the structure did provide the opportunity to create jobs and put new people in the newly created positions. But we have seen that implementation of ED was largely in the hands of individuals who did not believe that structure makes much difference. Thus, the people that reorganization brought to power generally did not take advantage of the opportunities for reordering power relationships that reorganization affords. They did little to institutionalize or restabilize the organizational units they headed. This was especially true in those units in which there were clear expectations of change attached to the structural reorganization efforts.

THE CULTURE OF ANALYSIS VS THE CULTURE OF POLITICS

In his discussion of the conflict between literary intellectuals and physical scientists, C. P. Snow has written: "Between the two a gulf of mutual incomprehension—sometimes (particularly among the young) hostility and dislike, but most of all lack of understanding. They have a curious distorted image of each other. Their attitudes are so different that, even on the level of emotion, they can't find much common ground."[8]

This case study of the development of ED suggests that the conflict between analysts and politicians is not unlike the clash that Snow has described between scientists and non-scientists. Like Snow, we believe that this conflict is best understood as resulting from two different views of the world. We find that the lack of common ground between the two sets of actors is accurately described—at least in metaphorical terms—as a conflict between cultures. Each of the types of actors has shared standards for perceiving, predicting, judging and acting on and about the world. And these standards, within each set of actors, pushes it in directions and towards goals that are very different from those that are pursued by the other.

This case study provides us with some data with which to describe the two cultures. The culture of analysis, not unexpectedly, revolves around the pursuit of information. The collection of information is at the core of the perceived role; the more information that is collected, the better it is. This leads to a sense that information is collected for its own sake. It is as specific and clear as possible. It assists in the specification of cause and effect relationships. The search for information takes place in a setting which is protected; one believes that it is better to consider all alternatives than to preclude consideration of a possibility prematurely. The negative consequences of simply considering a volatile possibility are minimized as one seeks—as much as possible—to replicate the closed atmosphere of the scientist's laboratory. The expertise of the analyst is usually acknowledged through formal training and credentials and by the trappings of analytical methods. This culture values change and wants to place the burden of proof on its participants to show why change is not needed. As we have noted, analysts want as much time as they can muster within their resources to engage in this search for "correct" solutions.

The culture of politics, by contrast, revolves around the search for agreement. It operates in an environment of uncertainty and ambiguity. It treats information as a political resource that will be used in an advocacy mode. If the information does not meet the needs of political actors, it is often diagnosed as irrelevant. Like the legal system which uses information to build a case and, strategically, to anticipate the positions of the opposition, this culture values information only when it is attached to specific positions in a decision-making arena. It acknowledges expertise based on an analyst's past track record of "success" rather than deference based on credentials or methodological rigor. At the same time, political actors want to put their own imprint on decisions and do not want to accept the advice that was given to others.

The political approach places many different levels of meaning on information, recognizing both symbolic and literal interpretations of actions and positions. It does not search for cause and effect relationships because it believes that this search is futile and does not assist in the achievement of agreement. Indeed, it values the ability of actors to finesse positions and to allow room for bargaining and maneuvering.

Within this culture there is a belief that all information has a political context and even the simple consideration of an alternative may give others the impression that the alternative is being taken seriously. It attempts to minimize the scope of change and, indeed, places the burden of proof on participants to show why change is needed. For the actors within this culture, time is a precious commodity that can be used either to assist or detract from achieving agreement.

Through the analysis of this case, we have seen that it is extremely difficult for actors from these two cultures to learn to live with one another. In part, this occurs because both cultures contain different types of actors within them; neither is monolithic. When one describes the culture of analysis in this case, we are talking about analysts who looked at education issues, at structural issues, at legal problems and at budget questions. We have also described analysts who operate in different organizational settings. This suggests that while all of the analysts may share certain predominant values and approaches, their particular task or organizational setting pushes them to emphasize different issues. Similarly the culture of politics is not monolithic. We described actors within the White House (particularly the Domestic Policy Staff), HEW, the interest groups and the Congress who all operated from the political paradigm but did so to achieve somewhat different ends.

As we have implied, however, to say that there are two cultures does not mean that the actors in one "world" line up neatly against the actors in another in terms of their conclusions and recommendations. Most organizational settings have their own mix of the two cultures in some form or another and find that actors come to similar conclusions for quite different reasons, reflecting different dominant criteria in the decision-making process.

While analysts know that they are dependent on others because they are always in an advisory role, this case indicates that the relationship between analyst (adviser) and client (decision-maker) is often an uneasy one. The difficulties faced by the analysts in the PRP are the most striking example of these problems. The analysts knew that political feasibility assessments were essential in their work. Yet when they sought to gather information about levels of support and opposition to various proposals, they expected others to be forthcoming with their opinions. The elaborate consultation process with interest groups was an extremely frustrating experience for the PRP staffers because they approached it believing that the interest groups would lay out their positions and provide the analysts with explicit data about the possibilities. Similarly, because they viewed information in a literal rather than symbolic fashion, the PRP had difficulty understanding the meaning of sponsorship of the Senate bill. After all, if nearly 70 members signed onto the bill, why should one expect members of the Senate to make significant changes in it?

Political actors in the White House, particularly the Domestic Policy Staff, had biases that were equally as strong. Their intuitive assessments of what would garner support were based on past experience and existing relationships of trust. They resented the intrusion of individuals who had no track record and yet tried to propose new ways of looking at issues. When given the opportunity, they devised schemes to close those individuals out of the decision process.

Throughout this account we have described the ways in which Jimmy Carter appeared to give conflicting signals to those engaged in the politics and analysis of ED. Although Carter was personally attracted to the style of the analyst, his goals were never clearly understood by the analysts who, thus, were limited in ability to focus their analysis on a specific range of issues. Although Carter was attracted to discrete technical matters, he was also a politician (of his own variety) and could be brought around to that point of view. As a result, the analysts found it difficult to predict the way that these two elements would be balanced in Carter's mind.

The conflict between the two cultures in this case was thus exacerbated by Carter's personal style. He was unable to articulate a vision of change that legitimated both sets of actors. He was unable—or at least unwilling—to confront conflict among his advisers. And he did not demonstrate a sustained awareness of the political significance of his actions.

INTEREST GROUPS AND ISSUE NETWORKS

Throughout this volume we have emphasized the important role played by interest groups in the development of ED. Had it not been for the NEA and the campaign promise, it is likely there would not have been a department.

The 1.8 million members of the NEA, spread across most of the 50 states, averaging 4,000 members to every congressional district, were a potent political force. The large Washington based staff was extremely articulate and able to influence the political process on Capitol Hill, in the Executive Office, and, when necessary, to mobilize grass roots support. This influence came into play not only when ED was created but also when the existence of ED was attacked by the Reagan administration.

But this case suggests that political resources of this type are not always an asset. Both the NEA and the administration were sensitive to the perception of the department as a captive of political support. NEA's strength was a double-edged sword and the perception of too much power was an issue at many points in the process. NEA helped create the Education Coalition to broaden the perceived base of support for the department and to present ED as more than a bill of indebtedness to a single organization. Throughout the process, Carter sought to present the proposal as something much more than a campaign promise to the NEA. His willingness to call for a study of the issue of the department at the beginning of his administration was motivated in part by a concern that his commitment would not be seen as a payoff to a special interest political supporter. His appointment of Hufstedler (and the subcabinet) signalled a message that NEA did not have automatic access to the door of the Department. Indeed, it appears that at times the administration went out of its way to limit the access of the NEA to the decision-making process.

This case study also sheds some light on the nature of the ways that the education interest groups operate and influence the policy process. We have seen that the concept of the iron triangle—where control is found in relationships linking executive bureaus, congressional committees and their staffs, and interest groups—while applicable in some cases, does not adequately describe the ways that the interest groups operated around this issue. Hugh Heclo's view of fluid issue networks seems to represent the process more accurately than does the iron triangle theory. The reorganization issue, as it took form, involved more than one set of interest groups, agencies and—potentially—congressional committees and subcommittees. In this case, it was clear that education interest groups were not a monolith; they included a number of overlapping triangles and even some separate sets of relationships. While the various groups might agree to work together on some education issues, they would also disagree on others. The disputes between the NEA and the AFT and the higher education and elementary and secondary education groups are evidence of this diversity.

In addition, the configuration of interest groups also varies depending on the way that an issue is framed. We have shown that certain groups may have supported ED when it was proposed as a general question. But as soon as specific issues were debated, then different clusters of interest groups became involved. Some education issues would probably unite all of the groups that are involved in education (resembling the coalition of support that existed when the 1965 Elementary and Secondary Education Act was passed), but ED was not one of them.

These events lead one to real appreciation of the role that the interest groups play in the policy process. We have noted that interest groups provided the linkages between the various stages, serving as communication paths for information. We also noted that these groups serve to provide regular sources of support and information for the day-to-day activities of the career bureaucracy, with well-worn paths of influence, regular consultation, and provision of information about the impact of programs at their point of delivery. These provide a thread of continuity for programs but, at the same time, evoke a sense of distrust among the existing groups when new actors come on the scene. In the case of the PRP, these actors were not only new but their scope of authority and power was not known. Why, then, should interest groups have trusted them?

Throughout this account, we have emphasized the role played by interest groups. We have seen that they are diverse in character and employ varying strategies to achieve their multiple agendas, such as maintaining budget allocations for their programs, building alliances, maintaining existing alliances, and developing new coalitions.

EDUCATION POLICY AND THE FEDERAL ROLE

We have observed that the controversy over the role of the federal government in education was never far from the debate about the creation of a federal department of education. It appears that it is not possible to debate any issue related to education without opening up the question of the limits of federal power in this field. The level of social agreement on the appropriate role of the federal government in education is, indeed, fragile and tends to vary from one education policy area to another.

As one reviews the activities involved in the creation and early implementation of ED, it appears that neither analysts nor political actors were adequately sensitive to this fragility. "Potomac myopia" did appear to be a problem throughout; it was difficult for individuals in Washington to focus on intergovernmental issues in ways that would lead to a resolution of historic problems. The PRP was not prepared for the House debate on the federal role in education. Even when the jurisdiction for the proposal was in the hands of the House Government Operations Committee, the concerns about ED could not be limited to questions about efficiency for its own sake. Hufstedler and her top aides did not appear to be sufficiently aware of the implications of federal-state relationships when the *Lau* regulations were developed and disseminated.

While the PRP was not unaware of the historic tensions regarding the federal role, it tended to see these issues not as a political problem but as a condition of "creative tension" between states and localities on the one hand and the federal government on the other. The reorganizers' "solution" was to establish a special unit within the department that was charged with advising on intergovernmental questions. The issues involving the federal role in education were complex political problems and did not yield to organizational solutions at one level of government.

LESSONS FOR THE FUTURE

Retrospective case studies are valuable because they allow us to reap the benefits of hindsight. In our quest to understand this complex policy issue, we have attempted to draw lessons for those who will be engaged in similar pursuits in the future. Our Lessons for the Future are presented to two different (though related) audiences: policy analysts and reorganizers.

Lessons For Policy Analysts

Policy analysts will, inevitably, find themselves in conflict with those who live in the world of politics. As we have noted, the two perspectives are not naturally compatible. Indeed, we believe that the conflict between the two worlds is not only inevitable but, if used effectively, a way of moving toward more creative policy development. The challenge is both to acknowledge the tension between the two perspectives and to find ways of building bridges between them.

At least part of that bridge-building can begin when policy analysts hold a realistic view of the policy environment in which they are working. For most federal domestic policies, that environment is best described as turbulent and uncertain; the boundaries between the policy under review and other issues are unclear and difficult to define. Interrelationships between seemingly unrelated issues are to be anticipated—but are not often predictable. The institutions involved in policy development have their own imperatives; people in those institutions may have perceptions about organizational survival that may seem irrational to the analyst but, nonetheless, these perceptions motivate the behavior of those affected by organizational change. These individuals want to be consulted ... whether or not they are willing to give information. Policy analysts must be willing to engage in the ritual dance of consultation, even though that dance may resemble shadow boxing.

The policy analyst searches for coherence, explanation and simplification of the complexity of the policy environment. But this can be risky when the analyst attempts to make political feasibility assessments. Symbolic action is not like other forms of action; while it has its own rationale, the explanations of that form of behavior call on quite different meaning than other forms of action.

The policy analyst must also be sensitive to the locus of the analytic activities. The analysis that is performed in a temporary office is less likely to be encumbered by a tradition of past victories or defeats and past relationships with individuals and units affected by the analysis. At the same time, it comes into the fray without institutionalized procedures and relationships. The new or temporary office is more likely to come up with an idea that accentuates change; the institutionalized office is more likely to come up with an answer that can be implemented.

Acknowledging the political environment that surrounds the activity can also help the analyst understand the difficulties involved in working in a "fish bowl" environment. It is difficult to protect the analyst from political scrutiny; even the consideration of an idea is a signal to the outside world that the alternative (however unpopular or hypothetical) is being taken seriously.

Finally, this case study has accentuated the difficulty involved in developing a relationship between analysts and their clients. In a fragmented decision process, the "real" client for an analysis is not always obvious. Analysts must be aware of the various stages of the public policy process and be clear about the immediate client for the work. As we have seen, it is difficult to develop an analysis for a client who does not have the authority to make the actual decision or who will not (or cannot) be clear about the goals being sought.

All of these elements accentuate the importance of one strategy. If they are to be effective (that is, if their advice is to be taken), policy analysts must have modest expectations about what they can accomplish. The larger the scope of their task (with attendant complexity of actors and issues), the more difficulty they will have developing ways to bridge the two cultures.

Lessons for Reorganizers

The lessons for reorganizers also call for modesty. We have seen that structure can make a difference, but rarely the type of difference promised with grand expectations for change. We, as have others[9], remind reorganizers that shifts in organizational structures are political choices, not mechanistic shifting of boxes. Reorganization in the federal government begins with the acknowledgement of limited ability of the President to make major structural changes, given the checks and balances embodied in the American political structure and the historical conflict between the legislative and executive branches of government.

One can anticipate that reorganization will provoke opposition. There is a sense that change in federal agency structure will have a "domino" effect. There is a strong perception that structural changes in the bureaucracy will produce changes in the organization of Congress, will dramatically alter the ways that interest groups interact with the bureaucracy, and will modify the internal standard operating procedures within the bureaucracy. Whether or not one accepts these perceptions as an accurate prediction of the effects of reorganization, it appears that such fears will be raised. Reorganizers should include examination of those concerns in their deliberations.

While one acknowledges the limitations of reorganization, it continues to be one of the few things that a leader can do to imprint an agenda and approach on the executive branch. It is one of the few manifestations of change that is tangible. If the reorganization is to be more than a message of authority, however, it cannot be bureaucratically removed from other day-to-day administrative decisions or from the political agendas related to the issue. The further removed the leader is from the day-to-day application and institutionalization of rewards and sanctions within the organization, the more difficult it becomes to accomplish change. Because the reorganizing activity takes up so many resources (attention and time are, perhaps, the most precious), it appears that reorganization must be viewed as a limited strategy. It is not sensible to view it as an on-going operation; there is no such thing as a self-reorganizing organization no matter how "logical" new arrangements are asserted to be.

Analysis on reorganization is a formidable task. First, it is never clear what is to be accomplished because reorganization is proposed so frequently as a surrogate for other sorts of change. Second, specialists in the public administration field are not clear about which organizational strategies either "work" or are "desirable". One can find some "expert" within the public administration community to argue for centralization and another for decentralization on almost any given issue. Concepts like "span of control" are elusive and difficult to define without a specific context.

Third, the difficulties of measuring outcomes of reorganization stem not only from the fuzzy and multiple goals of the effort but from the difficulty in collecting and analyzing information about those goals. In domestic policy areas in which state and local governments actually deliver federally funded services, the boundaries of the changes desired are problematic. In such a case, if one changed the organization structure at the federal level to make a program more effective, would one measure the success of such a change by focusing inside the federal bureaucracy or by looking to the point of service delivery? How can one predict the consequences of future actions which are intended to reorder relationships and priorities? The more comprehensive the proposal, the more improvement is anticipated; at the same time, the more comprehensive the proposal, the less reliable the analysis of possible outcomes.[10]

As this case study has indicated, changes in organization structure are also closely linked to changes in internal processes and new personnel policies that bring an infusion of new blood into an organization. All three arenas provide useful mechanisms for change and are most effective when they are used to reinforce one another.

We conclude our *Lessons to Reorganizers* by stressing a theme of the volume: there is much that reorganization cannot do. The grander the scheme, the less likelihood there will be of it achieving success. At the same time, because any other technique of change has similar significant limitations, it is a tool worth learning how to use.

NOTES

1. Murray Edelman, *Politics as Symbolic Action* (Chicago: Markman, 1971), p. 7; see also Murray Edelman, *The Symbolic Uses of Politics* (Urbana: University of Illinois Press, 1967).
2. Jack Knott and Aaron Wildavsky, "Jimmy Carter's Theory of Governing," *Wilson Quarterly* (Winter 1977): 49-67.
3. Michael Cohen, James March and Johan Olsen, "A Garbage Can Model of Organizational Choice," *Administrative Sciences Quarterly* 17 (March 1972): 1-25.
4. Ibid.
5. Eugene Bardach, *The Implementation Game* (Cambridge, Mass.: The MIT Press, 1977), p. 31.
6. Herbert Kaufman, *The Limits of Organizational Change* (Alabama: The University of Alabama Press, 1971), p. 8.
7. Peter Szanton, *Federal Reorganization: What Have We Learned?* (Chatham, New Jersey: Chatham House Publishers, Inc., 1981), p. 2.
8. C. P. Snow, *The Two Cultures and a Second Look* (Cambridge: Cambridge University Press, 1963), p. 4.
9. See, for example, Szanton, Ibid., and Herbert Emmerich, *Federal Organization and Administrative Management* (Alabama: University of Alabama Press, 1971).
10. J. Conant, "Reorganization and the Bottom Line," *Public Administration Review* Vol. 46, No. 1 (January/February 1986): 48-56.

 # BIBLIOGRAPHY

PUBLISHED WORKS

Graham Allison, *Essence of Decision* (Boston: Little, Brown and Company, 1971).

James E. Anderson, *Public Policy-Making* (New York: Praeger, 1975).

Stephen K. Bailey and Edith K. Mosher, *ESEA: The Office of Education Administers a Law* (Syracuse, N. Y.: Syracuse University Press, 1968).

Alan P. Balutis, "The Restructuring of HEW in 1977," Paper presented at the Annual Meeting of the American Society for Public Administration, San Francisco (April 1980).

Michael P. Balzano, *Reorganizing the Federal Bureaucracy: The Rhetoric and the Reality* (Washington, D.C.: American Enterprise Institute for Public Policy Research, 1977).

Eugene Bardach, *The Implementation Game* (Cambridge, Mass.: The MIT Press, 1977).

Larry Berman, *The Office of Management and Budget and the Presidency—1921-79* (Princeton, N.J.: Princeton University Press, 1979).

Elizabeth Gray Bowden, *The Gubernatorial Administration of Jimmy Carter,* MA Thesis (University of Georgia, 1980).

Gary D. Brewer and Peter deLeon, *The Foundations of Policy Analysis* (Homewood, Ill.: Dorsey Press, 1983).

Joseph A. Califano, "Statement," *HEW NEWS* (March 8, 1977). Testimony to the Senate Appropriations Committee (February 2, 1978). *Governing America: An Insider's Report from the White House and the Cabinet* (New York: Simon and Schuster, 1981).

Nathan Caplan, "A Minimal Set of Conditions Necessary for the Utilization of Social Science Knowledge in Policy Formulation at the National Level," in Carol H. Weiss, editor, *Using Social Research in Public Policy Making* (Lexington, Mass.: Lexington Books, 1977): 183-197.

Jimmy Carter, *Why not the Best?* (New York: Bantam Books, 1975).

A Government as Good as its People (New York: Simon and Schuster, 1977).

"My Personal Commitment to Education," *Today's Education* (January-February 1977).

Presidential Papers: Executive Committee on Reorganization (June 2, 1977). "State of the Union Address," *Vital Speeches of the Day*, Vol. 45, No. 8 (February 1, 1979).

Keeping Faith: Memoirs of a President (New York: Bantam Books, 1982).

"Statement to the National Education Association," (October 1975), from *Some Selected Statements by President Jimmy Carter Concerning the Creation of a Separate Cabinet-level Department of Education,* 1975-79.

"Interview with the Iowa Teachers," (Waterloo, Iowa, November 1975).

Roger W. Cobb and Charles D. Elder, *Participation in American Politics: The Dynamics of Agenda Building* (Boston: Allyn and Bacon, Inc., 1972).

Michael Cohen, James March and Johan Olsen, "A Garbage Can Model of Organizational Choice," *Administrative Sciences Quarterly* 17 (March 1972): 1-25.

J. Conant, "Reorganization and the Bottom Line," *Public Administration Review,* Vol. 46, No. 1 (January/February 1986): 48-56.

Murray Edelman, *Politics as Symbolic Action* (Chicago: Markman, 1971).

The Symbolic Uses of Politics (Urbana, Ill.: University of Illinois Press, 1967).

Terry D. Edgmon, "Energy as a Disorganizing Concept in Policy and Administration," *Policy Studies Journal*, Vol. 7, No. 1 (Autumn 1978): 58-67.

Eugene Eidenberg and Roy D. Morey, *An Act of Congress: The Legislative Process and the Making of Education Policy* (New York: W. W. Norton and Company, 1969).

Herbert Emmerich, *Federal Organization and Administrative Management* (Alabama: University of Alabama Press, 1971).

Gary M. Fink, *Prelude to the Presidency* (Westport, Conn.: Greenwood Press, 1980).

Charles E. Gilbert, "Preface: Implementing Governmental Change," *The Annals of the American Academy of Political and Social Science*, Vol. 466 (March 1983): 15-18.

Willis D. Hawley and Beryl A. Radin, "The Presidency and Domestic Policy: Organizing the Department of Education," in Michael Nelson, editor, *The Presidency and the Political System* (Washington, D.C.: Congressional Quarterly Press, 1984): 449-470.

Hugh Heclo, "Issue Networks and the Executive Establishment," in Anthony King, editor, *The New American Political System* (Washington, D.C.: American Enterprise Institute for Public Policy Research, 1979): 87-124.

"The Changing Presidential Office," in Arnold J. Meltsner, editor, *Politics and the Oval Office* (San Francisco: Institute for Contemporary Studies, 1981).

Ben W. Heineman, Jr. and Curtis Hessler, *A Memorandum for the President: A Strategic Approach to Domestic Affairs in the 1980s* (New York: Random House, 1980).

Richard Hofferbert, *The Study of Public Policy* (Indianapolis: Bobbs-Merrill, 1974).

Irving Janis, *Groupthink, Second Edition* (Boston: Houghton-Mifflin, 1982).

Charles O. Jones, *An Introduction to the Study of Public Policy* (Belmont, Ca.: Wadsworth Publishing Company, Inc., 1970).

Thomas J. Kaplan, "The Narrative Structure of Policy Analysis," *Journal of Policy Analysis and Management*, Vol. 5, No. 4 (1986): 761-778.

Herbert Kaufman, *The Limits of Organizational Change* (Alabama: University of Alabama Press, 1971).

John W. Kingdon, *Agendas, Alternatives and Public Policies* (Boston: Little, Brown and Company, 1984).

Jack Knott and Aaron Wildavsky, "Jimmy Carter's Theory of Governing," *Wilson Quarterly* (Winter 1977): 49-67.

Paul C. Light, *The President's Agenda: Domestic Policy Choice from Kennedy to Carter* (Baltimore: The Johns Hopkins University Press, 1982).

Charles Lindblom and David K. Cohen, *Usable Knowledge* (New Haven and London: Yale University Press, 1979).

Lawrence E. Lynn and David deF. Whitman, *The President as Policymaker: Jimmy Carter and Welfare Reform* (Philadelphia: Temple University Press, 1981).

James G. March and Johan P. Olsen, "Organizing Political Life: What Administrative Reorganization Tells Us About Government," *American Political Science Review* No. 77 (1983): 281-96.

Judith V. May and Aaron B. Wildavsky, editors, *The Policy Cycle* (Beverly Hills: Sage Publications, 1978).

Daniel A. Mazmanian and Paul A. Sabatier, *Implementation and Public Policy* (Glenview, Ill.: Scott, Foresman and Company, 1983).

Arnold J. Meltsner, *Policy Analysts in the Bureaucracy* (Berkeley, Ca.: University of California Press, 1976)

Editor, *Politics and the Oval Office* (San Francisco: Institute for Contemporary Studies, 1981).

Rufus E. Miles, Jr., *The Department of H.E.W.* (New York: Praeger Publishers, 1974).

A Cabinet Department of Education: Analysis and Proposal (Washington, D.C.: American Council on Education, 1976).

"Considerations for a President Bent on Reorganization," *Public Administration Review* (March/April 1977): 155-62.

Robert T. Nakamura and Frank Smallwood, *The Politics of Policy Implementation* (New York: St. Martin's Press, 1980).

Roger B. Porter, *Presidential Decision Making: The Economic Policy Board* (Cambridge: Cambridge University Press, 1980).

Jeffrey L. Pressman and Aaron Wildavsky, *Implementation, Third Edition* (Berkeley, Ca.: University of California Press, 1984).

Patricia Rachal, *Federal Narcotics Enforcement: Reorganization and Reform* (Boston: Auburn House Publishing Co., 1982).

Beryl A. Radin, *Implementation, Change and the Federal Bureaucracy* (New York: Teachers College Press, Columbia University, 1977).

"Evaluation on Demand: Two Congressionally Mandated Education Evaluations," in Ron Gilbert, editor, *Making and Managing Policy* (New York: Marcel Dekker, Inc., 1984).

Emmette S. Redford and Marlin Blissett, *Organizing the Executive Branch: The Johnson Presidency* (Chicago: The University of Chicago Press, 1981).

Randall B. Ripley and Grace A. Franklin, *Congress, The Bureaucracy, and Public Policy* (Homewood, Ill.: Dorsey Press, 1976).

Francis E. Rourke, "Grappling with the Bureaucracy," in Arnold J. Meltsner, editor, *Politics and the Oval Office* (San Francisco: Institute for Contemporary Studies, 1981).

Harold Seidman and Robert Gilmour, *Politics, Position, and Power, Fourth Edition* (New York: Oxford University Press, 1986).

Allan P. Sindler, Editor, *Policy and Politics in America* (Boston: Little, Brown and Company, 1973).

C. P. Snow, *The Two Cultures and a Second Look* (Cambridge: Cambridge University Press, 1963).

David Stephens, "President Carter, the Congress and the NEA: Creating the Department of Education," *Political Science Quarterly,* Vol. 98, No. 4 (Winter 1983-84): 641-663.

Peter Szanton, *Federal Reorganization: What Have We Learned?* (Chatham, N.J.: Chatham House Publishers, Inc., 1981).

Norman C. Thomas, *Education in National Politics* (New York: David McKay Co., Inc., 1975).

Jack L. Walker, "The Origins and Maintenance of Interest Groups in America," *American Political Science Review* 77, (1983): 390-406.

J. McIver Weatherford, *Tribes on the Hill* (New York: Rawson, Wade Publishers, Inc., 1981).

Carol H. Weiss, *Evaluation Research: Methods for Assessing Program Effectiveness* (Englewood Cliffs, N.J.: Prentice-Hall, Inc., 1972).

Editor, *Using Social Research in Public Policy Making* (Lexington, Mass.: Lexington Books, 1977).

Joseph A. Wholey, *Evaluation and Effective Public Management* (Boston and Toronto: Little, Brown and Company, 1983).

GOVERNMENT PUBLICATIONS

Education and Public Welfare Division, Congressional Research Service, *Proposals to the U.S. Congress for the Creation of a Department of Education and Related Bills Offering Similar Proposals* (Washington, D.C.: Library of Congress, June 1971).

Establishing a Department of Education: Message from the President of the U.S. (Washington, D.C.: U.S. Government Printing Office, 1979).

Papers Relating to the President's Departmental Reorganization Program: A Reference Compilation (Washington, D.C.: U.S. Government Printing Office, 1971).

U.S. Congress, House Committee on Governmental Operations, *Hearings Before a Subcommittee of the House Committee on Governmental Operations on Establishing a Department of Education, H.R. 13778,* 95th Congress, Second Session (Washington, D.C.: U.S. Government Printing Office, March and April 1979).

U.S. Congress, House Committee on Government Operations, *Department of Education Organization Act, Hearings Before a Subcommittee of the House Committee on Government Operations on H.R. 2444,* 96th Congress, First Session, (Washington, D.C.: U.S. Government Printing Office, March and April 1979).

U.S. Congress, Senate Committee on Government Affairs, 95th Congress, *Hearings on Department of Education Act of 1977,* Part Two, 20-21 March; 14, 18, 27 April; and 8, 16-17 May 1978.

U.S. Congress, Senate, *Department of Education Organization Act of 1978, Senate Report 1078 To Accompany S. 991,* 95th Congress, Second Session (Washington, D.C.: U.S. Government Printing Office, 1978).

U.S. Congress, Senate Committee on Government Affairs, *Department of Education Legislation* (Washington, D.C.: U.S. Government Printing Office, 1978).

U.S. Congress, Senate Committee on Labor and Human Resources, *Hearings on the Nomination of Shirley Hufstedler to be Secretary of Education* (Washington, D.C.: U.S. Government Printing Office, 1979).

PRESS ACCOUNTS

Albequerque Journal, "LULAC Unhappy at Choice for Ed Secretary," (October 31, 1979).

Daniel J. Balz, "Carter's Honeymoon on the Hill—How Long Can it Last," *National Journal* (November 13, 1977): 1618-23.

Dom Bonafede, "Carter Staff is Getting Itchy to Make the Move to Washington," *National Journal* (October 30, 1976): 1542-47.

"Carter's Relationship with Congress—Making a Mountain Out of a 'Moorehill,'" *National Journal* (March 26, 1977): 456-63.

"Political Scientists Issue Their Report Card to the President," *National Journal* (September 16, 1978): 1464-67.

David Breneman and Noel Epstein, "Uncle Sam's Growing Clout in the Classroom," *Washington Post* (August 6, 1978): D1.

Congressional Quarterly, "Education Department Survives Crucial Test," (June 16, 1979).

"Education Department Bill Delayed; Amendments Stir New Opposition," (June 23, 1979), p. 1247.

"Education Department Wins Final Approval," (September 29, 1979), p. 2112.

Richard Corrigan and Joel Havemann, "The Issues Teams: The People Who Prepare Jimmy Carter for the Presidency," *National Journal* (August 21, 1976): 1166-72.

Education Daily, "Califano Suggests Under-Secretary as Alternative to Education Department," Vol. 11, No. 36 (February 22, 1978). "Senate Agriculture Committee Protests Shift of Food Programs to Education Department," Vol. 11, No. 78 (April 21, 1978), p.1.

"School Boards Break Ranks on Education Department," Vol. 12, No. 31 (February 13, 1979).

Education USA, "Education Groups 'Construct' Secretary," (October 15, 1979), p. 54.

C. M. Fields and L. Middleton, "Secretary of Education Hufstedler Hit for Failure to Name Civil Rights Aide," *Chronicle of Higher Education* (April 21, 1980), p. 13.

E. Fiske, *New York Times* (May 11, 1980).

Joel Havemann, "Reorganization—How Clean Can Carter's Broom Sweep," *National Journal* (January 1, 1977): 4-8.

"Carter's Reorganization Plans—Scrambling for Turf," *National Journal* (April 20, 1978): 788-94.

Eugene H. Methvin, "The NEA: A Washington Lobby Run Rampant," *Readers Digest* (November 1978): 97-101.

Lorenzo Middleton, "Who Will Be the First U.S. Secretary of Education?" *Chronicle of Higher Education* (June 25, 1979), p. 14.

National Farmers' Union, Washington Newsletter, Vol. 25, No. 29 (July 21, 1978), p. 1.

NEA Reporter, "NEA Gets Plum; AFT Munches Sour Grapes," (undated), p. 3.

New York Times, Editorial, "The High Price of Cheapening the Cabinet," (January 16, 1978).

"Include Head Start Out," (June 14, 1978).

"An Illusion of Education Reform," (January 16, 1979).

Lynn Olson, "Education Agency Added to Cabinet by Carter Signing," *The Baltimore Sun* (October 18, 1979).

Robert Pear, "Hispanic Leaders Rap Carter for Choice for Ed Secretary," *Washington Star* (October 31, 1979).

Spencer Rich, "Education Department is Approved," *Washington Post* (May 3, 1979): A1.

"Congress Passes Bill to Establish Education Department," *Washington Post* (September 28, 1979): A1.

Bill Richards, "New Education Chief Knee-Deep in Territorial Wrangling," *Washington Post* (December 11, 1979): A2.

"Thousands Seek Non Existent Jobs at Education Department," *Washington Post* (February 2, 1980): A5.

Mark A. Shiffrin, "Promises to Keep: Will Carter Really Create an Education Department," *Washington Post* (August 14, 1977): B.3.

Skee Smith, "The United States Department of Education," *American Education* (undated).

Michael J. Sniffen, "Search for Education Secretary Widens; Ex-Gov. Apodaca Said Out of Running," *Washington Post* (October 20, 1979).

Rochelle Stanfield, "Getting the E Out of HEW—The Trauma Has Only Just Begun," *National Journal* (October 6, 1979), p. 1649.

Time, "Carter's Choice: a Judge for Education," (November 12, 1979).

Washington Post, Editorial, "The Hufstedler Nomination," (October 31, 1979): A20.

Editorial (May 7, 1980).

Beverly T. Watkins, "Separate Department of Education Nears Final Approval in Congress," *Chronicle of Higher Education* (September 24, 1979).

Steven R. Weisman, "Carter Signs Measure Creating a Department of Education," *New York Times* (October 18, 1979).

Betty Anne Williams, "Reaction to Shirley M. Hufstedler," Associated Press Story (November 1, 1979).

Karen J. Winkler, "Separate Department of Education Not Among Carter's Top Priorities," *Chronicle of Higher Education* (January 17, 1979), p. 13.

UNPUBLISHED SOURCES

American Association of School Administrators, Legislative Alert, "Crucial Nominations to Come Soon: Time to Act is Now," (undated).

American Federation of Teachers, Department of Legislation, "Deficiencies in Federal Department of Education Legislation," (March 1979).

Richard C. Atkinson, Director, The National Science Foundation, Letter to the President (April 10, 1978).

Rosalyn H. Baker, National Education Association, Letter to Harrison Wellford on Behalf of 12 Education Groups (October 25, 1979).

Joseph A. Califano, Memorandum for the President, "Subject: The Administration's Proposal for a Cabinet-Level Department of Education," (circa April 10, 1978).

Memorandum to the President (June 1977).

Memorandum to the President (July 11, 1977).

Howard Carroll, National Education Association, Memorandum to Roz Baker, "Subject: Department of Education Media Campaign," (March 10, 1978).

W. S. Dinsmore, OMB, "Notes on Implementation of New Agencies," (September 1974).

Marian Wright Edelman, Memorandum to Vice President Mondale, "Reasons Why Head Start Should Not Be Included in the Department of Education or Placed Under Educational Auspices in Such a Department," (undated).

Letter to Vice President Mondale, "Re: Reorganization of HEW—What are the Goals?" (December 4, 1977).

Letter to Harrison Wellford (March 21, 1978).

Letter to Congressman Jack Brooks on Behalf of the Education Coalition (February 26, 1979).

Stuart Eizenstat, Memorandum for Hamilton Jordan and Jim McIntyre, "Subject: Cabinet-Level Department of Education," (January 9, 1978).

Patsy Fleming, Memorandum to Harrison Wellford and Pat Gwaltney, "Re: Congressional Action on Legislation to Create a Department of Education," (August 18, 1978).

Gary Fontana and Carroll Thornton, Memorandum to Jim McIntyre and Hubert Harris, "Re: Analysis of Department of Education Vote," (July 14, 1979).

Hendrik D. Gideonese, Memorandum to Planners for a Carter Presidency, "Re: Executive Summary—Improving the Federal Establishment: Crucial Supplements to Reorganization," (September 22, 1976).

Patricia Gwaltney, President's Reorganization Project, Note to Ben Heinemann and Fred Bohen, HEW (May 20, 1977). Memorandum to OMB Chief McIntyre (November 28, 1977). Memorandum to Les Francis, "Subject: Committee Jurisdictions over Programs that Might be Included in the Education Department," (February 21, 1978).

Bill Hawley, Memorandum to Patricia Gwaltney, "Subject: Speculation on the Program Content of a New Department of Education," (February 3, 1978).

Shirley M. Hufstedler, Memorandum to Staff Members, "Subject: Selection Process for Presidential Appointees," (undated). Memorandum, "Subject: Regulations Process for the New Department," (February 7, 1980).

Nicole Jeffers, Memorandum to Bill Hawley (December 23, 1977).

Nancy LeaMond, Memorandum to Harrison Wellford, "Subject: Implementation of the Department of Education," (October 3, 1979).

Memorandum to Harrison Wellford, "Subject: Meeting with HEW Regarding Department of Education Implementation," (October 15, 1979).

Memorandum to Patricia Gwaltney McGinnis (undated).

Memorandum to Burt Gindler, "Subject: Thoughts on Implementation," (November 28, 1979).

Ray Marshall, Secretary of Labor, Memorandum for the President, "Subject: Employment and Training Programs and the New Department of Education," (April 10, 1978).

Brian McGovern, PRP, Memorandum to Terry Straub (December 2, 1977).

John McGruder, OMB, Memorandum to Don Boselovic, PRP, "Preliminary Draft Plan for Activation of the Department of Education," (April 17, 1979).

James T. McIntyre, Jr., Memorandum to the President, "Subject: Next Steps on Education Reorganization," (January 7, 1978).

Memorandum to the Vice President, Hamilton Jordan, Stuart Eizenstat and Frank Moore, "Subject: Secretary Califano's List of Agencies Considered for New Education Department," (February 24, 1978).

Memorandum to President Carter, "Subject: Department of Education Initiative," (May 10, 1978).

and Frank Moore, Memorandum to the President (August 17, 1978).

Memorandum to the President (January 25, 1979).

and Stuart Eizenstat, Memorandum for the President, "Subject: Establishment of a Cabinet Department of Education," (undated).

Keith M. Miles, Memorandum to President's Reorganization Project Assistant Director Peter Szanton (November 22, 1977).

Walter Mondale, Speech to the NEA Convention (June 26, 1976).

Cover Memorandum to Presidential Decision Memo to President Jimmy Carter (June 1977).

Remarks: Meeting of Ad Hoc Committee on the Department of Education, Old Executive Office Building (January 24, 1979).

Education Staff, National Council of State Legislators, Memorandum to Patricia Gwaltney (February 26, 1979).

Office of General Counsel, Education Division, Memorandum, "Suggestions for Department of Education Regulations Management System," (December 31, 1979).

Michael O'Keefe, "Draft Paper: Policy Formulation and Implementation," (December 7, 1979).

James Pickman, Deputy Commissioner for Resources and Operations, Memorandum to Stewart Baker, Special Assistant to the Secretary, "Position Paper on Reorganization of the Regulations Development Process," (January 4, 1980).

President's Reorganization Project, "Plan for Conducting Federal Government Reorganization and Management Improvement Program, Discussion Outline," (March 1977).

Memorandum to Patricia Gwaltney (July 15, 1977).

Paper, "The Purposes and Program Content of a New Department of Education," (July 18, 1977).

Memorandum to the President (November 1977).

Paper, "Outline for a Political Strategy for Establishing a Department of Education," (February 6, 1978).

Staff Paper, "Education and the National Science Foundation," (undated).

Presidential Decision Memorandum to President Jimmy Carter (June 1977).

Senator Abraham Ribicoff, Letter to Native American Groups (April 14, 1978).

Paul Royston, Memorandum to POIG Task Force Leaders, "Subject: Task Force Work Plans and Schedule," (December 28, 1979).

Memorandum to Richard Beattie, "The Report and Recommendations of the Public Consultation Team Regarding Tab B and the Beattie Memoranda Issues," (February 21, 1980).

Senate Committee on Agriculture, Nutrition and Forestry, Letter to Senator Abraham Ribicoff (April 18, 1978).

Albert Shanker, President, American Federation of Teachers, Letter to Senator Abraham Ribicoff (May 1977).

Thomas A. Shannon, Executive Director, National School Board Association, Cover Letter to Report on Department of Education Implementation Task Force Meeting (January 21, 1980).

John Shattuck, Karen Christiansen and Laura Murphy, ACLU Washington Office, Letter to Congressman Jack Brooks (June 12, 1979).

Arthur Sheekey, Memorandum to Willis Hawley, "Subject: Meeting with Frank Press on Science Interests," (February 10, 1978).

Memorandum to Patricia Gwaltney (December 13, 1978).

Ted Sky, Office of General Counsel, Note to Stewart Baker, "Re: Suggestions for Regulations Management System," (December 31, 1979).

Terry Straub, Memorandum to Shirley Hufstedler, "Re: Hill Visitations," (November 7, 1979).

Jane Stutsman, "Establishment of a Department of Education: A Current Policy Issue," Paper for Course in Policy Analysis, University of Southern California, Washington Public Affairs Center (December 1978).

Patricia Wald, Assistant Attorney General, Letter to James T. McIntyre, Jr. (April 10, 1978).

Congressman Robert Walker, "Letter to Colleagues: Lesson #1," (May 16, 1979); "Lesson #2," (May 17, 1979); and "Lesson #3," (May 21, 1979).

Harrison Wellford, Testimony to House Appropriations Subcommittee on Department of Treasury, Postal Service and General Government, "Supplemental Request for OMB," (February 24, 1977).

INDEX

ABOUT THE
AUTHORS

Beryl A. Radin is Professor of Public Administration at the Washington Public Affairs Center of the University of Southern California. She has taught at the University of California at Berkeley as well as the University of Texas at Austin. In addition to her academic work, she has served as a staff member or consultant to a number of federal government agencies. Her publications include books and articles on issues related to federal policy implementation, human services policy, and education policy.

Willis D. Hawley is Dean of the Peabody College and Professor of Education and Political Science at Vanderbilt University. He is the author of numerous books and articles dealing with educational policy, school reform, urban politics, and organizational change. He has been a faculty member at Yale and Duke as well as a consultant to a number of local, state, and federal agencies concerned about education and urban policy issues.